Who Should Be Liable?

A Guide To Policy For Dealing With Risk

A Statement by the
Research and
Policy Committee of
the Committee for
Economic
Development

CED

Library of Congress Cataloging-in-Publication Data

Committee for Economic Development. Research and
   Policy Committee.
   Who should be liable?

   1. Torts — United States. 2. Insurance, Liability —
United States. 3. Torts — Economic aspects — United
States. I. Title.
KF1250.C56   1989   346.7303   89.7171
ISBN   0-87186-789-3   347.3063
ISBN   0-87186-089-9 (pbk.)

First printing in bound-book form: 1989
Paperback: $10.50
Library binding: $12.50
Printed in the United States of America
Design: Rowe & Ballantine

COMMITTEE FOR ECONOMIC DEVELOPMENT
477 Madison Avenue, New York, N.Y. 10022
(212) 688-2063
1700 K Street, N.W., Washington, D.C. 20006
(202) 296-5860

CONTENTS

RESPONSIBILITY FOR CED STATEMENTS ON NATIONAL POLICY

The Committee for Economic Development is an independent research and educational organization of over two hundred business executives and educators. CED is nonprofit, nonpartisan, and nonpolitical. Its purpose is to propose policies that will help to bring about steady economic growth at high employment and reasonably stable prices, increase productivity and living standards, provide greater and more equal opportunity for every citizen, and improve the quality of life for all. A more complete description of CED appears on page 176.

All CED policy recommendations must have the approval of trustees on the Research and Policy Committee. This committee is directed under the bylaws to "initiate studies into the principles of business policy and of public policy which will foster the full contribution by industry and commerce to the attainment and maintenance" of the objectives stated above. The bylaws emphasize that "all research is to be thoroughly objective in character, and the approach in each instance is to be from the standpoint of the general welfare and not from that of any special political or economic group." The committee is aided by a Research Advisory Board of leading social scientists and by a small permanent professional staff.

The Research and Policy Committee does not attempt to pass judgment on any pending specific legislative proposals; its purpose is to urge careful consideration of the objectives set forth in this statement and of the best means of accomplishing those objectives.

Each statement is preceded by extensive discussions, meetings, and exchange of memoranda. The research is undertaken by a subcommittee, assisted by advisors chosen for their competence in the field under study. The members and advisors of the subcommittee that prepared this statement are listed on page ix.

The full Research and Policy Committee participates in the drafting of recommendations. Likewise, the trustees on the drafting subcommittee vote to approve or disapprove a policy statement, and they share with the Research and Policy Committee the privilege of submitting individual comments for publication, as noted on page 168 of this statement.

Except for the members of the Research and Policy Committee and the responsible subcommittee, the recommendations presented herein are not necessarily endorsed by other trustees or by the advisors, contributors, staff members, or others associated with CED.

CED RESEARCH AND POLICY COMMITTEE

*Voted to approve the policy statement but submitted memoranda of comment, reservation, or dissent. (See page 168.)

SUBCOMMITTEE ON RISK MANAGEMENT, DISPUTE RESOLUTION, AND INJURY COMPENSATION

ADVISORS

PROJECT DIRECTOR

PROJECT COUNSELOR

PROJECT ASSOCIATE

EDITORIAL ASSOCIATE

PROJECT STAFF

Purpose of This Statement

Our nation's tort liability system is designed to resolve disputes over personal injury or financial loss by affording injured parties an avenue for suing for damages. It is intended to deter misconduct and compensate injury. But new social and technological demands have strained the tort system so that it neither effectively deters nor efficiently compensates. At the same time, it imposes heavy costs on business, government, and consumers.

Our economic system also contains other effective means that can help to control risk and compensate loss. Important alternatives are market forces for controlling risk and public and private insurance for providing compensation. Further, government regulation contributes to the same end. Also, under the wing of the tort system, various alternative dispute resolution mechanisms such as arbitration, mediation, and mini-trials are evolving.

Each of these alternatives, including tort liability, has its own strengths and weaknesses. Unfortunately, as the tort system and these alternatives are used today, they are ill-fitted together and often not used to best advantage for purposes of risk management, injury compensation, and dispute resolution. The uncontrolled and uncoordinated expansion of tort liability not only burdens U.S. business firms, service organizations, and individuals with burgeoning legal fees, court awards, and insurance costs, but also threatens to detract from our national economic well-being by raising prices, deterring the provision of certain vital goods and services, discouraging product and service innovation, and damaging U.S. international competitiveness. These seriously adverse consequences have led the Committee for Economic Development (CED) to make this careful study of tort liability, in the context of other systems of risk control and compensation, and to search for effective reforms.

THE ECONOMIC RATIONALE FOR REFORM

CED has long been concerned with enhancing U.S. competitiveness. In recent years, it has explored a number of key domestic and international policy areas that affect U.S. international competitiveness, such as education, labor market issues, and trade and budget deficits.

It is important for policy makers and business leaders to understand the impact that the current liability system has on the competitiveness of U.S. firms. For example, the United States pays much greater liability insurance costs than many of its trading partners, including Japan, West Germany, France, Great Britain, Canada, Italy, and Australia.

Although society benefits from some of this expenditure, consumers, workers, and businesses ultimately pay a high cost for what they receive. A more efficient U.S. liability system would not only strengthen U.S. competitiveness, it would also help ensure a higher standard of living for Americans.

If well designed and well managed, our courts, regulatory agencies, and social insurance programs should be able to mesh with one another and with market forces to jointly control risk and compensate injury efficiently– that is, provide the best combination of benefits relative to costs. We believe the recommendations developed in this policy statement point the way toward such a more efficient system.

ACKNOWLEDGMENTS

On behalf of the Research and Policy Committee, I would like to commend Theodore A. Burtis, retired chairman of the board and now a director of Sun Company, Inc., for his dedicated leadership as chairman of the CED subcommittee that prepared this study. I would also like to thank John H. Filer, former chairman of Aetna and now a partner at Tyler, Cooper & Alcorn, for his expert guidance as subcommittee vice chairman, and to acknowledge the contributions of the distinguished group of business and academic leaders who served on the subcommittee.

In addition, I would like to recognize the extraordinary expertise brought to this study by Professor Patricia M. Danzon of The Wharton School, The University of Pennsylvania, who served as project director, and Jack A. Meyer, president of New Directions for Policy, who served as project counselor. Special thanks also go to Project Associate Katherine E. Jones, CED Information Staff Associate Cynthia Rice, and Deputy Secretary of CED's Research and Policy Committee Lorraine M. Brooker.

I would also like to thank the many scholars and practitioners whose work in this area helped CED formulate its recommendations. The research papers commissioned by CED, a list of which can be found on page 175, helped us to grapple with particularly difficult aspects of the problem. We are also grateful for the guidance we received from participants in two conferences CED cosponsored, "Risk, Compensation, and Liability: The Policy Choices," cosponsored with the Yale School of Organization and Management in April 1986, and "The Impact of U.S. Product Liability Laws on U.S. Export Trade and International Competitiveness," cosponsored with the Fletcher School of Law and Diplomacy at Tufts University and the Council on Competitiveness in October 1987.

Finally, I would like to thank the following organizations for the generous support that made possible the development of this study and its two preparatory conferences: The Andrew W. Mellon Foundation, The Pew Charitable Trusts, Pfizer Inc., RJR Nabisco, Inc., The Prudential Foundation, Travelers Corporation, Exxon Corporation, The Procter & Gamble Fund, G. D. Searle & Co., USX Corporation, Dow Chemical Company, Aetna Life & Casualty Company, AT&T Foundation, E.I. du Pont de Nemours & Company, The Ford Foundation, Ford Motor Company Fund, Mobil Corporation, Liberty Mutual Insurance Company, and Delta Air Lines, Inc.

Dean P. Phypers
Chairman
Research and Policy Committee

CHAPTER 1
Introduction and Summary of Recommendations

The purpose of this policy statement is to evaluate in a broad context the tort liability system that has evolved in the United States. Tort liability involves noncontractual claims against someone – an individual, a corporation, a municipality, an organization, a physician, an accountant, or other professional – for compensation for personal injury or financial loss. Such claims arise out of injuries from myriad different causes, including faulty products, medical and other professional negligence, automobile accidents, toxic substances, and accidents occurring at public facilities. Our main focus is product liability, but much of our analysis and many of our recommendations are quite general and apply equally to other areas of tort liability.

In 1985 and 1986, the U.S. economy experienced what many termed a *liability crisis.* Many corporations, municipalities, not-for-profit organizations, and professionals were faced with huge increases in liability insurance costs, and for some, coverage became simply unavailable. This crisis reverberated throughout the economy, raising prices and disrupting the supply of a wide range of goods, services, and activities.

Although the crisis has eased, its root causes have not been resolved. Until they are, liability insurance costs will remain high, availability may be limited in some sectors, and the risk of recurrent crises will persist. These problems in liability insurance markets have focused attention on more fundamental problems in the underlying tort liability system.

The tort liability system in the United States is intended to perform two main functions: deterrence and compensation. Most obviously, tort liability provides compensation to persons injured by the actions of others. In addition, the anticipation of liability is intended to deter such injuries. Both are very valid objectives. But our liability system was designed in an earlier era. It has subsequently been extended to handle new circumstances and perform functions for which it is ill designed. One purpose of this study, therefore, is to suggest ways to overhaul and modernize the liability system to enable it to do a better job of meeting its proper goals.

Evaluation and reform of tort liability should not take place in a vacuum. Liability is only one of the forces operating in the economy to achieve the twin social goals of deterring harm and compensating victims of injury. For example, market forces and government regulation also play key roles in the control of risk. On the compensation side, private health and disability insurance, social insurance, and workers' compensation systems far exceed the tort system in the aggregate compensation they provide for injuries, and they also cost far less to operate. Each has its own strengths and weaknesses, costs and benefits, and each has a useful role to play. Thus far, these systems have developed independently of one another, with little attention to focusing each one on areas where it could be used most cost-effectively. Consequently, liability and regulation often create overlapping and conflicting standards of deterrence, and the liability system often duplicates compensation by other private and social insurance programs. Better coordination of these different systems and elimination of conflicts are major goals of our recommendations.

But our concern is not simply with the waste caused by duplication. Our more fundamental concern is that if tort liability is inappropriately designed and used, it fails to provide socially efficient deterrence and compensation.[1] Furthermore, under these conditions, if excessively relied upon, it becomes a drag on the economy by raising costs of production and consumer prices, causing the withdrawal of valuable goods and services from the marketplace, and harming U.S. productivity and international competitiveness.*

There are no hard data on the total costs and benefits of the liability system. Liability insurance premiums are certainly only a fraction of the total cost. Much harder to measure are the indirect costs of loss of productivity and international competitiveness and the loss to consumers from goods and services that are withdrawn or simply not produced. Some of the changes induced by liability surely do produce safer products, as intended. Unfortunately, these benefits – in terms of deterrence and compensation – are equally hard to measure.

To wait for hard data on all elements of costs and benefits would be to postpone action indefinitely and allow the current drift in the liability

---

*See memorandum by JAMES Q. RIORDAN (page 168).

system to continue unchecked. We believe the partial data and practical experience available today permit us to reach some reasonable judgments on ways of improving our systems of risk management and deterrence. We believe such improvements are well worth enacting now, even as further research proceeds on the unresolved issues.

We are convinced that tort liability has an important place along with other policy mechanisms for dealing with risk. But those features that are counterproductive must be reformed and revised to achieve more efficient and equitable deterrence and compensation while fostering a growing and productive economy that is competitive in world markets.

SYMPTOMS OF THE PROBLEM

The number of tort claims and the size of awards have increased sharply in the past decade, leading the insurance industry to raise prices and, in some cases, refuse to grant coverage altogether, and resulting in enormous national expenditures on litigation. In part, it is the world that has changed. The U.S. tort system was simply not designed to resolve the increasingly complex issues and disputes that now arise. At the same time, society's standards of acceptable risk and fair compensation have risen. But the tort system is also being used to pursue social goals for which liability is an ill designed vehicle, resulting in a misallocation of resources that is both wasteful and cumbersome.

NUMBER AND SIZE OF CLAIMS

The tort liability system addresses noncontractual claims for personal injury and financial losses in a vast range of different circumstances. From 1981 to 1985, the total volume of tort claims grew only 3 percent annually (after adjusting for population growth), a fairly modest increase.[2] However, this aggregate figure can be misleading. Although automobile accident claims, roughly half the total, have remained stable, some other types of claims have skyrocketed. Automobile claims are typically rather routine cases, mostly between individuals, and the rules governing the disposition of such claims have remained stable (except for the shift to no-fault laws in some states), as has the number of claims.

But there has been a dramatic increase in the number of claims for nonauto torts, including liability regarding products, professionals, municipalities, and not-for-profit entities. For example, even excluding the huge surge of asbestos-related claims, the number of product liability cases increased fivefold between 1975 and 1985.[3] The greatest growth has occurred in the area of the so-called mass toxic torts, which involve thousands of claims against a single product, notably asbestos, Agent Orange, and the Dalkon Shield. By 1986, more than 325,000 Dalkon Shield claims had been submitted.[4]

Trends in the size of jury awards (adjusted for inflation) also differ dramatically by type and size of case. The typical (median) award for auto cases has remained stable in constant dollars, but the typical award for product and medical malpractice cases has risen sharply. Awards in the very highest-paying cases have risen most rapidly, resulting in even more dramatic increases in the average (mean) than in the typical, particularly for nonauto cases. In two sample jurisdictions, between 1960-1964 and 1980-1984, for example, the average award for product liability and medical malpractice suits increased between 200 and 1,000 percent (see Table 2.1, page 20). Over those two decades, the average personal injury award rose from $59,000 to $187,000 (in inflation-adjusted 1984 dollars) in Cook County, Illinois, and from $66,000 to $302,000 in San Francisco. For almost every type of case, the plaintiff's probability of winning increased.[5]

PRICE AND AVAILABILITY OF LIABILITY INSURANCE

Since 1984, rates have increased sharply for both commercial and professional liability insurance. Medical malpractice premium rates increased 25 to 40 percent a year.[6] Rates rose several hundred percent over the space of one or two years for such diverse groups as municipalities, public transit operators, toy manufacturers, corporate directors and officers, architects and engineers, and day-care centers.[7] At the same time, many buyers report being unable to obtain the amount of coverage they would prefer.[8]

Three factors appear to have contributed to the rising costs and unavailability of liability insurance. First and most fundamental is the growth in the number of claims, size of awards, and associated litigation costs. Second, in the mid-1980s, insurance prices for risks of long duration (the long-tailed lines), which include general liability and medical malpractice and which fluctuate with interest rates, reached a peak in their seemingly cyclical pattern. Third, unanticipated increases in claim costs resulting in part from retroactive changes in law and judicial reinterpretations of contracts have caused unanticipated losses on past policies. These unfunded losses seriously depleted the capacity of the insurance industry and contributed to the sharp price increases and lack of availability of coverage in high-risk lines.

Because the scope and duration of liability and the size of awards have become virtually unbounded, risk cannot be accurately priced.

Since this court-imposed risk affects all policyholders alike, it is not readily diversifiable through traditional insurance pooling, which requires that risks be independent. Some policyholders are responding to higher insurance prices and lower availability by simply bearing more risk, retaining higher deductibles and lower limits of coverage, or forming captive insurance companies and risk-retention groups. But these are accommodations rather than solutions to the underlying problem of unbounded and unpredictable liability.

THE COST OF LITIGATION

Of the $19.5 billion spent on nonauto cases in 1985, $11 billion went to litigation costs, including attorneys' fees and time costs of the litigants, leaving only $8.2 billion as compensation to plaintiffs. If liability insurance overhead costs are added, the plaintiff's share is even smaller. On average, the litigation process for nonauto cases absorbs roughly 57 percent of total expenditures through the tort system.[9]

In litigation, private rational behavior is often at odds with social efficiency. Legal activity that is not necessary to establish the facts but that is undertaken to gain strategic advantage in settlement or trial represents a waste of societal resources from a public perspective. Although it is individually rational for each litigant to spend money in an attempt to influence the outcome of the trial or settlement, such expenditure only exacerbates the unpredictability of the court system, creating a cycle that encourages more litigation. Furthermore, the high cost of litigation distorts out-of-court settlements because defendants are willing to pay higher settlements in order to avoid even higher court costs.

In search of ways to prevent, manage, and resolve disputes more cost-effectively, the private sector has developed a range of alternative dispute resolution (ADR) mechanisms, including pretrial mediation, arbitration, and mini-trials. These voluntary strategies typically bring in a neutral third party to arbitrate or simply advise the key decisionmakers from each side. Agreement is often reached with much less cost and delay than through traditional litigation.

The search for more efficient methods of dispute resolution is most urgent for mass torts related to a single product. The traditional legal system is particularly ill designed to handle such cases, which can involve thousands of claimants with similar injuries and raise duplicative issues and murky questions of general and specific causation, as well as multiple defendants, primary insurers, and reinsurers for each plaintiff. Courts and private parties have adopted various ADR mechanisms to aggregate and resolve claims regarding asbestos, Agent Orange, and the Dalkon Shield, but costs remain high.

CAUSES OF THESE PROBLEMS

Although social, economic, and technological forces may be the underlying causes of these trends in litigation, the primary immediate cause lies in the evolution of law and legal rules and in the subtle changes in the implementation of these rules. In the area of product-related injuries, the shift from contract to tort law has been followed since the 1960s by a shift from fault-based standards to strict liability and, in some cases, to absolute liability. Increasingly, a manufacturer is liable even if all reasonable precautions were taken given the state of knowledge at the time. Manufacturers have been found liable even if the plaintiff wantonly misused the product, if other parties contributed to the injury (e.g., by removing safety devices) and even if no connection has been established between a defendant's actions and a plaintiff's injuries.

The intent of the courts in expanding liability has often been to create incentives for risk reduction by internalizing the cost of injuries to contributing parties and to provide compensation. Although the value of deterrence and compensation is beyond question, we believe that the scope of the liability system has been expanded beyond what the system can cost-effectively accomplish.

Consider first the goal of deterring injury by making responsible parties pay the costs of those injuries. Imposing liability where a defendant has taken all reasonable precautions serves no positive deterrent function; on the contrary, it undermines the incentive for other parties to take appropriate care and so may actually increase the number of future injuries. In addition, it encourages inefficient defensive strategies and leads to the withdrawal of products and services as the only sure way to avoid such liability.

Consider next the goal of compensation. Expanding liability in order to compensate is grounded in the mistaken belief that defendants can spread this risk without cost, smoothly passing it on through liability insurance and ultimately through higher prices for goods and services. In fact, such a transfer is not automatic and is far from smooth when the unpredictability of tort law disrupts the supply of liability insurance. Furthermore, the costs to be passed through are unnecessarily high.

Tort liability is an extremely inefficient form of social insurance. In fact, compensation through tort liability is less efficient than virtually any other form of private first-party or social insurance. Overall, plaintiffs receive only 40 cents for each dollar spent on product liability or malpractice insurance, whereas workers' compensation pays the plaintiff roughly 62 cents per insurance dollar, and private first-party health insurance pays over 80 cents per dollar.[10]

Other factors compound the inefficiency of tort liability as a system of compensation. Awards in the tort system vary widely in amount and are often received only after years of litigation. Other forms of private and social insurance come much closer to the ideal of providing a steady, smooth flow of income immediately following a loss. By attempting to "make the plaintiff whole," the tort system attempts to provide compensation for losses that cannot be compensated by money. On the other hand, tort compensation for wage loss and medical expenses often duplicates other private and social insurance payments, because coordination of benefits is costly and imperfect.

Finally, using tort liability to extend compensation is a major contributor to problems of cost and availability of liability insurance. The judicial view of tort as a vehicle for extending compensation without regard for the reasonableness of the defendant's actions leads to distortions in out-of-court settlements and makes the liability risk essentially unpredictable.

THE FUNDAMENTAL ISSUES

Several fundamental issues underlie our society's approach to handling risk. One such issue is the divergence between public and expert views of risk and what constitutes reasonable risk. Polling data indicate tremendous public concern about risk, particularly regarding chemicals and environmental hazards. Reflecting these views, recent legislation, such as the Safe Drinking Water Act and the 1986 Superfund revisions, set goals of zero risk, although such goals are simply not feasible for the foreseeable future because of the costs and technological barriers.

The public view of risk often includes broader and more complex issues such as the potential for catastrophe, who wins and loses, risks to future generations, and who is in control. Technical experts work with quantitative measures of probability and magnitude.[11] Neither approach is wrong, and sound public policy must encompass and weigh all these considerations. Better education and mutual communication concerning risk are critical to developing sound public policy toward risk so that the technical measures more explicitly account for distributional effects, and public perceptions are better informed about the quantifiable dimensions and the costs and benefits of reducing risk.

Zero risk is simply not feasible; our limited resources force us to make inevitable choices. By not facing up to the need to make choices, we in fact often end up making worse decisions. We are continually faced with trade-offs between risk reduction and other social goals, such as promoting economic growth, maintaining international competitiveness, and producing needed goods and services.

The challenge is to achieve the best balance we can between risk reduction and other social goals and to produce whatever level of safety and health we choose in the most cost-effective manner. Achieving the most efficient balance for society in delivering risk reduction, compensation, and dispute resolution will not be possible until we accept the need to make choices.

Each day, people make hundreds of choices about risk in the course of their daily activities. Consumers are not willing to expend infinite effort on reducing risk; in general, each successive increment of risk reduction is worth less to the consumer; at the same time, it becomes more expensive to achieve. Where consumers and workers understand the risks involved, and where producers face costs that accurately reflect full social costs, market forces will produce efficient solutions to the problems of risk.

But markets can fail when injuries are latent and hard to assess, or when there are hazards to parties whose preferences are not reflected in the market. In cases of severe market failure, government intervention through regulation or the tort system may be warranted in order to control risk, but such intervention imposes costs of its own. For example, it is costly for courts and regulators to obtain information required to make good decisions and to administer the decision-making process. Both courts and regulators are prone to random mistakes and systematic bias. Thus, regulation and liability should be designed with care and implemented only when there is significant market failure.*

SUMMARY OF RECOMMENDATIONS

Our study has led us to formulate recommendations for how our society can improve the handling of risk. These recommendations will not remedy all the problems with the present system, but we believe they would lead to a significantly improved balance of benefits relative to costs.

Because our recommendations focus on the tort system and its interaction with alternative systems of deterrence and compensation, we have not attempted to make a comprehensive, thorough review and detailed recommendations for reform of regulatory agencies and insurance programs. However, because we do recommend greater reliance on regulation and insurance for some purposes, we have made a limited number of general recommendations with respect to those programs.

---

*See memorandum by JOHN DIEBOLD (page 168).

Although our main focus in this statement is on product liability, many of our recommendations regarding the tort system apply equally to all areas of tort law, including personal, professional, and municipal liability. We have tried to minimize our use of terms peculiar to the legal and insurance industries, but because some terms are ingrained in the policy debate, we provide a glossary of a limited number of terms on page 170.

CHOICE OF INSTITUTIONS

- **We should rely on market forces in cases where the parties are aware of the risks and transaction costs are low.***(See Chapter 5.)

- **Courts should honor contractual agreements between reasonably well-informed parties.** This would include disallowing liability where risks are obvious and adhering to liability insurance and other commercial contracts and contractual agreements to use alternative dispute resolution. (See Chapter 5.)

- **Standard setting through existing regulatory agencies – such as the Occupational Safety and Health Administration (OSHA), Environmental Protection Agency (EPA), and Food and Drug Administration (FDA) – should be the primary instrument for controlling environmental hazards, chemical hazards, pharmaceuticals, and medical devices. Compliance with regulatory standards of product design or warning should be a bar to tort liability except in cases of fraud or suppression of evidence.** Regulation is more efficient than tort liability for controlling mass hazards with potentially long-latent effects. Adding tort liability creates conflicting standards that are unlikely to be more efficient, and it generates wasteful litigation. The proposed regulation defense would apply only to those aspects of a product that are in compliance with regulatory standards.* (See Chapter 5.)

- **Workers' compensation (WC) should be restored to its original role of sole remedy for work-related injuries and diseases where occupational exposure is the predominant cause.** The current combination of market forces, OSHA regulation, and workers' compensation provides strong incentives for controlling risk in the workplace. Workers' compensation benefit schedules should provide adequate benefits-replacement of after-tax earnings and reasonable medical and rehabilitation expense. Benefit levels should be indexed to keep pace with inflation. Superimposing tort liability for product-related workplace injuries is costly and inefficient. (See Chapter 6.)

---

*See memoranda by RODERICK M. HILLS (page 169).

REFORM OF THE TORT SYSTEM

GENERAL PRINCIPLES

- **Tort liability should be designed to create efficient incentives for control of risk. Deterring excessive risk should override concern for compensation if these two goals conflict.** Compensation can be provided much more cost-effectively through properly designed private first-party insurance or social insurance programs. (See Chapter 6.)

- **Liability should be based on a notion of fault, responsibility for harm, or failure to take reasonable or cost-justified precautions.** This principle is designed to provide incentives for all parties who are potential contributors to risk to take care. (See Chapter 5.)

- **Compensatory awards should be structured along the same lines as private first-party and social insurance programs**. Tort compensation, which aims at full compensation for all monetary and nonmonetary loss, is far more generous than any other form of private or social insurance. Full compensation is typically not worth its social cost, particularly for nonmonetary losses and in situations of moral hazard where full compensation discourages individuals from taking proper care to prevent or minimize the loss. (See Chapter 6.)

- **Specific guidelines should be set by statute for both monetary and nonmonetary loss.** By narrowing the range of discretion left to the courts, this would make awards more equitable across different cases, reduce incentives for litigation, and increase predictability. (See Chapter 6.)

- **Compensation for monetary loss should aim to replace after-tax wages (with special provisions for persons not in the labor force) and cover reasonable medical, rehabilitation, and special educational expenses.** The responsible parties should be encouraged to provide for such compensation through the purchase of annuities, private health and disability income policies, or other financial instruments. (See Chapter 6.)

- **Payments for nonmonetary loss should be reasonable and made according to a schedule based on the plaintiff's age and severity of injury.** Such a schedule is preferable to single caps, which tend to be unfair to young, severely injured plaintiffs. (See Chapter 6.)

- **Statutory benefit levels should be indexed for inflation.** This is essential to preserve adequate compensation. (See Chapter 6.)

- **Further study is needed to determine the best method of coordinating tort and nontort insurance coverages.** For purposes of deterrence, requiring tort defendants to pay full damages while reducing payments from other insurers is preferable to the alternative of reducing the amount paid by the tort defendant by the amount payable from other insurance benefits. However, the first alternative may cost more to implement. (See Chapter 6.)

- **Punitive damages should be awarded only in cases of willful misconduct and should be limited to a modest multiple of the compensatory award.** Exposure to unpredictable and potentially bankrupting punitive awards, which fails to create sound deterrence incentives, would thus be limited while preserving incentives for prudent attention to risk. Under these conditions, legislatures, courts, regulatory agencies, and insurance companies may be inclined to disallow insurance for punitive damages as a matter of public policy. (See Chapter 5.)

- **Punitive damages should be coordinated across different cases relating to the same issue, to the extent that this is feasible.** In general, in class actions that are voluntary with respect to compensatory damages, participation should be mandatory with respect to punitive damages. (See Chapter 5.)

- **Joint and several liability should be eliminated.** Joint and several liability violates the principle of assessing costs to responsible parties. It tends to encourage the frivolous naming of deep-pocket defendants because they can be liable for the entire award even if only minimally responsible. It discourages cooperative activities in the control and disposal of hazardous waste. By limiting the ability of an insurer to perform an accurate risk assessment, joint and several liability has undermined the market for pollution liability insurance. (See Chapter 5.)

- **A state-of-the-art defense and a reasonable standard of repose are required to prevent retroactive applications of new knowledge and new standards of liability.** Liability imposed retroactively for unknowable risks cannot be a useful deterrent. It inevitably generates unfunded liabilities that force defendants into costly litigation in attempts to shift those liabilities. Moreover, retroactive liability discourages the production of goods and services that are long-lived or have long-latent possible risks. (See Chapter 5.)

PRODUCT LIABILITY (See Chapter 5.)

- **A federal product liability statute is needed to ensure a predictable standard of liability.** The diversity of state standards causes costly and inefficient uncertainty.

- **Courts should disallow or modify liability if a product is unreasonably misused, altered, or used in a way that the manufacturer explicitly warned against.** In such cases, liability should be in proportion to fault. These measures would provide all parties with incentives to take cost-justified care.

WORK-RELATED INJURIES (See Chapter 6.)

- **Tort actions against product suppliers and employers for work-related injuries should be disallowed.**

- **Workers' compensation should be the sole remedy for injuries and diseases where occupational exposure is the predominant cause.** Drawing a line between claims that are only remotely connected to occupation and those for which occupation is the predominant cause will inevitably be difficult, particularly for occupational disease claims. However, enforcing this distinction is essential to prevent the workers' compensation system from expanding into a general system of social insurance.

- **WC benefits should provide for replacement of after-tax earnings, medical and rehabilitation expense.** It is critical that benefit levels be indexed to keep pace with inflation, in order to maintain an adequate real standard of compensation.

- **Improved management of the workers' compensation system is essential.** Litigation costs are absorbing more and more of the dollars paid into the system. Benefit levels and eligibility criteria should be set by statute at the state level, to the extent possible, to minimize litigation on individual cases.

NONOCCUPATIONAL MASS TORTS (See Chapter 6.)

- **Further study is required to determine the best way of handling the mass tort cases not preempted by any new rules barring liability where the products comply with existing regulatory standards. Our tentative recommendation is for such claims to be permitted only where the contribution of the defendant exceeds some threshold. Alternatively, damages paid by the defendant should be reduced by the percentage contribution of other factors.** Because of the difficulty of determining both general and specific causation and apportioning damages appropriately when there are multiple contributing factors, these cases will continue to pose severe problems in terms of litigation costs, deterrence, and coordination of benefits. Further research in this area is imperative in order to develop practical and timely solutions.

INTERNATIONAL RIGHTS AND RESPONSIBILITIES (See Chapter 5.)

- **All U.S. courts should deny access to foreign litigants for injuries incurred outside the United States, as most federal courts already do.** Our aim here is to achieve a more level playing field between foreign-based and domestic-based sellers of products.

- **Foreign sellers of products in the United States should be subject to financial responsibility requirements as stringent as those applied to U.S. firms.** This will assure U.S. consumers the same tort rights against foreign-based suppliers as against domestic firms.

STANDARD SETTING THROUGH REGULATION (See Chapter 5.)

- **A goal of regulatory standards should be to achieve roughly equal benefits (in terms of life-years saved) per dollar spent for all types of hazards.** This standard is designed to achieve the maximum benefit for the cost incurred. Any other standard implies an inefficient allocation of resources.

- **Performance standards should be defined in terms of target quality or risk levels.** Government's comparative advantage is in assessing risk and setting standards. Industry's comparative advantage is in finding the least costly methods to achieve these standards. Regulations mandating specific process standards destroy incentives for developing new methods that can achieve the desired result at lower cost.

SOCIAL INSURANCE PROGRAMS (See Chapter 6.)

- **In general, expanding our existing broad social insurance programs as needed is preferable to creating new programs targeted to specific injuries.** Existing private and social insurance systems already provide extensive coverage of medical expense and wage loss. To the extent that certain groups are not adequately covered, changes in existing broad programs are preferable to creating new programs.

- **The benefit structure should provide reasonable compensation (e.g., replacement of lost after-tax wages) while preserving incentives for rehabilitation and return to active life if possible.**

- **There is a critical need to control the relentless rise in health care costs, which contributes to the escalating costs of private health insurance, workers' compensation, tort liability, and social insurance programs.** All these programs should attempt to prevent overuse of medical resources through such devices as copayment, case management, utilization review, selective contracting, prepayment, and capitation forms of reimbursement.

RESOLUTION OF DISPUTES (See Chapter 4.)

- **Parties should be permitted and encouraged to contractually adopt alternative dispute resolution (ADR) systems such as arbitration, mediation, and mini-trials, provided that such contracts clearly state where rights to jury trial are being waived.** The search for cost-reducing ADR mechanisms is particularly critical for multi-party mass litigation and Superfund-related disputes. There is a need to better educate law students, judges, corporate management, and general counsel on the benefits of ADR.

- **The effects of class actions and bankruptcy proceedings to handle mass claims require further study.** Such research is necessary in order to develop a sound base for efficient reform of the handling of mass claims.

- **Aggressive judicial management of cases can prevent strategic abuse of pretrial and trial tactics.** Judges should disallow unsubstantiated testimony of expert witnesses, should be more willing to grant summary judgment, should send to the jury only those issues that are truly within the jury's realm of expertise, and should consider reduction of excessive awards.

- **Further study is needed of the effect of the so-called English rule for awarding costs (whereby the losing party pays the legal fees of the winning party).** Some variant of this rule could be useful in deterring frivolous litigation.

JUMP-STARTING THE LIABILITY DEBATE

As we tackle the challenge of modernizing both regulation and liability to meet changing circumstances, we need to recognize the twin ingredients of success: the knowledge of what to do and the political will to do it. Over the past fifteen years, major breakthroughs have been achieved in understanding how to design regulation more efficiently, and as a result, some important changes have been made.

We think it is fair to say that the debate over tort liability has lagged far behind the regulation debate in this respect. The aim of this policy statement is to jump-start the debate over tort liability by laying out our recommendations for change. There have been some signs of progress over the past few years – in better judicial management as well as state efforts at statutory reform. By 1988, thirty-seven states had enacted changes in their tort systems, some along lines similar to those we recommend.[12] We encourage such efforts but feel that a great many changes are still needed.

Many of the reforms proposed here require fundamental revisions in our systems of risk management, compensation, and dispute resolution. Change is essential in order to arrest the trends of the liability system that have developed in recent years, which force the system to perform functions it is not designed to perform and which can be achieved more efficiently through other means.

Making the necessary changes will require extensive efforts by many parties. Reform of the tort system and of regulation requires action by Congress and state legislatures. The courts and the legal profession have a critical role to play in implementing the rules and managing cases efficiently. Private parties – manufacturers, insurers, and others – can and should do more to control litigation costs by using ADR mechanisms. If well designed, our courts, regulatory agencies, and social insurance programs can mesh well with each other and with market forces and can jointly control risk and compensate injury. But if they remain poorly designed and uncoordinated, these potentially useful corrective forces can generate wasteful distortions from which we all lose in the long run.

CHAPTER 2
Evolution of the Liability System: Trends in Law and Litigation

In recent years, the potential liability of businesses and individuals in all walks of life has expanded. This expansion has occurred both through new interpretations of old rules of law and through the introduction of radically new rules, primarily by the courts and to a lesser extent by legislatures.

This chapter will examine the trends in number of suits and size of awards and some of the major changes in law and legal interpretations that underlie these trends. Later chapters will examine the wider implications of these legal changes for our society's ability to manage risk, resolve disputes, and compensate injuries efficiently, and their effects on the price and availability of liability insurance.

Liability for personal injury has expanded from a fault-based standard to one in which a defendant can be found liable on the basis of at most a remote connection between his or her action and the injury to the plaintiff. Manufacturers can be held liable for risks that were scientifically unknowable at the time of production. Under the rule of joint and several liability, one defendant can be responsible for the full damages even if that defendant's contribution was minor, relative to that of other parties. Employees covered by workers' compensation have been allowed to sue in tort although the intent of the compensation program, which provides compensation without regard to fault, was to replace such tort suits. New and broader concepts of damages have greatly expanded payments, particularly for pain, suffering, and mental anguish.

Although the erosion of fault as a legal basis for compensation has been of primary importance in expanding the scope of liability, other developments have also played a role. The advance of scientific knowledge has permitted us to trace increasingly remote risk factors that contribute to injuries and diseases, thereby vastly expanding liability to new sources although often not permitting a precise determination of the relative role of multiple contributing factors. Implicit and sometimes explicit attempts by judges, juries, and legislators to increase incentives for injury prevention and provide more complete compensation have also been a driving force. In addition, non-economic factors, such as the desire to prove one's case and punish a guilty party, certainly play a role in many suits.

But if injury prevention and more complete compensation are the primary objectives of this expansion in legal rules and interpretations, we believe that the current drift in legal rules fails on both counts. The tort system with a rule of absolute liability is highly inefficient for purposes of both deterrence and compensation. It is also inequitable. Consequently, we believe the case for basic reform is becoming both logically and practically compelling.

TRENDS IN LITIGATION

NUMBER OF SUITS[1]

In recent years, an intense debate concerning reform of the U.S. liability system has been based in part on divergent views of the available statistics on litigation. Some analysts say that the United States is undergoing a litigation explosion; others deny the claim.

For example, the 1987 report of the U.S. Department of Justice Tort Policy Working Group noted a 758 percent increase between 1974 and 1985 in the number of product liability actions filed in federal district court, an almost threefold increase in the rate of malpractice claims per physician in the last decade, and substantial increases in tort claims filed against municipalities (e.g., a 375 percent increase in New York City between 1979 and 1983).[2]

On the other hand, a 1986 report by the National Center for State Courts found virtually no increase in tort filings in state courts between 1978 and 1984 after adjusting for population growth. The report identified a 9 percent increase in filings, which roughly parallels the 8 percent population growth in the states studied.[3] Based on these data, some have denied the existence of a litigation explosion, arguing that the sharp rise in product liability claims in federal courts may simply reflect a shifting of these claims from state to federal courts, rather than an increase in the total volume of filings.

The conclusion that emerges from a review of this and other evidence[4] is that although the aggregate number of claims has increased only moderately, there has been an enormous increase in some types of cases. The total number of tort claims shows a fairly modest rate of growth of 3.9 percent a year (or 3.0 percent after adjusting for population growth), over the 1981-1985 period. However, these figures are dominated by automobile-related claims, which have remained stable or even fallen in some states because of a decrease in auto-related injuries and the adoption of no-fault laws that remove some claims from the courts.

By contrast, there has been a rapid increase in other areas of litigation, notably product liability and, to a lesser extent, medical malpractice. Even excluding the huge surge of asbestos-related claims, there was an increase of almost 500 percent in federal court product liability suits between 1974 and 1984, and this cannot be attributed to removal of cases from state to federal courts.[5] The greatest growth has occurred in the area of so-called mass toxic torts, involving harm believed to be caused to thousands of individuals by single products. For example, between 1981 and 1986, the number of Dalkon Shield claims increased fortyfold, from 7,500 to 325,000. Over the same period, the number of asbestos claims doubled, from 16,000 to 30,000.[6] These mass toxic cases present the greatest challenge to the liability system because of the enormous complexity of the scientific, legal, administrative, and social issues they raise and the huge number of parties typically involved on both sides of such cases.

SIZE OF AWARDS

The available knowledge base for measuring trends in size of payments to plaintiffs is quite limited and the debate has been equally acrimonious. For the great majority of cases that are settled out of court, the records are dispersed among literally hundreds of insurance companies and self-insured entities, plaintiff attorneys, and some courts. There is also no central comprehensive repository of data on jury verdicts from all jurisdictions.

Evidence of trends in the size of jury awards is available for particular jurisdictions, notably Cook County, Illinois, and San Francisco, California, for the period from 1960 to 1985.[7] Although jury verdicts represent only a small fraction of all cases (less than 10 percent in product liability and medical malpractice), these verdicts are a vital indicator of all awards because they set the norms and expectations that subsequently influence both cases settled out of court and nonlitigated insurance claims.[8] Jury verdicts are also an important barometer of trends because they account for a disproportionate percentage of dollars paid out. However, because cases in which a verdict is reached tend to be atypical both in the size of the stakes and the complexity of the issues, generalizations from such data need to be made with caution. Trends in average award size can be very much affected by changes in case-load composition. For example, the trends reported below for San Francisco verdicts are certainly upwardly biased (but to an unknown degree) by the introduction of mandatory arbitration of small cases and the increase in the lower courts' jurisdictional level in California in the late 1970s.[9]

The data on jury awards from Cook County and San Francisco paint a picture of trends in awards that parallels the trends in number of suits: a reasonably stable aggregate, dominated by automobile claims, that masks dramatic increases for medical malpractice, product-related, and other business-related cases. For example, since 1960, the typical (median) award for all suits has been remarkably stable, after adjusting for inflation and other relevant factors. For product-related and medical malpractice cases, however, the inflation-adjusted median award has more than doubled.

This trend is even more pronounced in the average (mean) awards. The overall average award for all tort cases increased over 300 percent since 1960 in both Cook County and San Francisco, after adjusting for inflation. The mean award for auto cases increased less than 200 percent, but average product-related and medical malpractice awards show much larger increases (see Table 2.1).[10]

The sharper increase for mean awards than for median awards in both auto and nonauto cases reflects much-higher-percentage increases for the very highest awards than in the smaller awards. High-stakes awards now account for a very large proportion of the total money awarded. Between 1980 and 1984, million-dollar verdicts in Cook County accounted for 2.8 percent of personal injury verdicts but 65 percent of all dollars awarded; in San Francisco, they accounted for 3.8 percent of cases and 47 percent of dollars awarded.[11]

The trends referred to so far are based on cases won by the plaintiff. They do not reflect the average plaintiff's expected award, taking into account the uncertainty of the plaintiff prevailing. The percentage of tried cases that were won by the plaintiff in both jurisdictions increased from roughly 50 percent in 1960-1964 to just over 60 percent in 1980-1984.[12] Taking into account both the probability of winning and the size of the award if successful, the mean expected award for product-related cases increased in constant dollars, between 1960-1964 and 1980-1984, from $56,000 to $575,000 in San Francisco and from $76,000 to $414,000 in Cook County.[13]

Awards for punitive damages have also grown in number and size in both jurisdictions (see Table 2.2).[14] Again, there are important differences by type of case. Punitive damage awards have increased in frequency but remain relatively rare for personal injury cases brought on grounds of negligence or strict liability. Less than 6 percent of all defendants in California or Cook County who were sued on grounds of negligence or strict liability were assessed punitive damages in 1980-1984.

Measuring trends in punitive awards in these jurisdictions is tentative because of the small sample size. Punitive damages were awarded in only four product liability cases in San Francisco and two in Cook County over the twenty-five years from 1960 to 1984. The fact that three of the four cases in San Francisco occurred between 1980 and 1984 suggests an

TABLE 2.1

Trends in Jury Verdicts in San Francisco, California, and Cook County, Illinois, 1960 to 1984

(in 1984 Dollars)[a]

Type	County	Mean 1960-1964	Mean 1980-1984	Percent Change
Aggregate[b]	SF	$74,000	$302,000	308
	CC	57,000	252,000	342
Automobile	SF	46,000	131,000	185
	CC	37,000	88,000	138
Common carrier	SF	56,000	107,000	91
	CC	61,000	89,000	46
Personal injury (total)	SF	66,000	302,000	358
	CC	59,000	187,000	217
Products	SF	99,000	1,105,000	1,016
	CC	265,000	828,000	212
Malpractice	SF	125,000	1,162,000	830
	CC	52,000	1,179,000	2,167

[a]All dollar figures are adjusted for inflation by use of the Consumer Price Index.

[b]Includes business/contract cases not involving personal injury.

SOURCE: Mark A. Peterson, *Civil Juries in the 1980s: Trends in Jury Trials and Verdicts in California and Cook County, Illinois* (Santa Monica, Calif.: The RAND Corporation, R-3466-ICJ, 1987), pp. 22, 24, 35, 29, 30.

increase in frequency, from less than 1 percent of trials with compensatory liability before 1980 to 12 percent after 1980. Moreover, in some recent product liability cases, punitive damages have been awarded without a finding of willful misconduct, a trend we find very disturbing. Even more dramatic is the increase in the number and size of punitive damage awards in business tort and breach-of-contract cases, particularly in California, where almost one-third of such cases with positive compensatory awards also had punitive awards in the 1980s.[15]

Because both compensatory and punitive damage awards are frequently reduced by post-trial actions (settlements, remittiturs, and appellate court decisions), these jury verdict data overstate the amount ultimately paid to some plaintiffs. In a sample of cases from Cook County and

TABLE 2.2

Trends in Punitive Damage Awards in San Francisco, California, and Cook County, Illinois, 1960 to 1984

(in 1984 dollars)[a]

Jurisdiction and Period	Number	Percent of Trials with Compensatory Award	Median Award (thousands)	Mean Award (thousands)	Total (thousands)
Cook County:					
1960-1964	3	0.2	$ 1	$ 7	$ 20
1970-1974	25	1.2	29	62	2,000
1980-1984	75	3.9	43	729	55,000
San Francisco:					
1960-1964	14	2.0	17	166	2,000
1970-1974	36	4.6	31	209	8,000
1980-1984	51	13.6[b]	63	381	19,000

[a]All dollar amounts are adjusted for inflation.

[b]Affected by change in composition of case load, particularly growing percentage of trials involving business and contract cases and intentional torts, where punitive damage awards are most frequent.

SOURCE: Mark Peterson, Syam Sarma, and Michael Shanley, *Punitive Damages: Empirical Findings* (Santa Monica, Calif.: The RAND Corporation, R-3311-ICJ, 1987), pp. 9, 15.

a diverse set of California counties, 15 percent of jury verdicts were reduced by post-trial action; in these cases, the average cut was roughly 50 percent, from $635,000 to $335,000. Proportionately larger cuts occurred in large awards and in cases with punitive awards. The overall reduction in payouts is about 25 percent.[16] Although these post-trial actions reduced amounts ultimately received by plaintiffs in some cases, the larger original verdicts are important because they make outcomes less predictable, add to litigation costs, and often have a significant influence on out-of-court settlements.

TRENDS IN TORT LAW

Although many factors may have contributed to this dramatic increase in filings and awards, we believe that changes in legal rules governing the liability of individuals and institutions are a major contributing factor.

THE OLD REGIME: FAULT-BASED STANDARDS

Before the 1960s, the standard of liability in most personal injury cases was negligence or fault. A plaintiff could collect damages only if he or she could prove that the defendant had violated a duty of care and that the defendant's action was the cause of the plaintiff's injury. The scope of liability was further constrained by other common law doctrines. A plaintiff who was contributorily negligent (had contributed to his or her own injury) could not recover damages, even if the defendant was also negligent. If risks were obvious, the plaintiff was barred from recovering damages because it was presumed that there was a voluntary assumption of risk. Statutes of limitations curtailed the duration of liability to one or two years from the date of injury. Doctrines of governmental and charitable immunity barred suits against government entities and not-for-profit organizations such as voluntary hospitals. While these traditional doctrines were not always an absolute bar to successful tort suits, in practice they constituted very significant obstacles. Although the standard of compensable damages was full compensation, traditionally this was limited to measurable out-of-pocket costs such as lost wages and medical expenses.

In the area of product-related injuries, a plaintiff's recovery was governed chiefly by contract law rather than tort law, which traditionally governed accidents involving strangers. The notion of privity of contract applied. The purchaser of a defective product could recover from the seller with whom he was in privity of contract, under the terms of the express product warranty or implied warranty of merchantability, but could not recover directly from the manufacturer. In 1916, in *MacPherson v. Buick,* the court overrode the privity restriction and allowed a suit grounded in negligence directly against the manufacturer.[17] In the four decades following *MacPherson,* courts increasingly allowed an action for negligence to be brought by a victim not a party to the contract, but such actions were usually limited to specific products, notably foodstuffs and products that were imminently dangerous.

The first major departure from a fault-based standard of liability occurred with the workers' compensation statutes enacted in the early 1900s. These statutes were intended to remove work-related injuries from the tort system. Employers became strictly liable, regardless of fault, for injuries "arising out of or in the course of employment." Under the workers' compensation statutes, workers forfeited their right to sue in tort in return for increased certainty of compensation. An administrative agency determines awards according to a statutory formula or schedule that provides compensation for monetary but not nonmonetary loss.

In general, a fault-based standard of liability provides both equitable and efficient grounds for and limitations on claims for compensation. The notion of fault is solidly grounded in principles of justice. It also corresponds roughly to a requirement to take economically efficient levels of care. As defined by Judge Learned Hand, negligence occurs only if a defendant fails to take precautions that cost less than the damages that would be expected to occur if such precautions are not taken.[18] This weighing of costs and benefits corresponds to the economic measure of efficient investment in injury prevention.[19]

FROM FAULT TO STRICT LIABILITY

An inevitable consequence of a fault-based standard is that some unfortunate individuals who suffer injuries through no fault of another party may go uncompensated if they also lack sources of private or public insurance. A desire to expand compensation and to internalize the cost of injuries for purposes of deterrence has been among the dominant forces in the evolution of legal rules in recent years.[20] Major changes in legal rights and responsibilities have occurred, sometimes by statute but more often by judicial decisions. [21]

During the 1940s and 1950s there was further erosion of the doctrine of privity of contract, a change of profound significance because it vastly expanded the scope of potential liability of corporations, professionals, and others; undermined the ability of potential defendants to control their exposure through contractual terms; and hence undermined predictability of losses. For example, the potential liability of manufacturers now extends beyond immediate purchasers to third- and fourth-hand users of products. Accountants have been sued successfully by users of financial statements which the accountants prepared for clients. (See "Accountants' Liability," below.)

The foundation of modern products liability law was laid by the Restatement of Torts (Second) Section 402A, drafted by the American Law Institute in 1965. The majority of states subsequently adopted 402A by judicial decision, a few adopted it by statute.[22] How far the restatement simply codified an existing trend in judicial decisions[23] and how far it reflected an innovative influence of a few highly respected legal scholars is an important issue still under debate.[24] The fact that it was adopted with so little opposition may reflect widespread concurrence; but it may also reflect failure to anticipate its far-reaching effects, which even the drafters of the restatement probably did not anticipate.

The restatement approach, if strictly interpreted, falls far short of absolute liability. Liability for a product-related injury was to occur only where a product was found to be both defective and unreasonably dangerous. These vague principles have been interpreted by subsequent courts to yield three bases for liability: a manufacturing defect (occasional deviation from standard specifications within a production run), a design defect (which makes all items of a production run equally defective), and a defect in warning or labeling of potential hazards.

In theory, a strict liability standard (with appropriate defenses) can

---

ACCOUNTANTS' LIABILITY

In *H. Rosenblum, Inc. v. Adler* (1983), accountants were held liable to stockholders of a corporation whose financial statements had been audited by the accountants. This case greatly expanded the types of third parties who can sue and recover damages from accountants and contributed to several similar decisions.[25] However, the original standard of accountants' liability set forth in 1931 in *Ultramares v. Touche Ross* was recently reaffirmed in *Credit Alliance Corp. v. Arthur Andersen & Co.* (1985), in which the New York Court of Appeals refused to hold the accountants liable to third parties without a relationship to the accountant approaching that of privity.[26] Recently passed privity legislation in Illinois, Kansas, and Arkansas will obligate courts in those states to apply a *Credit Alliance* standard. Thus, although the overall trend appears to be toward increased liability for accountants, standards of liability now vary, depending upon the jurisdiction.

provide efficient incentives for risk management in some cases;[27] but in practice it can generate very inefficient results. Strict liability in practice has proved imprecise, unpredictable, and costly to implement, particularly in cases of design defect and failure to warn. For example, in claims alleging design defects, courts have attempted to weigh risks and utilities of alternative product designs. In principle, an accurate weighing of costs and benefits could yield an economically efficient standard of liability. In practice, the issue readily degenerates into a conflict between expert witnesses over complex technological feasibilities that existed many years earlier, to be resolved ultimately by juries, often with the wisdom of hindsight. Moreover, a strict liability standard cannot, even in principle, provide efficient incentives for risk management in circumstances where efficient risk control requires care by multiple parties, particularly product users as well as product manufacturers, unless defenses of contributory negligence and assumption of risk are allowed.[28]

The rejection by some courts of the state-of-the-art defense and the retroactive application of new technological and legal standards effectively abandons an attempt at an efficient deterrence basis for liability and substitutes an unprincipled search for a deep-pocket (wealthy) defendant from whom to obtain compensation. In *Beshada v. Johns-Manville* (1982), for example, the New Jersey Supreme Court held that even if the danger at issue was scientifically unknowable at time of production, defendant asbestos manufacturers were still liable for having failed to warn of an unknowable risk.[29]

The rejection of the state-of-the-art defense and the application of standards of absolute liability are particularly devastating to the goals of efficient risk management and insurability when combined with long statutes of limitations (time allowed to sue), as apply in many product-related and medical malpractice cases. For contracts and most tort disputes, limitations are often set at one or two years, reflecting a compromise between the desire to give plaintiffs reasonable time to assemble their case and the desire to protect potential defendants from indefinite exposure. Short statutes appear particularly unfair to plaintiffs in the case of injuries that lie latent for many years (e.g., some birth defects and cancers). Courts and legislatures have therefore ruled that for product-related and medical malpractice claims, the statute of limitation runs from the discovery of the injury, rather than from the action of the defendant that allegedly caused the injury. Such discovery-based statutes clearly provide better protection to plaintiffs, but they expose producers to the risk of retroactive application of new standards, as scientific advances develop new and improved technologies or allow us to measure minute exposures to numerous substances that may have toxic effects. Equally important, new legal standards of liability and compensable damages are applied in situations where such liability could not have been anticipated at the time of the injurious act. We believe such retroactive application of new technological and legal standards serves no useful deterrent function; on the contrary, it may overdeter. It can also be inequitable and tends to create an uninsurable risk.[30]

EROSION OF CAUSE AS A NECESSARY CONDITION FOR LIABILITY

Proof that the defendant's action was the proximate or immediate cause of the plaintiff's injury was one of the essential steps in proving negligence. The notion of cause, a concept that has absorbed philosophers and lawyers for centuries, has become even more elusive with modern technologies and increasingly complex chains of social interaction. It is now possible to detect minute levels of innumerable substances which may raise the probability that an individual will contract cancer or other diseases. However, it is currently – and for the foreseeable future is likely to remain – often impossible to establish conclusively that a particular substance caused a particular individual's cancer. Our understanding of the complex interactions of environmental, genetic, and behavioral factors in causing cancer is still in its infancy. At most, we can say that certain carcinogens increase the probability of contracting cancer, but estimates of specific dose-response effects are often necessarily based on tenuous extrapolations to humans from tests on laboratory animals. Even where the carcinogenic effects of a particular substance are reasonably well established, it may be impossible to identify which manufacturer produced the batch to which a particular plaintiff was exposed.

The inability of the legal system and its concept of cause to handle these new scientific and social realities lies at the heart of the new generation of toxic tort cases, which account for a large fraction of current litigation and a potentially expanding volume in the future.[31] Faced with the plaintiffs' inability to determine which of several DES manufacturers produced the particular tablets alleged to have caused cancer in a particular individual, a California court held that if it were proved that DES caused the injury, DES manufacturers would be liable in proportion to their market share.[32] Although market-share liability without proof of cause assures compensation, at least as long as some producers stay in the market, it undermines incentives for manufacturers to improve the safety of their products because their liability depends on the care exercised by their competitors as well as on their own care.

The elusiveness of proof of cause appears in many of the mass toxic cases. At the conclusion of the Agent Orange litigation, Judge Jack

Weinstein declared to the plaintiffs' lawyers: "In no case have you shown causality for the health effects alleged." Nevertheless, the case was settled for approximately $180 million in damages. The profound problems raised by these cases is aptly summarized by Peter Huber:

> None of the plaintiffs in Love Canal, Jackson Township, Woburn, Triana, or Times Beach [five recent mass toxic tort cases] had a strong positive case linking cause and effect [of toxic pollution], nor could the defendants irrefutably prove the negative. Indeed, the only convincing defense in lawsuits of this kind involves a demonstration that some other factor or set of factors accounts for the plaintiffs' illnesses and complaints, a contention that always presents equally difficult questions of proof.[33]

JOINT AND SEVERAL LIABILITY

The rule of joint and several liability originally applied primarily to cases where multiple defendants acted in concert and the negligence of any one alone was sufficient to cause the plaintiff's injury. In such cases, the plaintiff could collect 100 percent of damages from any one of the parties found liable, who might then seek contribution from the others in a separate suit.

Recently, joint and several liability has been applied not only where defendants acted in concert but also where it is impossible to show the percentage of fault of any single defendant. Aside from obvious questions of equity, such a rule can seriously distort efficient incentives for risk management and destroy insurability if parties with assets or adequate insurance are likely to end up paying a disproportionate share of the award. The rule also creates incentives for plaintiffs to name deep-pocket defendants in suits because even if they are found to have contributed only marginally to the injury, they may be liable for the entire award.

In addition to its expansion by the courts in product cases, the concept of joint and several liability is applied under the Superfund legislation to cleanup of hazardous waste sites. All parties that have contributed to a particular waste site are considered jointly and severally liable for the entire cost of cleanup. This ruling is a major factor in the collapse of the market for environmental liability insurance.

BREACH OF THE WORKERS' COMPENSATION BAR TO TORT SUITS

Since the 1960s, the sole remedy principle of workers' compensation has been undermined. Suits against third-party manufacturers (i.e., suppliers of products used in the workplace, by workers or their employers) were the first tort actions brought for work-related injuries and are still by far the most numerous. A more limited number of suits by workers against their own employers have been allowed on novel grounds of dual capacity (as manufacturer of products used in the workplace, as well as employer) or willful misconduct.

Many of these work-related tort suits are for occupational diseases rather than injuries. Many occupational diseases are particularly hard to handle within the confines of the workers' compensation system because of the difficulty of proving the contribution of occupational exposure to diseases of everyday life such as cancer, especially where there is a long delay between exposure to the toxic substance and manifestation of the disease. Also, workers' compensation benefit levels are less than potential tort awards.[34] By 1982, the Manville Corporation alone had 16,500 asbestos suits pending, and over 100,000 additional suits against the company are anticipated. Paul MacAvoy has estimated that the ultimate liability of the asbestos industry will be $38.2 billion; but depending on the incidence of the disease and trends in litigation, the cost could be as low as $7.6 billion or as high as $87.1 billion. Thus, the cost could exceed the net worth of the asbestos industry ($25.6 billion) and even of the entire property and liability segment of the insurance industry ($52 billion).[35] The unprecedented confusion, expense of litigation, and extent of unfunded liabilities that surround the asbestos claims arise in part because the risks were not scientifically well established at the time of exposure; further, at that time, any work-related claim would have been handled through workers' compensation, not through tort.[36] Because the tort liability was unforeseen, liability insurance contracts were worded in a way that left the coverage of long-latent diseases ambiguous, and insufficient premiums were collected to cover the liability that has subsequently emerged.

COMPENSABLE DAMAGES
The intent of tort damage awards is full compensation or to "make the plaintiff whole." Traditionally, this meant payment of measurable out-of-pocket losses due to wage loss and medical expense. Some of the recent growth in awards may be due to more accurate measurement of these losses.[37] But in addition, over time, the categories of compensable damages have been expanded to include such nonpecuniary losses as pain and suffering, loss of consortium (the fellowship and company of a spouse), and mental anguish. The absence of any compelling rules for quantifying these unmeasurable losses and determining appropriate compensation for these essentially uncompensable losses is a major source of unpredictability of liability awards.

NEW DUTIES WITHIN OLD RULES: EXPANSION OF NEGLIGENCE ACTIONS

Explicit adoption of rules of strict liability is by no means a necessary condition of expansion of liability. Within the rubric of negligence law, the responsibilities of individuals in all walks of life has been vastly expanded through court decisions.[38] For example, medical malpractice claims have grown at a rate of 10 percent a year over the past decade,[39] without major explicit departures from the negligence standard of liability. This suggests that simply restoring a fault-based rule of liability in product cases as recommended by some commentators,[40] is by itself unlikely to restore predictability or stem the tide of litigation.

Because any rule of liability necessarily leaves considerable discretion to the courts, the effect of any rule in practice depends critically on how it is applied by the courts. Many observers of the tort system believe that judges are granting increasing latitude to juries and that this generates expanded liability within rules that are formally unchanged. We believe that judges' increasing latitude is certainly a factor. It is also possible that the fundamental forces driving the expansion of liability may lie deeper. The adoption of legal standards of strict and sometimes absolute liability may be merely symptoms of more profound underlying causes.

IMPACT OF MODERN SOCIAL AND TECHNOLOGICAL CHANGES

The role of social and technological forces in driving the evolution of modern tort law are not yet fully understood.[41] Certainly, consumer expectations seem to have risen along with incomes. Increasing government responsibility for individual well-being may also have created an atmosphere in the United States in which potential liability could expand with little opposition, although countries with more advanced welfare states have not had a parallel expansion.

At the same time that social forces have taken effect, the growing complexity of product design and mass production and distribution systems has undermined the ability of traditional contract law to appropriately handle relationships between manufacturers and consumers.[42] Another interesting hypothesis is that the unique procedural rules of the U.S. legal system have facilitated the doctrinal expansion.[43]

Many scholars argue that modern technologies have undermined the moral force of the notion of fault as a basis of liability. The adoption of strict or absolute liability has been grounded on the alternative notion of internalizing costs to parties in a position to take measures to reduce risks. In simple cases where control of risks is within the hands of one party, this argument has powerful intellectual force. However, it breaks down in cases of multiple contributing parties, which constitute the overwhelming majority of cases. In cases with multiple contributing parties, a standard of strict or absolute liability violates principles of efficient incentives for injury prevention by ignoring the role of the consumer in preventing product-related injuries, the role of the employee in preventing work-related injuries, and the excessive burden placed on tort defendants when they are held liable for injuries and diseases with multiple contributing causes, including life-style and genetic factors. Thus, we believe that to the extent the current trend in liability rules is inspired by a search for efficient management of risk, it is defective in application.

The desire to provide compensation and distribute losses is often identified as the single most important factor underlying the evolution of modern tort law. Just how closely the expansion of liability by courts and legislatures is linked to the availability of liability insurance is hard to document.[44] But again, a principle that is well founded in intent is violated in implementation because the tort system has evolved in directions that have made it inefficient and inequitable as a system of compensation (see Chapter 6). The costs of using the tort system are several times higher than the costs of other systems of compensation; the tort system is often less fair to similarly situated victims (see Chapter 4).

ROLE OF TORT LAW IN OUR SYSTEMS OF INJURY PREVENTION AND COMPENSATION

Improving safety and health is a major goal of any society and indeed seems to acquire increasing importance as higher levels of economic well-being are achieved. But at some level, the social cost of additional risk reduction begins to rise very sharply. Because we do not have unlimited resources, we are always faced with a trade-off between risk reduction and other social goals, such as economic growth, job creation, and maintaining international competitiveness. The challenge we face in this situation is twofold: to achieve the best balance between risk reduction and these other social goals and to produce whatever level of safety and health we choose in the most cost-effective manner. The search for cost-effectiveness must also apply to our institutions for delivering compensation and resolving disputes.

In evaluating the liability system, it is important to view it as one among several approaches to achieving these goals of risk management, compensation, and dispute resolution. Market incentives and public regulation play vital roles in the control of risk. For purposes of compensation, private health and disability insurance, social insurance, and workers' compensation far exceed the tort system in magnitude; they also pay more promptly, with greater equity, and cost less to operate (see Chapter 6). Because none of these alternative systems are perfect, there is a role for the liability system. Our goals should be to improve the cost-effectiveness of each of these component systems of deterrence and compensation, and to ensure their efficient integration into an overall system for dealing with risk.

CHAPTER 3
Liability Insurance: Problems of Cost and Availability

In recent years, there has been a tremendous increase in the price and and lack of availability of liability insurance. Some have called it a "crisis"; others say this is too strong a word. But it is clear to most observers that the sharp increases in insurance premiums and the lack of availability of insurance coverage have presented major problems for many sectors of society. For many businesses, municipalities, professionals, corporate directors and officers, and not-for-profit entities, the cost of coverage more than doubled within the space of one or two years. Many have been able to obtain insurance only with higher deductibles, exclusionary clauses, or limits on coverage, and some have been unable to obtain insurance on any terms.[1]

Three factors appear to have contributed to this upheaval in insurance markets.[2] First and most fundamental is the upward trend in the frequency and severity of claims and litigation expense. Second, adjustment to these trends has been exacerbated by the insurance underwriting cycle, in which periods of "soft" markets with very low rates and ample availability are followed by "tight" markets with abrupt rate hikes and rationing of coverage. Third, the unpredictability of costs has caused the recent cycle to be far more extreme than previous cycles, particularly for the long-tailed lines, such as commercial general liability and professional liability. In these long-tailed lines, the insurer's ultimate liability is not known for many years after the policy is written because claims may be filed many years after the act causing the alleged injury.[3] Shorter-tailed lines, such as private passenger automobile insurance, have for many years experienced more moderate cyclical movements in prices and profits, often linked to interest rate changes or price regulation and subsequent corrections.[4] The distinguishing feature of this crisis in long-tailed commercial lines appears to be increased uncertainty in predicting future costs, due to both unanticipated trends in tort law and novel interpretations of insurance contracts.

Since 1986, the atmosphere of crisis has subsided. Prices have steadied, and insurance is more widely available.[5] However, pockets of unavailability remain, notably for pollution coverage, and rates are still at much higher levels than before the crisis. Moreover, the problems of cost and availability were resolved in part by shifting risk from insurers to policyholders. Policyholders have accepted policies with higher deductibles and lower policy limits (the maximum the insurer promises to pay over the term of the policy), and have resorted to self-insurance mechanisms such as captives, risk-retention groups, and mutuals. There has also been some shift to a claims-made policy form, which shifts from the insurer to the insured the risk associated with claims filed after the policy period.

Under all these changes, policyholders retain more risk than under the more traditional form of occurrence coverage purchased from commercial companies. Because the underlying exposure of potential defendants has increased rather than contracted in recent years, such a reduction in the spreading of risk through insurance markets represents at best an accommodation to the problem rather than a solution. This accommodation is symptomatic of the fundamental difficulties created by current trends in tort law for the operation of insurance markets.

This chapter reviews the dimensions of the recent crisis in cost and availability. We then discuss the causes of the crisis, including trends in claim costs, the insurance cycle, and uncertainty in pricing when liability is of long duration. Next, we turn to a review of the market and regulatory responses to this crisis. We conclude that price increases and reduced availability of insurance may be recurrent phenomena in liability insurance markets, as long as tort law is subject to the unpredictable changes described in Chapter 2. Until the problems in the tort system are addressed, suppliers and buyers of liability insurance will remain vulnerable to major market disruptions.

The acute experience of directors' and officers' insurance illustrates the problems that have arisen to varying degrees in most areas of general liability insurance. (See "Directors' and Officers' Liability Insurance," pages 34-35.)

Because our primary concern is with the role of the liability system in deterrence and compensation of injuries, this chapter does not attempt to provide a complete analysis of the liability insurance crisis. But an evaluation of the liability system cannot ignore the interaction between liability rules and liability insurance markets. Having access to a stable supply of liability insurance at reasonable rates has become a necessary part of doing business for most corporations, professionals, and other entities that routinely interact with the general public. But as long as liability rules remain unpredictable, the supply of liability insurance may be unstable, and prices will remain high. In expanding liability, courts

---

DIRECTORS' AND OFFICERS' LIABILITY INSURANCE

The experience of directors' and officers' (D&O) liability insurance clearly illustrates the increase in claim costs and how unpredictable legal rules undermine insurance markets. D&O is a subline of general liability coverage that insures corporate officers and directors against claims brought by shareholders, employees, consumers, clients, or businesses. Shareholder suits are the most frequent type of claims.[6] There are good data on D&O insurance from the biannual surveys of business organizations published by the Wyatt Company.[7]

For the largest firms in the survey, those listed in the top 1,000 by *Fortune* magazine, the probability of one or more D&O suits during the prior nine years almost doubled from 21 percent in 1978 to 41 percent in 1986. Claim frequency (defined as the total number of claims per participating firm during a nine year period) increased even more dramatically, from 3.1 claims for every 10 firms in 1978 to 9.1 in 1986. The average cost per paid claim, excluding legal expenses, rose from $877,361 in 1980 to $1,988,200 in 1986. Even when there is no payout to the claimant (over half of all claims), there are legal costs. Average defense costs in 1986 were estimated at $592,000 (including open claims), up from $318,255 in 1980.

Between 1985 and 1986, over half the firms surveyed experienced premium increases of over 200 percent, but the effective rate of increase is much greater because new policies have higher deductibles and provide less coverage. Based on a premium index that incorporates these changes in coverage, the cost of coverage increased from an index value of 100 in 1974 to 682 in 1986. In addition to traditional exclusions for losses caused by dishonesty or personal profit, policies now commonly exclude losses related to mergers and acquisitions, tender-offer resistance, and securities transactions. These exclusions tend to eliminate from coverage shareholder claims which are a major reason for purchasing insurance. Extended-discovery provisions have also been reduced, which limits

have assumed – incorrectly – that costs imposed on defendants can be readily spread through liability insurance. Insurance markets cannot be expected to function smoothly when liability rules and judicial interpretation of liability insurance contracts are unpredictable. In such circumstances, liability becomes a very imperfect and costly mechanism for spreading risk.

the policyholders' protection for claims filed after the policy period.

This crisis in D&O insurance reflects many of the same factors that have plagued commercial liability in general, but some factors are either unique or particularly severe for D&O.

First, business conditions in the 1980s, particularly the wave of mergers and acquisitions, the increase in public offerings, and the rash of business failures, have contributed to the increase in claims. Defining liability for financial losses raises difficult questions because most financial decisions involve judgment in the absence of perfect information. So far, courts have for the most part applied the traditional business judgment rule, which gives directors who are informed and act in good faith the benefit of the doubt for their decisions in duty of care cases.[8] It is critical that courts steadfastly apply the business judgment rule.

Second, in their reading of D&O insurance contracts, courts have frequently rewritten the contracts to the disadvantage of the insurer.[9] Courts have also construed D&O policies as placing the risk of all unspecified perils on insurers. The recent spate of cases in which banks have directly sued officers and directors for negligently approving what, with hindsight, were bad loans in order to recover from the D&O insurance policy illustrates this tendency. Such claims could not have been anticipated by insurers because a corporation suing its employees for negligence was theretofore unthinkable.[10] The traditional insurance law maxim – that ambiguity in the contract is construed against the insurer – is sensible in the case of a standard form contract purchased by a relatively uninformed individual. But in the D&O context, where professional brokers negotiate individualized policies, such protection is unnecessary and is indeed counterproductive. If insurers cannot bound their liability, they cannot price it accurately, and that makes a risk uninsurable. The response in D&O insurance has been even broader policy exclusions, limited availability, particularly for excess limits, and higher premiums.

DIMENSIONS OF THE LIABILITY INSURANCE CRISIS

Since 1984, there have been sharp rate increases for both general liability insurance (which includes product and other liability coverages for businesses, not-for-profit organizations, municipalities, and other entities) and for professional liability insurance for physicians, accountants, and other professionals. Because there are literally thousands of subclassifications within the commercial liability lines, each with its own rate schedule, no overall figure is meaningful. However, rate increases of 300 percent or more over the space of one or two years have been reported for such diverse groups as municipalities, public transit operators, toy manufacturers, machine tool manufacturers, corporate directors and officers, accountants, architects and engineers, and day-care centers, to name only a few.[11]

Although these extreme hikes were relatively rare, most policyholders faced very substantial rate increases. Moreover, the increase in premiums paid often understated the increase in costs for a given level of coverage because policy limits were reduced in many cases. Even the increase in rates for given policy limits understates the increase in the cost of a given level of real financial protection because higher limits of coverage are needed to offset the increase in exposure of policyholders.

In general, the premium increases are not nearly as dramatic when viewed over a longer time frame. In the late 1970s and early 1980s, premiums were relatively stable and, indeed, for some lines declined in real terms.[12] Most of the rate increase over the decade was compressed into two or three years. In the case of medical malpractice, despite annual premium increases of between 25 and 40 percent since 1984, over the period 1976 through 1984 as a whole, malpractice premiums for physicians in the lower risk medical specialties have risen at roughly the same rate as other components of the medical price index.[13] The *New York Report of the Governor's Advisory Commission on Liability Insurance* reached a similar conclusion for other insureds.[14]

However, the longer-term view understates the disruptive effect of the price increases. In the short run, commercial enterprises cannot readily pass large liability insurance cost increases on as higher prices, nor can municipalities obtain offsetting budget increases nor charitable organizations obtain additional donations. Thus, in the short run, suppliers of goods and services bear the cost through lower net revenues or exposure to uninsured loss. Some share of the cost will be shifted to the public through price increases; where this is not feasible, goods and services may be withdrawn. In the longer run, provided the rate of insurance price increase modifies, the production of goods and services will resume and higher liability insurance rates will be passed on to consumers through higher product prices. However, to the extent the increase in liability applies retroactively to goods and services already marketed, the cost falls on producers and their insurers and cannot be passed through to consumers.

In the shorter term, the reduced availability of insurance has been at least as disruptive as the increased cost. Although total lack of insurance availability has been relatively rare, policy cancellation or nonrenewal and difficulties finding alternative sources of coverage have been common.[15] Most prevalent has been partial unavailability, with policyholders being unable to obtain the limits of coverage they would prefer to purchase. Of course the distinction between a problem of affordability and availability is partly a question of perspective. Very high premiums may make coverage effectively unavailable for some policyholders, even if such coverage could be obtained, perhaps only after extensive search in the surplus lines market.

Lack of availability has been and remains a particularly severe problem for pollution coverage.[16] The issue of whether coverage for gradual pollution was included in previously issued general liability policies providing sudden and accidental pollution coverage or only in separate policies providing environmental impairment liability coverage (EIL) is the subject of continuing litigation. However, the trend now by insurers is to exclude virtually all pollution coverage from their new general liability policies. Very few insurance firms are currently providing EIL coverage.[17]

Although both theory and survey evidence suggest that price of liability insurance is currently a more serious and widespread problem than lack of availability, regulation of either rates or solvency margins could create severe shortages of coverage. Regulation of rates below levels considered adequate by insurers was a major factor in the massive withdrawal of commercial insurers from the medical malpractice insurance market in 1975, and it remains responsible for the continued absence in some states of a market in which insurers voluntarily write coverage.[18] Although general commercial liability insurance has so far been less subject to prior approval of rates, it could become a more significant issue in the future.

CAUSES OF THE INSURANCE CRISIS

RISING COST OF INDEMNITY AND LITIGATION EXPENSE

The fundamental cause of the rising cost of liability insurance is the increasing cost of both components of the risk covered by insurance: payments to plaintiffs and litigation expense.

38

The most readily available measure of trends in total costs is insurance-incurred losses, including the costs of handling claims (loss-adjustment expense). As shown in Figure 3.1, losses incurred on general liability policies rose steadily from roughly $3 billion in 1975 to $8 billion in 1983 but increased sharply to $14 billion in 1985.[19] One study estimates that losses incurred grew at a rate of over 40 percent a year between 1984 and 1986.[20] Critics point to the fact that losses incurred include a large measure of subjective estimate by insurers. Technically, losses incurred in any year include those actually paid plus the change in loss reserves from the previous year for claims that have been reported but not closed and for claims that have not been filed – the so-called incurred but not reported (IBNR) reserves. Critics have argued that losses, especially IBNR losses, have been artificially inflated in order to justify the price hikes sought. The accuracy of recently reported insurance losses will not be finally resolved for many years because delays in claim filing and claim disposition mean actual losses from the mid-1980s will not be known for several decades.[21] Several analysts who have attempted to assess the accuracy of insurance reserves have concluded that as of 1985, insurers may still have been underreserved for the accident years 1980 through 1985, with the possible

FIGURE 3.1

Trends in Premiums and Losses: General Liability

Billions of Dollars

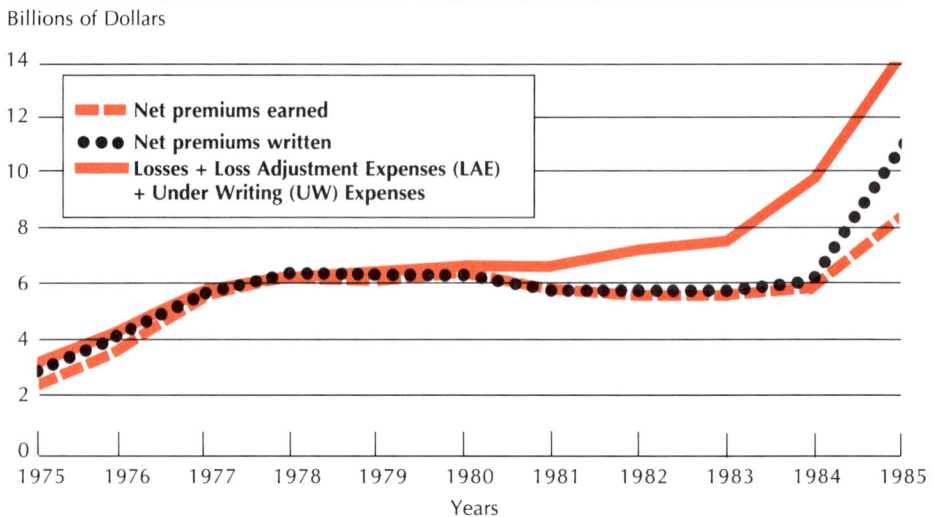

Legend:
- Net premiums earned
- Net premiums written
- Losses + Loss Adjustment Expenses (LAE) + Under Writing (UW) Expenses

Years: 1975 1976 1977 1978 1979 1980 1981 1982 1983 1984 1985

SOURCE: Best's Insurance Management Report, December 30,1985, as reported in U.S. Department of Justice, *Report of the Tort Policy Working Group on the Causes, Extent, and Policy Implications of the Current Crisis in Insurance Availability and Affordability* (Washington, D.C.: U.S. Government Printing Office, February 1986), p. 24.

exception of 1985.[22] There are also obvious disadvantages to insurers in overstating losses. Market valuation of company stock may be adversely affected. Ability to raise premiums may not increase and could even decrease.[23] Even if data on paid claims were available, such data would be of limited value because the experience to date for the most recent policy years provides a very incomplete picture of ultimate losses because of the long tail of claims.

With these limitations in mind, Figure 3.2 shows trends in the number of claims in various size classes, from under $25,000 to over $250,000, for all municipal classes for the years 1980 to 1984, as reported by the Insurance Services Office.[24] These data show that the rate of increase in number of claims accelerated sharply after 1982, with by far the most dramatic rise for the largest category (over $250,000), where there was almost an eightfold increase over the four-year period.[25]

The cost to insurers of handling claims adds roughly 30 percent over and above loss payments to plaintiffs. Loss adjustment expense and year-to-year volatility of this expense has grown in recent years.[26] Litigation over policy interpretation and bad-faith claims against insurers adds further to total overhead costs.

FIGURE 3.2

**Trends in Number of Claims, by Size of Class:
New York Municipalities 1980-1984**

Index (12/31/80 = 1.00)

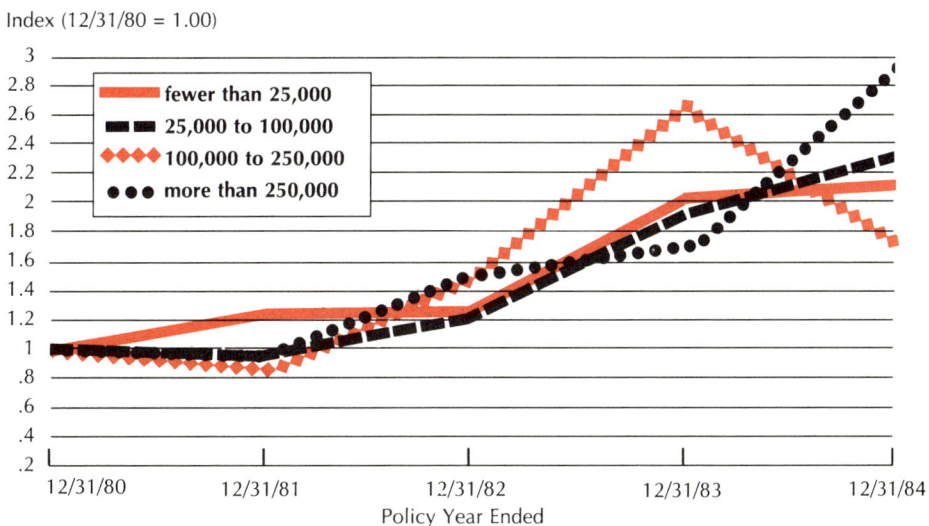

Legend:
— fewer than 25,000
■ ■ 25,000 to 100,000
◆◆◆ 100,000 to 250,000
●●● more than 250,000

Policy Year Ended

SOURCE: *Insuring Our Future: Report of the Governor's Advisory Commission on Liability Insurance* (New York: April 7, 1986).

UNDERWRITING CYCLE

Adjustment to the upward trends in the frequency and severity of claims and of litigation expense has been exacerbated by the insurance underwriting cycle. The property/liability insurance industry has for several decades exhibited a loosely cyclical pattern of prices, underwriting profits, and return on equity. On the pricing side, periods of sharp premium increase and limited availability in some lines are followed by periods of stable or falling premium rates and ample availability. This is mirrored by cycles in underwriting profits[27] and return on equity.[28] The most recent cycle of the early 1980s has been longer, and the peaks and troughs of price and profits have been more extreme than usual, particularly for long-tailed commercial lines.

The causes of this apparent cyclical pattern of insurance prices, particularly the extreme recent cycle, are still not fully understood. Lack of competition is not a particularly plausible explanation.[29] The large number of firms, low concentration, and ease of entry indicate that the structure of the property/liability insurance industry is very unlikely to support non-competitive behavior. This is particularly true in the commercial lines, where the feasibility of self-insurance and formation of mutuals, captive insurers, and risk-retention groups acts as an added competitive constraint on the commercial insurance industry.[30]

Interest rates are one factor contributing to fluctuations in insurance prices and reported underwriting profits in long-tailed lines. High interest rates tend to attract new capital into the industry, putting increased competitive pressure on prices. In addition, insurance premium rates move inversely with interest rates, reflecting the fact that insurers earn investment income over the period between collection of premium and payout on claims. The longer the payout period on claims the greater this interest sensitivity of premiums. When interest rates are high relative to the expected rate of inflation of claim costs, insurers reduce premiums. This is often called cash flow underwriting and interpreted as if companies discount insurance prices simply to obtain cash to pursue lucrative investment opportunities. But, for the most part, the pricing discounts in response to high interest rates reflect competitive pressures to pass on the expected investment income to policyholders.[31] However, although interest sensitivity of premiums can explain some fluctuations in insurance prices, it cannot explain the recent rate hikes of 300 percent or the lack of availability of some coverages.

Another factor that has contributed to price volatility is the difficulty in making accurate cost forecasts when legal rules and interpretations are continually changing. For any line of insurance, the price must be set before the costs are known. In lines with only brief delays in filing and paying claims, the experience on the prior year's policies provides a current and reasonably accurate basis for pricing. But for a line with long delays in filing and disposition of claims, the most current fully mature policy year may be at least ten years old.[32] When pricing a policy in 1985, the 1975 experience cannot provide an accurate guide if liability exposure is changing.

Longer-tailed lines need not present a problem if the loss distribution is either stable over time or undergoing gradual or predictable change. Actuarial methods are used to develop immature experience, estimate trends, and project future losses. Although some authors have suggested that these techniques could lead to profit cycles,[33] it seems unlikely that this is a major cause of persistent underwriting cycles; competitive pressures would surely lead firms to abandon techniques that result in systematic forecasting errors. It is also unlikely that flawed actuarial methods would cause price shocks of several hundred percent and lack of availability of coverage.

Fluctuations in insurer capital and surplus that result directly from unexpected losses also contribute to insurance cycles. In 1984, huge unanticipated losses on past policies resulted in an unprecedented loss of insurer capital, masked to some degree by gains on the investment side of the business. Shrinking capacity in the worldwide reinsurance market further limited the ability of primary insurers to take on new liability exposures.[34]

Insurers hold capital to offset unexpected losses. When this buffer capital has been eroded, insurers require higher premium rates in order to keep the risk of insolvency down to an acceptable level and may cut back the coverage they offer in the highest risk lines. At that very high price, the policyholder may prefer to self-insure entirely or at least to retain a larger fraction of the risk through a higher deductible or lower limits of coverage, creating the pockets of unavailability that have been observed.[35]

In the longer run, as existing insurers' capital is replenished and new firms or self-insurance mechanisms enter the market, premiums fall, and availability increases until another major unanticipated surge of losses occurs. But as long as changes in tort law and the interpretation of insurance contracts remain volatile, insurers are subject to large, unanticipated losses that cannot be averaged out over policyholders. These shocks deplete insurer surplus and translate into shocks in prices and availability of coverage for the riskiest activities and levels of coverage.

In addition to the voluntary reductions in coverage that may be induced by an unexpectedly large loss of insurer surplus, solvency regulations may induce further withdrawal from high-risk lines. Regulators monitor premium-to-surplus ratios as a measure of leverage and hence as one among several indicators of insurer solvency.[36] Regulators and rating agencies become concerned if an insurer's premium-to-surplus ratio reaches 3 to 1. If strictly enforced, such a ceiling on the allowable premium-to-surplus ratio in effect sets an implicit price ceiling that could deter the insurer from implementing the rate increases necessary to assure availability following a large underwriting loss and shock to surplus.[37] But since premium-to-surplus ratios are not rigidly enforced, particularly when fluctuations in the ratio are industry-wide and clearly related to the underwriting cycle, it seems more plausible that voluntary rather than regulatory constraints have been the primary cause of rationing coverage in unpredictable lines.

UNPREDICTABILITY OF FUTURE COSTS

Insurance losses have not only risen in magnitude but have also apparently become much less predictable – although this is necessarily very hard to document.[38] As we described in Chapter 2, the scope of corporate liability has expanded with the shift from negligence first to a narrow definition of strict liability and now to a broader notion of absolute liability in some cases. Each expansion of liability for losses beyond the control of the insured undermines the predictability of claim frequency. For example, judicial decisions that are based explicitly on the public purpose of providing compensation to injured parties can be used to justify virtually unlimited liability of defendants. It has also been used to nullify attempts by insurers to limit their exposure through exclusion clauses in the insurance contract. In *Summit Associates Inc. v. Liberty Mutual,* the New Jersey Superior Court ruled that consideration of broader public policy overrode literal interpretation of the insurance contract.[39] Moreover, under occurrence-based insurance contracts, insurers are exposed to a risk of indefinite duration that reflects the indefinite duration of liability of policy holders under discovery-based statutes of limitations.

This unpredictability of claim frequency is exacerbated by unpredictability of size of awards as long as there are no limits on the amounts that can be awarded, particularly for pain and suffering and punitive damages. The evidence on jury verdicts suggests that the most dramatic increases in awards have occurred in the very high-stakes cases (see Chapter 2). Although they are only a small percentage of all cases, these large cases account for a very large fraction of the total dollars paid out and hence exert powerful influence over the price insurers must charge for coverage. Moreover, higher standards of payments for high-stakes cases may feed back into higher payments for the majority of lower-stakes cases and increased claim frequency if claimants anticipate a higher payoff to filing a claim.

The shift toward absolute liability, the dramatic growth in awards, the judicial reinterpretations of insurance contracts, and the liabilities created by the Superfund legislation could not have been fully anticipated. Failure to anticipate these and other expansions of liability contributed to the underpricing of insurance in the early 1980s and the subsequent need for large corrective premium increases.[40] Thus, as long as judicial standards and the interpretation of liability insurance contracts are unstable, policy-holders are at risk of large swings in price and availability of coverage.

Moreover, unpredictability of standards of liability and size of awards has created a type of risk that cannot be readily diversified through the insurance mechanism. The basic principle of insurance is that, through the law of large numbers, an insurer can spread risk by pooling a large number of independent events. If the underlying distribution is stable over time, the mean loss for the group as a whole can be accurately predicted. This mechanism breaks down when unstable standards of compensation and legal rules of liability create a sociolegal risk that tends to affect large classes of risks equally, undermining the principle of diversification through pooling risks that are independent.[41] For example, a single adverse ruling regarding liabilities for design defect or failure to warn may lead to a surge of claims from other users of the product. A change in the interpretation of insurance contracts may expand the insurer's liability on all prior policies. The longer the insurer's exposure under the policy, the greater the range of possible changes within the term of the policy and the higher the premium the insurer will have to charge. Thus, sociolegal risk raises the average cost of coverage over the cycle, in addition to amplifying the magnitude of the cycle. A shift from the occurrence policy form to claims-made and an increase in self-insurance are rational responses to an increase in this nondiversifiable sociolegal risk.[42]

RESPONSES TO THE INSURANCE CRISIS

Private insurance markets have adjusted to the crisis in several ways. In addition, government agencies and legislatures in some states have increased the regulation of rates, increased data reporting requirements, and have required the formation of residual market mechanisms to assure availability of insurance to persons unable to obtain coverage.

SWITCH FROM OCCURRENCE TO CLAIMS-MADE

Until recently, occurrence coverage was the most common form of commercial and professional insurance. An occurrence policy covers all claims arising out of incidents occurring in the policy year, regardless of when in the future the claims are filed, thereby providing the greatest protection to the policyholder. In response to the medical malpractice crisis of 1975, most insurers switched to the claims-made form for medical providers. Claims-made has also become the standard insurance policy offered to attorneys and to corporate directors and officers, and the crisis of the mid-1980s led to the introduction of the claims-made form for some high-risk general liability lines. A claims-made policy covers claims filed within the policy period that arise out of incidents that occurred in the policy period or within the retroactive period defined by the policy.[43] Although the insurer typically guarantees the availability of coverage for claims that may be filed after the policy period but that arise from occurrences within the policy period, the price of the future coverage is not guaranteed.[44] Thus, uncertainty about the cost of future liability is shifted from the insurer to the insured. Claims-made insurance exposes the policyholder to the risk of an increase in the cost of insurance that reflects an unanticipated increase in liability for prior acts. With occurrence coverage, by contrast, the insurer assumes this risk.

CAPTIVES, RISK-RETENTION GROUPS, AND MUTUALS

One response of policyholders to the lack of commercial insurance or to its high price has been to form self-insurance groups such as captive insurers, risk-retention groups, and mutuals. Following the 1975 malpractice crisis, many hospitals joined to form captives, often with commercial reinsurance. Physicians in most states formed mutuals or reciprocals, which have grown and now account for over half the market for physicians' professional liability insurance nationwide, and even more in some states. The importance of this trend toward self-insurance is apparent in directors' and officers' insurance; two of the newly formed policyholder insurer groups are among the top four insurers in that line (measured by premium volume).[45] The oil industry recently formed a risk-retention group to provide pollution coverage.

The growth in use of these risk-sharing alternatives has been facilitated by the 1986 amendments to the 1981 Product Liability Risk Retention Act, which expanded the range of insurance options available to smaller businesses, professionals, not-for-profits, and state institutions. The 1981 Act permitted the formation of risk-retention groups to provide product liability coverage but was little used. The 1986 amendments extended the scope of the Act to all commercial liability risks, except workers' compensation and personal coverages such as private passenger automobile and homeowner's insurance. The Act facilitates the formation of these groups by preempting state insurance regulation except in the state where the group is chartered.[46] Previously, a group had to be licensed as an admitted or surplus lines insurer in every state where a member was located. In response to this federal legislation, several states have enacted special enabling statutes to facilitate the formation of these groups, although lack of coordination among states has remained an obstacle to full implementation of the Act.[47]

These self-insurance options have some advantages. At the height of the insurance crisis, they provided otherwise unavailable coverage. Over the longer term, they increase competition and may protect their members from the shocks of the insurance cycle, although this is less true if they rely on commercial reinsurance. Self-insured firms may also have greater incentives for aggressive risk management and efficient claims defense.[48] By being more selective, risk-sharing groups may be able to offer lower-priced coverage to low risks; however, that would cause higher prices for higher risks in the conventional market.

Overall, it seems unlikely that these self-insurance options offer large net savings to society when compared with large, diversified commercial insurers except for some savings in regulatory costs. Perhaps their main long-term advantage lies in facilitating after-the-fact adjustments in price when future liability is very hard to predict accurately. If loss projections turn out to have been too pessimistic and therefore premium levels were too high, a captive or a mutual can return the excess to its members in the form of a dividend or lower premiums in later years. By contrast, if premiums charged by a commercial insurer turn out to be unnecessarily high, the excess is kept by the insurer as profit. Thus, a captive or mutual can have lower initial premiums because, in principle, any inadequacy can be recouped later through an assessment or required contribution to surplus.

However, because in practice it may be hard for self-insured groups to assess their members to cover unfunded losses, there is legitimate concern that some of these self-insurance arrangements offer less real protection. This insolvency risk is borne by their policyholders, potential claimants, and other insurers. Because mutuals are typically covered under state guaranty funds, the risk of insolvency accrues primarily to other insurers, who are assessed to cover the costs of guaranty fund operations, and ultimately to their policyholders. Claimants against the insolvent company may be inconvenienced by delays in receiving compensation. On the other hand, some groups, such as offshore captives and risk-retention groups, are not covered by state guaranty funds and are also subject to less stringent capitalization requirements and solvency surveillance by state regulators. Because in general they provide less real insurance to policyholders and to potential claimants against these policyholders, these self-insurance options are a less than perfect solution to the underlying liability problem.

It is not easy to determine the optimal degree of regulation of such nontraditional insurance mechanisms. More stringent capitalization and other solvency requirements might reduce the insolvency risk. The sharp increase in number of insolvent insurers in 1984 and 1985 is evidence that insurer solvency is a real concern.[49] But increasing solvency regulation also tends to act as a barrier to entry and raises the cost of coverage.[50] This could be counterproductive if policyholders would respond by buying less coverage or none at all. Simply extending guaranty fund protection to these nontraditional mechanisms, without raising solvency requirements, is also unlikely to be an efficient solution. Because guaranty funds effectively provide insurance to insolvent insurance companies, they tend to create moral hazard, like any other form of insurance (see Chapter 6). Specifically, guaranty fund protection tends to undermine the incentives of policyholders and insurance regulators to monitor the solvency of the insurers. Thus, extending guaranty fund protection to these nontraditional mechanisms could significantly increase the risk of their insolvency.[51]

RATE REGULATION

Some states have responded to the rising cost of insurance by directly regulating rates, particularly for medical malpractice and to a lesser extent for commercial general liability. The result of such regulation has been the predictable effect of price controls in any competitive market: the withdrawal of supply. But unlike regulation of automobile insurance rates, which typically limits availability of coverage for only a minority of high-risk drivers, price controls have virtually destroyed the voluntary market for malpractice insurance in states such as New York, Rhode Island, and Massachusetts. In contrast, commercial carriers remain a major source of malpractice coverage in states that have not applied heavy rate regulation.

Regulation of rates for general commercial liability or municipal liability is less common than for medical malpractice. Because general liability requires a detailed and complex classification system of manual rates for smaller risks and individual rating for many large risks, rate regulation is much less feasible. In addition, the policyholder-protection rationale for rate regulation is weaker in commercial lines than for personal coverages, since commercial policyholders generally have greater understanding of insurance contracts and are repeat purchasers.

In view of the lack of economic rationale for rate regulation, its impracticality, and its proven adverse effects on availability, rate regulation is unlikely to prove an efficient solution to the problem of high insurance costs. Nevertheless, several states have considered greater scrutiny of rate increases. New York and several other states are moving toward a system of flex-rating, in which the magnitude and frequency of rate changes in both directions would be limited.

JOINT UNDERWRITING ASSOCIATIONS

States that have undermined the voluntary market through rate regulation have been forced to adopt some mechanism to assure availability of coverage. The most common form of residual market mechanism is a joint underwriting association (JUA). All insurers writing property/casualty insurance in the state are required to participate in the JUA, which offers coverage at regulated rates. Losses are recouped through an assessment of participating insurers in proportion to their premium volume in other lines. Thus, a JUA in essence provides a hidden subsidy to the JUA policyholders from the insuring public in general. Such a program is subject to the usual economic objections that apply to any subsidy: costs are not fully attributed to the activities that generate those costs, which results in a distortion of relative prices and induces inefficient resource allocation. Specifically, such a subsidy undermines the deterrence purpose of the tort system and could be considered inequitable.[52] Subsidies through JUA mechanisms are particularly objectionable because they are hidden, rather than line items in public budgets. This makes it much harder to measure the amount involved and evaluate its impact.

DATA REPORTING REQUIREMENTS

Over twenty states have imposed new data-reporting requirements on insurance companies. Frustration at the lack of hard data to support the huge rate increases is understandable. But the fundamental problem is that even with the best data that could conceivably be gathered, predicting future liability costs and determining the acceptable markup for risk would necessarily remain a matter of judgment. It seems likely that the reported data will ultimately be used to justify rate regulation, which we have argued is an inappropriate solution to the problem of high liability insurance costs. Given the costs of data reporting – costs that must ultimately be passed on to policyholders – and the dubious benefits, the net effects of this approach should be further analyzed before additional reporting is required.

Obtaining meaningful data is made even more difficult by the trend toward self-insurance. Manufacturers, retailers, and others are retaining an increased share of risk, but the details of limits of coverage and policy exclusions vary greatly. Data on claims are meaningless without accurate data on the exposure generating the claims. But obtaining an accurate picture of the continually shifting liability costs would impose very significant costs on self-insured and partially self-insured firms, particularly smaller businesses, and these costs must ultimately be passed on to consumers.

BEYOND SHORT-TERM ACCOMMODATIONS

There are no easy solutions to the rising cost of liability insurance. The underlying cause of rising premiums is the rising cost of liability claims and litigation expense. The adjustment to higher levels of liability costs has been exacerbated by interest sensitivity of premiums for long-tailed coverage and by unanticipated changes in tort law and in judicial interpretation of insurance contracts. The combination of unanticipated liabilities on past policies and unpredictability of future loss trends has shocked the capacity of the insurance industry and restricted availability of coverage in high-risk lines. It seems likely that the upward trend in costs and that cyclical volatility will continue in long-tailed lines unless some limits are set on the drift in legal rules.

The increased use of self-insurance, captive insurers, and risk-retention groups has eased problems of availability, but there remains a need for better coordination and more consistent requirements at the state level to govern the administration of such programs. Moreover, these mechanisms provide less real insurance for policyholders and may expose others in the event of insolvencies. A shift to claims-made coverage, if adopted more widely, would somewhat reduce the interest sensitivity of premiums and the uncertainty facing insurers. But claims-made insurance does not eliminate the risk of unanticipated changes in liability; it simply shifts the risk to policyholders. Such changes in policy form represent an accommodation rather than a solution.

The fundamental problem lies in the fact that rules of third-party liability, which lack well-defined limits on the duration and scope of liability and on the size of awards, create a risk that is not readily diversifiable and cannot be accurately priced. Making the rules of liability more stable and predictable is essential if the tort system is to provide valuable deterrence and compensation. Reasonable stability and predictability are also critical to the smooth functioning of liability insurance markets. More specifically, the impossibility of accurately pricing liability that is of long duration and subject to sociolegal changes raises serious doubts about the efficiency of using the tort system for either deterrence or compensation of long-latent risks or those resulting from cumulative exposure. We return to this in Chapter 6.

CHAPTER 4

The Tort System as a Mechanism for Resolving Disputes

There is a growing mismatch between the nature of disputes over personal injury and our system for resolving these disputes. The U.S. system for resolving tort claims evolved at a time when there were fewer claims and the typical dispute was relatively straightforward, involving a clearly defined injury to a single plaintiff and, at most, two or three defendants. The traditional legal rules and procedures still work reasonably well for injuries of this type, such as automobile accidents, which account for over half of personal injury suits. But even for relatively straightforward automobile claims, the costs and delays of the tort system have led some states to adopt no-fault statutes that are intended to remove minor claims from the tort system and substitute a system that compensates without determining blame. Although these auto no-fault statutes have not always worked as their designers hoped, they are one possible policy response to the widespread frustration with the high costs of resolving disputes through the tort system.[1]

We are concerned here not with these relatively simple auto claims but with the far more complex nonauto suits that are increasingly ill suited to traditional methods of dispute resolution. Modern product-related and environmental litigation can involve hundreds of individual plaintiffs alleging similar injuries from the same product or event. Each plaintiff's case can involve multiple defendants, and each defendant may be claiming coverage under several insurance policies, so multiple insurers have a stake in each claim. The injuries alleged are often not sudden traumas that result from a single well-defined accident; today's courts must attempt to assign responsibility for diseases that are of uncertain origin, involving highly technical issues in determining causation and the due standard of care. Claims related to the professional liability of physicians, accountants, architects, engineers, and corporate officers and directors raise different but equally complex and technical issues.

Obviously, resolving disputes over complex issues will always entail some costs, and up to a point, that is an appropriate use of societal resources. From a societal point of view, expenditure on litigation is valuable to the extent that it generates the information and law enforcement that is essential for efficient compensation and deterrence. The public subsidy to the courts is one reflection of this public interest in litigation. Our goal should be to use the most cost-effective methods of resolving disputes and to expend resources on litigation only up to the point where the additional cost is justified by additional benefits, in terms of fair compensation and efficient deterrence. Many who are familiar with the day-to-day management of tort claims believe that much of the litigation expense incurred today contributes very little to accurate fact-finding and has minimal, if any, social value. Rather, such expense is incurred for strategic reasons, to influence the jury or to influence the amount the other side is willing to accept or offer in settlement, in order to avoid the even higher costs of continuing to litigate to verdict.

The current structure of dispute resolution tends to encourage a vicious cycle of litigation expense and unpredictable verdicts, which are costly to both individuals and society. If verdicts were highly predictable, determined by observable facts of the case, rational litigants would settle out of court for the expected verdict, thereby avoiding costly litigation. But when verdicts are unpredictable and can be influenced by the parties to the dispute, this creates incentives for the litigants to spend more on litigation in an effort to influence the outcome. Since both cannot win, much of this expenditure is waste from a private perspective to at least one of the parties. Increased expenditure encouraged by unpredictability also tends to generate changes in legal standards of liability and damages. The causes of the drift in rules of liability and damages over the past two decades (see Chapter 2) are many and complex. But the structure of our system of dispute resolution has surely been a facilitating factor. Thus, unpredictability induces expenditure on litigation, which in turn produces novel rulings, thereby reinforcing the chain of legal uncertainty and expenditure on litigation.

Heavy litigation expense has further social costs in distorting the filing and disposition of claims. Given the unavoidable fixed costs of entering the system, small but meritorious claims may not be worth filing. But, legally weak cases involving more severe injuries may be worth filing, in the hope that the defense will make a settlement offer in order to buy out of the even greater costs of defending a claim, even one that has little merit.

Such results provide neither equitable compensation nor efficient deterrence.

In this chapter, we document the costs of litigating nonauto tort claims and examine why these costs are so high. Then, we look at alternative, potentially lower-cost methods for resolving disputes, such as arbitration, mediation, mini-trials, and options for handling mass torts. The costs reported here are solely the direct costs related to litigating tort claims. Chapter 5 discusses the equally important indirect costs of the liability system, such as loss of productivity and withdrawal of products from the market. Similarly, the options discussed in this chapter are alternative mechanisms for resolving disputes within the current structure of tort liability. Chapters 5 and 6 discuss market and regulatory alternatives to the tort system for risk control and private and social insurance alternatives for compensation.

COSTS OF LITIGATION

The high litigation costs of the tort system are documented in a 1986 study by Kakalik and Pace.[2] Drawing on this study, Table 4.1 shows a breakdown of the costs of litigating an estimated 405,000 nonauto tort claims resolved in 1985 that involved lawsuits in federal or state courts. These claims include medical malpractice, product liability, and other types of personal injury and property damage covered under the insurance lines of general liability and commercial multiperil liability. They accounted for almost half (47 percent) of all tort claims and over four-fifths (84 percent) of claims in federal courts.[3]

The average gross payment to plaintiffs in these nonauto tort claims (including cases closed with and without payment to the plaintiff) was $31,600. Of this $31,600, the average plaintiff paid $9,383 in legal fees and expenses, or 30 percent of the gross compensation, and incurred additional time and other expenses estimated at $1,850. These averages conceal a great range among cases, with the typical case probably having much lower values but a relatively small number of very large cases pulling up the average.

Overall, defendants spent a very similar amount in legal fees and expenses: on average $9,416 per case, including both specifically allocated expenses and general (unallocated) claims-processing costs. The time and other expense costs of defendants were estimated at $5,863 per case, or over three times the amount spent by plaintiffs; however, the estimates of defendant time costs were based on interviews with insurers rather than the defendants themselves and so are of doubtful quality.[4] In

TABLE 4.1

Direct Cost of Litigating Non-Auto Tort Claims in 1985[a]

	Average Cost Per Case ($)	Total All Cases ($ billion)	% of Total Expenditures	
			Time Costs Excluded (%)	Time Costs Included (%)
Plaintiffs' Costs				
Legal fees and expenses	9,383	3.8	22	20
Time and other expense	1,850	0.7	—	4
Total	11,233	4.5	22	24
Defendants' Cost				
Legal fees and expenses (ALAE)	8,500	3.6	21	18
Unallocated claims costs (ULAE)	916	0.4	2	2
Time and other expenses	5,863	2.2	—	12
Total	15,329	6.2	23	32
Court Expenditures	741	0.3	2	2
TOTAL LITIGATION EXPENSE	27,303	11.0	47	57
Compensation Paid				
Total	31,358	12.7	—	—
Net of plaintiffs' legal expenses	21,728	8.8	53	—
Net of all plaintiff expenses	20,247	8.2	—	43
Total Expenditures (Litigation & Compensation)				
Excluding litigants' time costs	41,975	17.0	100	—
Including litigants' time costs	48,148	19.5	—	100

[a]Costs are for claims resolved in federal and state courts of general jurisdiction in 1985.
'Time costs' refer to litigant time costs. Indirect cost are excluded (see text).

SOURCE: James S. Kakalik and Nicholas M. Pace, *Costs and Compensation Paid in Tort Litigation* (Santa Monica, Calif.: The RAND Corporation, R-3391-ICJ, 1986).

addition to these expenses by the parties involved, the public costs of operating the courts averaged out to roughly $741 per case, after netting out the court fees paid by the litigants.

These estimates imply that litigation expense consumed between 47 and 57 percent of total funds spent resolving nonauto claims through the tort system. The higher figure (57 percent) applies if all time costs are included in total expenditures; the lower figure (47 percent) applies if time costs are excluded. In other words, between 43 percent and 53 percent of expenses incurred by the parties in resolving tort claims ultimately reached the plaintiffs as compensation.

Another way of viewing the costs of the tort system is to calculate the fraction of the liability insurance premium dollar that reaches the plaintiff as compensation. Such estimates generally conclude that the plaintiff nets 35 to 45 percent of the liability insurance premium dollar for medical malpractice and product liability, although some estimates are even lower. The value of this compensation to the plaintiff is reduced by the fact that it is often received months or even years after the injury occurred. By contrast, individuals net roughly 62 cents of the insurance dollar through workers' compensation and over 80 cents on the dollar through first-party health insurance.[5] These sources also pay more promptly. These numbers clearly show that if the only function of the tort system is to deliver compensation, this can be done more cost-effectively through other private or public insurance mechanisms. But of course a full evaluation must include the other indirect costs and benefits of the tort system.

Further confirmation of the magnitude of litigation expense of the tort system is provided by Schotter and Ordover.[6] They estimated that the administrative costs of the tort system, including both auto and nonauto claims, were in the range of $15 to $20 billion in 1984. This is similar to the total litigation costs of $16 to $19 billion in 1985 estimated by Kakalik and Pace.

Kakalik and Pace found that the costs of litigation consumed a larger share of total expenditures for nonauto claims than for auto claims. Auto claimants received 52 percent of the total including time costs, compared with 43 percent for nonauto claimants when time costs are included. The difference was accounted for by higher legal fees and time costs for defendants in the nonauto claims. Higher defense costs on nonauto claims, both in absolute terms and relative to the compensation to the plaintiff, is not surprising in view of the greater complexity of the issues and the fact that product liability and medical malpractice claims are more likely to involve multiple defendants and duplicative defense effort. The higher cost of nonauto torts is further evidence that the traditional legal system is less suited for the complex issues raised by such disputes than for more traditional, simple cases such as most auto accidents.

It is important to put the numbers reported here in perspective and note their relation to other commonly cited figures. First, these estimates of direct litigation costs do not include the indirect costs of the tort system in terms of products withdrawn or not introduced and other effects on productivity that are discussed in Chapter 5. Second, the figures in Table 4.1 relate to claims resolved, with and without payment to the plaintiff, in 1985. This understates the costs of litigation that are reflected in current liability insurance premiums because current premiums take expected future costs into account and these costs are continually rising.[7] Third, the costs of defending nonauto tort claims of $6.2 billion reported in Table 4.1 do not include many other corporate costs of litigation and so are not comparable to estimates of over $20 billion spent by corporations on legal expenses for all types of litigation,[8] of which tort claims are only one component. Fourth, whether or not the costs of litigation are regarded as excessive depends on the magnitude of the benefits relative to the costs. But regardless of the magnitude of the benefits, if the same compensation and deterrence benefits could be delivered at lower cost through other mechanisms such as those discussed below, then our current methods of dispute resolution are not the most cost-effective.

WHY IS LITIGATION SO COSTLY?

Litigation expenses reflect the voluntary choices of the parties involved based on the opportunities and constraints that they face. Any measure to reduce litigation expense must operate through these incentives and constraints.

The great majority of tort claims (over 90 percent) are settled out of court, but not before significant expenses have been incurred. Under the simple assumption of rational behavior, both parties can gain by settling immediately and thereby avoiding the costs of litigation. Consider a simple model of rational settlement behavior by parties who are risk-neutral (i.e., willing to take an even gamble). The minimum sum that a rational plaintiff would be willing to settle for would be the expected payoff in court (i.e., the probability of winning times amount of award if he or she wins) minus the costs of litigation. The maximum amount that a rational defendant would be willing to offer is the expected payout in court, plus litigation costs. Thus, the parties would tend to settle if their expectations of the outcome in court differ by less than the sum of their costs of pursuing litigation. Each side would invest in litigation only as long as the marginal expected payoff exceeds the marginal cost.

Obviously this model's assumption of rational, risk-neutral maximization of financial self-interest ignores emotional and nonfinancial factors that no doubt influence the behavior of the litigants in many cases. Litigants also have noneconomic motivations in bringing suits. The desire to prove one's innocence or another's guilt is the driving force behind many lawsuits. Plaintiffs who are very averse to risk will settle for less than the expected award. Similarly, risk-averse defendants sometimes settle rather than face even a small risk of a very large verdict that could result in adverse publicity or set a precedent for future cases. Also ignored by the simple model of rational settlement behavior is the fact that counsel for both the plaintiff and the defendant may not always act in the best interest of their clients. Nevertheless, studies of the disposition of malpractice and product liability claims indicate that the assumption of rational behavior goes far to explain average behavior and outcomes.[9]

The simple model of rational behavior in settlement and litigation decisions provides useful insights into the causes of expenditures on litigation and the possible effects of procedural reforms and alternative systems of dispute resolution. First, unpredictability in standards of liability and damages increases the possible range of honest disagreement and therefore makes settlement less likely unless the parties are very averse to risk. If either is very risk-averse, uncertainty tends to make that party more willing to settle, but the settlement amount may be quite far from the likely court award.

Second, unpredictable standards encourage expenditures to either influence the outcome in court or raise the costs for the other side and hence influence the amount for which they would be willing to settle. Pretrial procedures, often essential to establish the facts, can be used and abused to obtain tactical advantage, impose costs on the other side, and hence influence the other side's settlement strategy. Although it may not be practical to lay down broad rules limiting the use of pleadings, discovery, and motions, it is clearly important for judges to manage trials aggressively in order to control the potential abuse of pretrial tactics.

One of the potential side benefits of strict guidelines or schedules for determining both compensatory and punitive damages is that by limiting the range of possible outcomes at trial, such guidelines reduce incentives to incur expenses to influence that outcome, so should reduce litigation expense and encourage earlier settlements. (For a more detailed discussion, see Chapter 6.) Similarly, rules that make more predictable the standards of liability to be applied and the allocation of shares among multiple defendants should have the side benefit of reducing expenditures on litigation.

Another implication of viewing litigation expense as a response to financial incentives is that when the cost of litigating is reduced, people may "buy" more. For example, procedural reform that reduces the per unit cost of litigating may have smaller and possibly even positive effects on total expenditures, depending on the elasticity of response. This is analogous to the freeway phenomenon: when a new freeway is built to reduce congestion, more drivers take to the roads, and the reduction in congestion is often negligible. Similarly, a reduction in the cost of filing or pursuing tort claims tends to increase the number of claims filed and reduce the percentage settled out of court. There are several examples of this freeway phenomenon at work in litigation. Class actions in which a plaintiff can simply opt in to a certified class reduce the cost to each individual plaintiff of pursuing a claim and hence tend to increase the number of claims filed. Some observers believe that because arbitration reduces the costs of dispute resolution, it tends to increase the number of claims that are filed and to reduce the percentage that are settled by negotiation without recourse to adjudication by a third party. Others disagree. There is no hard evidence, and it probably depends on the type of dispute.

Of course even if procedural reform does attract more users into the system it may still be desirable. The net evaluation of such changes depends not only on their impact on litigation costs but also on their effects on the accuracy of the outcome and hence on the equity and efficiency of deterrence and compensation. But the potential for unintended consequences of procedural reforms must be acknowledged and anticipated, including the possibility of an increase in indemnity and litigation costs paid by defendants and perhaps even an increase in the public costs of operating the courts.

The role of judges in managing and controlling the predictability of trials deserves emphasis. In the U.S. legal system, the judge determines questions of law, including whether there is an adequate basis in law and sufficient factual evidence for the plaintiff's case to be taken to the jury. Many knowledgeable observers believe that some judges are increasingly reluctant to dismiss a case on a legal issue, and that unqualified "expert" testimony is often admitted with little basis in either scientific evidence or consensus of qualified experts. Thus juries are being called on to resolve cases in which both the legal and the factual bases are weak. Not surprisingly, different juries can come to radically different conclusions on essentially similar cases. Litigation involving the morning sickness drug

Bendectin, alleged to cause birth defects, illustrates this judicial inconsistency. As of July 1987, seventeen juries had considered the Bendectin birth defect link. The defendant, Merrell-Dow, had won twelve times, the plaintiffs five. In one case, a Massachusetts judge dismissed the case as lacking sufficient evidence to be taken to a jury. In another Bendectin case, a District of Columbia judge allowed it to go to the jury which awarded $20 million. Nevertheless, scientific studies provide no evidence of a link between Bendectin and birth defects.[10] If judges consistently exerted their existing powers to control what goes to the jury, this could significantly decrease the unpredictability of the current system and reduce expenditures on litigation.

Finally, the incentive system facing both the plaintiff and defense counsel surely contributes to the problem of unnecessary litigation expense. The United States is one of the few countries that permits a contingent fee for plaintiff attorneys. Both the hourly wage basis of payment of defense lawyers and the contingent fees of plaintiffs' lawyers have advantages and disadvantages. There is very little hard evidence of the effects of these and other methods of payment on the volume, cost, and delay in litigation. This is an important area requiring further study.

PRIVATE INITIATIVES TO REDUCE LITIGATION COSTS

In search for ways around the high costs of litigation, a wide range of alternative dispute resolution (ADR) mechanisms have been developed by such interested parties as court administrators, local court systems, individual judges, and the litigants and other private parties. Here we focus on private sector initiatives.[11] These alternatives may be undertaken informally by the litigants or with the assistance of one of the entities founded specifically to encourage and facilitate alternative dispute resolution, such as the American Arbitration Association, the Center for Public Resources, the National Institute for Dispute Resolution, EnDispute Inc., and others. The Center for Public Resources defines ADR as "a range of practices aimed at preventing, managing and resolving disputes cost-effectively." These include pretrial mediation, summary jury trials (brief trials before a judge and jury several months before the real trial is scheduled to start), and the mini-trial.

ADR mechanisms have been used to resolve a wide range of both tort and nontort cases. Certain procedures work better for certain types of cases.

ARBITRATION

Many commercial contracts contain clauses that provide for arbitration of a broad range of potential disputes. (See "Alternative Dispute Resolution Mechanisms," page 60.) Arbitration is also widely used for resolving labor-management disputes and insurance claims. The application of arbitration to personal injury disputes is more recent but growing. For example, several leading health maintenance organizations (HMOs) stipulate the use of arbitration for medical malpractice disputes as a condition of the health insurance contract, and courts have upheld these provisions. Arbitration agreements that are not part of the health insurance contract but are signed just before the course of medical treatment or at admission to a hospital have been struck down by some courts; other courts have required that a patient have the opportunity to rescind the agreement within 30 or 60 days after the execution of the agreement or the completion of the treatment, whichever comes later.

Although judicial concern over unequal bargaining power between producers and consumers may be warranted in markets where a producer has monopoly power, such circumstances are rare in modern markets. On grounds of economic efficiency and freedom of choice, a strong case can be made for permitting and encouraging potential litigants to enter into voluntary but binding arbitration agreements. When arbitration services are provided in competition with the publicly subsidized court system, there is a strong presumption that the rules and procedures of arbitration will be designed to maximize the value of the service to potential litigants.[12] Arbitration will be voluntarily adopted only where the parties consider that the savings in litigation costs exceed the benefits forgone by giving up the right to trial by jury. Potential plaintiffs can be protected from unknowingly giving up their rights to a jury trial by statutes, already in place in many states, that require large print and explicit language in arbitration agreements.

Denying producers the right to make arbitration a condition of offering a service or product forces all consumers to pay for legal protections that at least some may be willing to forgo in return for lower-priced products. Competition can work in the realm of dispute resolution just as it does in markets for other goods and services. If some consumers view arbitration or some other ADR mechanism as a more cost-effective option for resolving disputes for some products and services, producers should be legally permitted to offer this option. In other words, because the right to jury trial entails high costs as well as benefits, parties should be allowed to opt out of that right by adopting private contractual terms that stipulate alternative forms of dispute resolution.

MEDIATION

Mediation and binding arbitration have been used successfully in aiding timely resolution of third-party insurance disputes, the majority of which are routine cases of moderate value. (See "Alternative Dispute Resolution Mechanisms," page 60.) Thousands of such claims have been resolved in recent years, and both the number and the size of cases resolved by these procedures is reportedly growing.

Mediation as well as arbitration services are provided by both not-for-profit and for-profit organizations. These providers will review the referral made by the initiating party (usually the insurer), contact and persuade the other party(s) to participate in an ADR procedure, explain the available procedures to the parties, and administer the chosen procedure. On average, about 60 percent of noninitiating parties agree to engage in ADR, and, of these, three-fourths choose mediation.[13] According to the Center for Public Resources, often the very act of initiating an ADR process will result in a resumption of negotiation and a settlement even before a hearing or mediation conference occurs. When such a conference is held, more than 80 percent of the cases settle at or shortly after the conference, with substantial savings in time and transaction costs for parties.

MINI-TRIALS

Another mechanism that has worked well to speed settlement is the mini-trial. (See "Alternative Dispute Resolution Mechanisms," page 60.) It has been successfully used in a wide range of disputes, including commercial, transnational, employee, environmental, and personal injury conflicts. It seems to work best for disputes involving two or more corporate entities. It is often quicker and less costly than arbitration, perhaps because it is nonbinding and involves key decisionmakers on both sides, with the neutral advisor offering opinions and advice rather than arbitrating the dispute.

The fact that mini-trials are voluntary, take place before a mutually accepted advisor, and involve the key decisionmakers distinguishes this form of ADR in critical ways from the mediation panels that have been introduced in some states to screen medical malpractice claims. Mediation panels are intended to provide an expert but nonbinding evaluation of the merits of a case and hence expedite the dismissal of nonmeritorious claims and the settlement of meritorious claims. While the powers assigned to these pretrial screening panels and their success vary from state to state, in general, imposing involuntary, nonbinding screening simply adds another tier of costly litigation. Mini-trials, unlike these mediation panels, tend to succeed because key decisionmakers take part and the process is voluntary.

ALTERNATIVE DISPUTE RESOLUTION MECHANISMS

ARBITRATION

Arbitration is the submission of a dispute to one or more neutral persons for a final and binding decision. It is unique in that, in contrast with mediation and mini-trials, it usually displaces trial by judge or jury, although in some cases the arbitrator's award is only advisory. The parties mutually agree on the range of issues to be resolved by arbitration, on many of the procedural aspects of the process, and on the identity of the arbitrators, who are often selected for their expertise in the issues under dispute. The process is usually less formal than a court trial, although the substantive rules of law remain the same; it is private and often quicker, less costly, and less adversarial.

MEDIATION

Mediation is the submission of a dispute to a party-selected outside facilitator, often with subject matter expertise, for assistance in reaching a mutually acceptable settlement. The procedure is private, voluntary, and nonbinding, with the mediator having no power to impose a settlement. It is usually an informal and unstructured process with the emphasis on the disputants' relationship, not on adherence to or development of consistent rules. The attitudes and principled arguments of each party to support a decision in their favor are generally considered more important than the presentation of proofs by each party. The process is less adversarial than litigation and arbitration, although it can be conducted in a manner that allows for advocacy as well as conciliation.[14]

THE MINI-TRIAL

The mini-trial is described by James F. Henry, founder and president of the Center for Public Resources, as follows:

> The mini-trial is a non-binding settlement procedure, structured to convert a legal dispute back into a business problem. Lawyers make abbreviated presentations, exposing the strengths and weaknesses of the case not to a judge and jury but to business executives from both sides. These summaries are often also heard by a neutral adviser, who may be a retired judge or an authority on technical issues. The neutral adviser presides and may offer opinions. After hearing the case presented by attorneys for each party, executives meet without their lawyers to negotiate an agreement, which frequently resembles a practical business deal rather than a legal settlement. The procedure is effective because it allows businessmen to become educated about both sides of the case. For the first time they have the necessary information to make a clear assessment of the risks and costs of going to trial. With this information – and, of course, with the knowledge of their own objectives – they are well-equipped to negotiate a settlement.[15]

ALTERNATIVE PROCEDURES FOR RESOLVING MASS TORTS[16]

The mass toxic tort litigation that has proliferated in recent years has posed the greatest challenge to traditional methods of resolving disputes. Traditional tort procedures evolved to handle simple suits, typically involving a traumatic injury and one or, at most, two plaintiffs and defendants. By contrast, mass toxic torts can involve hundreds of thousands of claimants alleging similar injuries that arise from reactions to a common substance or device.

Table 4.2 lists the major instances of mass toxic tort litigation, most of which have been initiated within the last two decades. These instances of mass litigation share particular – and problematic – characteristics. Issues of general causation are often murky; for example, the toxicity of the product to humans may be in doubt. And even if general causation is established, as in the case of asbestos, the specific relation between the product of a particular defendant and the injury of a particular plaintiff may be impossible to establish. The long latency of injuries from toxic substances frequently compounds the difficulty and cost of establishing causation and raises complex questions regarding statutes of limitation.

Long latency also means that the insurance contracts written at the time of exposure did not contemplate some of the issues that have subsequently arisen. The two key issues that have generated extensive litigation and have not yet been conclusively resolved with respect to the old insurance contracts are: (1) What event triggers the coverage, the exposure to the toxic product or the manifestation of the injury? (2) Does the insurer have a duty to defend after the policy limits have been exhausted?

On the coverage issue, different courts have adopted different trigger theories: the exposure theory, the manifestation theory, and the triple-trigger theory, which is the most expansive and implies that all insurers who wrote coverage from the first exposure to the manifestation of the disease are at risk. These issues have pitted primary insurers against excess insurers (who write higher limits of coverage) and against manufacturers, compounding the complexity and the number of parties involved in each case. The result is delays in disposition that frustrate plaintiffs' needs for prompt compensation and defendants' needs for resolution of liabilities. Because many of the issues involved in each case are similar, much of pretrial procedure becomes duplicative and redundant. Separate trials result in different outcomes for similar plaintiffs, and the total award of punitive damages, aggregated over individual plaintiffs' cases, may be unfair to defendants and out of proportion to compensatory damages.

Lawyers and courts have developed formal and informal procedures to aggregate claims and avoid litigating thousands of similar claims

TABLE 4.2

Number of Cases and Use of Aggregate Procedures for Some Mass Torts

	MER/29	Tobacco	Asbestos	DES	Agent Orange	Dalkon Shield	Toxic Shock	Bendectin	MGM Grand	DDT (Alabama)	Salmonella
Number of cases	1,000	250	35,000	1,000s	250,000	325,000	100s	1,200	1,000	11,000	19,000
Litigation ongoing		●	●	●	●	●	●	●	●		●
Individual litigation	●	●	●	●		●	●	●			●
Consolidated actions			●							●	●
Ad hoc and aggregation	●		●			●					
Multi-district litigation					●	●		●	●		
Class actions			●		●					●	●
Bankruptcy			●			●					
Private ADR			●								

SOURCE: Mark Peterson and Molly Selvin, "The Resolution of Mass Torts: Toward a Framework for Evaluation of Alternative Procedures" (Research paper prepared for CED Subcommittee on Risk Management, Dispute Resolution, and Injury Compensation, June 1987).

involving overlapping litigants and similar issues. These procedures and the types of cases in which they have been used are shown in Table 4.2. For example, the traditional methods of consolidation of cases involving common questions of law or fact and ad hoc groupings of cases for negotiation have been widely used for asbestos cases.[17]

Class action has also been used, usually for subgroups of plaintiffs affected.[18] In the case of Agent Orange, which involved 250,000 claimants, a voluntary class was certified to decide common issues and a mandatory class was established for punitive damages.

The costs of litigation have led some corporations to take extreme measures. In 1982, Manville Corporation took what was then an unprecedented step for an otherwise profitable corporation by filing for reorganization under Chapter 11 of the Federal Bankruptcy Act as a way of resolving its open-ended liability. At that time, Manville faced 16,500 outstanding asbestos-related claims for $12.5 billion in damages and had already paid out $50 million. New suits were being filed at a rate of 500 per month. Manville estimated the present value of all future claims at approximately $2 billion, which exceeded its net worth of $1.1 billion.[19] Since that time, five other asbestos manufacturers have sought protection under Chapter 11, and the A. H. Robins Company entered Chapter 11 in 1985 to resolve claims connected with the Dalkon Shield. Bankruptcy proceedings are a drastic step taken in a search for a final resolution of the claims of current and potential future claimants, rather than face the open-ended uncertainty of paying claims as they come in.

Another novel private initiative to reduce the time and money costs of resolving the multiparty asbestos litigation was the Asbestos Claims Facility, which operated from February 1986 until its reorganization in June 1988. Its successor, the Center for Claims Resolution, began operation in October 1988.[20] The Facility was designed to provide a central place where asbestos claimants could file a claim without filing a lawsuit and going to court. The Facility acted as the sole agent for participating asbestos manufacturers and insurers and had exclusive authority and discretion to administer, evaluate, settle, pay, or defend all asbestos-related claims on behalf of participants. Although the Facility encouraged the use of settlement, arbitration, and other dispute resolution procedures, it in no way changed the substantive law. Plaintiffs could refuse an offer tendered by the Facility and pursue their claims in court. Participating producers and insurers agreed on rules for allocating costs among themselves. In June 1988, the U.S. members of the Facility agreed to dissolve the original structure and establish a new claims handling organization. Some manufacturers and insurers withdrew and opted to handle their own cases.

During the Facility's two and a half years of operations, it resolved more than 20,000 claims, compared with only 6,000 claims resolved by its members independently during the prior ten years. Thirty-four asbestos producers and 16 insurers participated, and the number of law firms involved in defense was reduced from over 1,000 to 60. Case filings at the Facility increased from approximately 500 a month to an average of 1,500 per month.[21]

Procedures for aggregating mass claims have undoubtedly expedited claim resolution and reduced at least some costs to some parties. In particular, the Asbestos Claims Facility and its successor could provide a blueprint for dealing with other complex, multiparty mass toxic cases involving hazardous wastes, chemicals, and possibly other products.

But many questions remain unanswered. A full evaluation of the various procedures for mass claim processing must await more experience and more thorough investigation of costs and benefits. Proponents argue that, in contrast with the capriciousness of individual trials, mass processing produces more equitable results, enables compensation to be allocated more rationally among individual plaintiffs and defendants, facilitates compromise compensation that reflects the uncertain probabilistic causal evidence relating an allegedly toxic substance to a particular plaintiff's injuries, and facilitates a more rational treatment of punitive damages.

Critics challenge the limitations on the individual plaintiff's procedural rights in class actions and in bankruptcy proceedings. For example, the Agent Orange settlement has been appealed on several grounds; it remains unresolved nine years after the first claims were filed. Class actions probably work to the disadvantage of the most severely injured plaintiffs, but marginal claimants probably gain from these procedures. The publicity that is required in order to consolidate plaintiffs as a class is likely to induce the filing of additional claims that would not otherwise have been filed, including a disproportionate number of claims of dubious merit. Such claims are not individually screened by plaintiffs' lawyers, whereas under individual contingent fee arrangements, plaintiff attorneys have some incentive to screen out nonmeritorious claims since the attorney is at risk for legal costs if the claim is dismissed without payment. Moreover, even if the capriciousness of individual trials is avoided, the outcome of mass processing is highly dependent on the few key individuals who happen to handle the case, particularly the judge and the plaintiffs' attorneys. It remains to be determined whether the benefits of these aggregation procedures, in terms of avoiding duplicative litigation and perhaps achieving greater equity of awards among some plaintiffs, outweigh the possible costs in terms of inequities to other plaintiffs and of encouraging nonmeritorious claims.

In the short run, as long as these questions remain unanswered, and as long as the fundamental problems of liability for mass toxic injuries remain unresolved, it seems best to allow and indeed encourage private parties to seek out and try alternative ways of resolving their disputes.

However, while private experimentation is to be encouraged, that should not distract attention from the need to devise a more efficient public policy toward managing the underlying risks, clearly defining the associated liabilities, and administering compensation. Moreover, important issues need to be resolved with respect to specific mass procedures currently in use. What limits, if any, should be put on an individual plaintiff's rights to opt in or out of a class action? Allowing opt-ins tends to increase the number of claims that are not subject to screening by attorneys with an incentive to weed out claims with little chance of success. Allowing opt-outs preserves a plaintiff's right to an individual trial, but at the cost of reducing the gains from aggregating cases. Class actions for compensable damages are usually voluntary. But a strong case can be made for disallowing punitive damages for plaintiffs who opt out of a class action. This principle was applied in the case of Agent Orange where a mandatory class was certified to decide punitive damages. [22] Finally, should limits be placed on the discretion of individual judges in handling these class actions?

DETERRING FRIVOLOUS CLAIMS AND FRIVOLOUS DEFENSES

By filing a suit, a plaintiff imposes costs on the defendant, who faces the alternatives of incurring costs of defense or buying out by a settlement offer. Conversely, by delay and other tactics, the defendant can impose costs on the plaintiff that may lead to the suit being dropped or acceptance of an unreasonably low settlement. To discourage such socially counterproductive strategic behavior, we believe that some variant of the English rule, which requires the losing party to pay the legal costs of both sides, merits serious consideration.

One advantage of such a rule is that it discourages the filing of frivolous claims where the chances of winning are low. On the other hand, there is a valid concern that imposing all costs on the losing party may go too far and would discourage risk-averse plaintiffs from filing claims that have at least an even chance of winning. Another concern is that the rule is one-sided in practice because a defendant can rarely collect costs from a losing plaintiff.[23] A possible remedy for both these practical objections is to permit the plaintiff's attorney to assume responsibility for the defendant's costs in the event that a suit is unsuccessful. This would be a simple extension of the standard contingent fee contract. A more extreme alternative would be to assess costs against the attorney of a losing plaintiff, rather than against the individual plaintiff. Even if the assessment were nominally against the plaintiff, permitting freedom of contract would probably result in attorneys assuming this risk in return for a higher percentage fee if the suit is successful. Such a sharing of risk would be efficient because the attorney is likely to be less risk-averse and is in a better position than is an individual plaintiff to assess the merits of a claim.

Although it is premature to recommend the adoption of the English rule for allocating costs, further study of the likely effects of alternative variants of such a rule is certainly warranted. It may offer an evenhanded way of discouraging strategic litigation tactics that are socially nonproductive and ultimately costly to all sides.

SUMMARY OF RECOMMENDATIONS

Our traditional systems for resolving tort claims are ill matched to the growing complexity of modern disputes. The result is very high costs of litigation.The problem is most severe for nonauto torts such as products, environment, and medical and other professional liability claims. We need to vigorously promote the use of formal and informal alternative dispute resolution mechanisms that encourage negotiation rather than litigation. Within the existing system, more active case management is needed to minimize costly delays, strategic behavior, and unpredictability. We offer the following specific recommendations:

- **Parties should be permitted and encouraged to contractually adopt alternative systems of dispute resolution and to experiment with new mechanisms. Such contracts should clearly inform the parties when they are waiving their rights to jury trial.**

- **Aggressive judicial management of cases is needed in order to prevent the unproductive use of pretrial tactics for purposes of delay and gaining strategic advantage. Judges should require that the testimony of expert witnesses be corroborated by either a reasonable body of scientific evidence or a consensus of a significant body of** experts. Summary judgment should be used more aggressively to dismiss unsubstantiated cases.

- Further study is necessary before specific recommendations can be made with respect to use of class actions and bankruptcy proceedings to handle mass claims.

- Where a broad class action is permitted that is voluntary with respect to compensable damages, the class should be mandatory with respect to punitive damages.

- Further study is needed of the effects of alternative strategies for deterring frivolous suits, such as variants of the English rule of awarding costs against the losing party. Further study of the effects of hourly and contingent fees is also needed.

CHAPTER 5

Recommendations for Change in Our Systems of Deterrence: Making the Best Use of Market Forces, Regulation, and Tort Liability

In a world of unlimited resources, we could afford to eliminate virtually all risk without sacrificing the consumption of other goods and services. But in the real world, resources are limited, and our overall risk management strategy should be designed to make the most cost-effective choices, by:

- First, allocating resources to risk reduction only to the extent that the marginal benefit exceeds the marginal cost.

- Second, using the most efficient technologies available to reduce risk.

- Third, and perhaps most fundamental, adopting an institutional structure that mixes market forces, regulation, and tort liability in a way best designed to achieve these goals.

Because the overall level of risk in our society is determined by literally trillions of decisions by millions of individual consumers and producers, no single governmental entity, legislative or judicial, has the omniscience to make optimal decisions. The best institutional design is therefore one that creates incentives for all individuals to make efficient decisions and that relies most heavily in each context on those best informed to make sound decisions.

Market forces, regulation, and tort liability play significant roles in controlling risk, and each system has unique advantages and disadvantages. The optimal mix depends primarily on who is best placed to assess risk and manage it optimally in a given circumstance. In general, both regulation and liability entail much higher overhead costs than markets, and often higher costs of obtaining the information required to determine optimal levels of risk reduction. Consequently, regulation and liability are often more prone to distortions and error than efficiently functioning markets. Where markets fail to provide proper incentives to control risk – but *only* where markets fail – there may be a useful role for regulation or tort liability. However, extensive control by both simultaneously is unlikely to be cost-effective.

In this chapter, we first review the circumstances in which market forces alone fail to provide adequate incentives for risk reduction, compare the relative advantages of regulation and tort liability as corrective mechanisms, and outline the necessary conditions for each to operate efficiently. Next, we discuss problems with the current regulatory and tort systems, which include overlaps and often conflicts between the systems, inherent institutional biases, inefficiencies in the design of regulation, and rules of liability and a structure of awards that result in excessive taxes on some activities and insufficient incentives for care in others. Next, we discuss the limited evidence available on the benefits and costs of regulation and tort liability, with particular emphasis on the often neglected indirect costs of liability, such as withdrawal of goods and services and damage to U.S. competitiveness. We then propose reforms, focusing on liability as one among several systems for controlling risk. Finally, we briefly discuss the unique problems of hazardous waste.

The compensation function of the tort system and its integration with other private and social insurance mechanisms are discussed separately, in Chapter 6.

OVERVIEW OF OUR SYSTEMS OF DETERRENCE

Activities of businesses can inadvertently cause harm to at least three groups: consumers, employees of the producing firm or other firms, and the general public.[1] Table 5.1 arrays some of the overlapping systems of the market, regulation, and tort liability that currently operate to control risk to these groups.

Market forces operating through prices and wages create strong incentives to control risk to individuals in their capacities as consumers and workers. In addition, a number of agencies regulate product safety. Industry-specific regulatory bodies, such as the Food and Drug Administration (food, drugs, and medical devices), the Federal Aviation Agency (airplanes), and the National Highway Transport Safety Authority (automobiles), have existed for decades. More recently, the Consumer Product Safety Commission (CPSC) has begun to regulate overall consumer product safety and has established standards for such diverse products as lawn mowers, children's clothing, and bicycles. Regulatory standards for purposes of risk control are typically set at the federal level, preempting state regulation in the interests of uniformity and fair competition in interstate commerce. Strict liability of producers for product-related injuries has recently been superimposed on this network of regulation. Since tort law is state-specific, this creates the potential for inconsistent judicial standards across jurisdictions, in addition to conflict with regulatory standards.

The forces operating on worker safety are even more complex. Since the early 1900s, employers have been strictly liable for work-related injuries under workers' compensation statutes. In addition, since the creation of the Occupational Safety and Health Administration (OSHA) in 1971 within the Department of Labor, every business in the country has had to comply with highly detailed federal safety standards.[2] Industry-specific standards have long existed in particularly hazardous industries such as mining. Specific regulations also control the use of such hazardous substances as radioactive and dangerous biological materials. These regulations are intended primarily to protect workers but also affect product safety and environmental emissions. Recently, however, the original

TABLE 5.1

Sources of Incentive to Control Risk

PARTY AT RISK	MARKETS	REGULATION	LIABILITY
Consumers	Product prices Warranties Professional standards Reputation	Consumer Product Safety Commission Food & Drug Administration Federal Aviation Agency National Highway Traffic Safety Administration	Tort liability
Employees	Wages	Occupational Safety & Health Administration	Workers' compensation Tort liability
Public at large (third parties)	Reputation (regulatory performance standards)	Environmental Protection Agency	Tort liability

intent that workers' compensation should be the sole remedy for job-related injuries has been eroded, and employers have been held strictly liable in tort for product-related injuries to their own workers and employees of other firms.

Risk to the public at large, other than in its capacity as consumers and employees, is less well controlled by market forces because there is no direct market interaction between the individuals potentially at risk and the firms that potentially create risk. Market-like forces often operate through reputation; for example, if a firm pollutes and incurs bad publicity, its sales are likely to suffer. But market forces are unlikely to adequately control risk to the general public. At the same time, tort liability tends to be prohibitively costly when damages are diffused over a large number of people and remote in time and place from the harmful cause. In the case of acid rain, for example, sulfur dioxide emissions from a number of plants or factories may cross state and even national boundaries to result in toxic harm to fish and wildlife hundreds of miles away. We believe that well-designed regulation is potentially more efficient than tort liability for controlling these environmental hazards.

In recent decades, in response to the shortcomings of market forces and liability in controlling environmental risk, a strong regulatory structure has been developed. The Environmental Protection Agency (EPA) is responsible for implementing and enforcing legislation governing environmental pollutants, such as the Clean Air Act, the Clean Water Act, the Toxic Substances Control Act (TOSCA), and Superfund. The EPA has been active in regulating sulfur dioxide, carbon monoxide, and other emissions, including discharges from factories and waste disposal sites. Although we believe regulation is the potentially more efficient method of controlling environmental risk, some reforms are still needed. Improved regulatory rules could stimulate the operation of market forces to control risk, for example, by using performance standards rather than mandating the adoption of specific technologies.

WHEN ARE MARKET FORCES SUFFICIENT?

We believe that the optimal level of safety is not that which eliminates all risk and all injuries. Rather, it is that level at which the marginal cost of attempting further risk reduction begins to exceed the marginal benefit. Benefits must of course be broadly defined to include nonfinancial as well as financial benefits of health and safety.

Critics of this view sometimes reject the principle of weighing costs and benefits simply because of the difficulty of quantifying the benefits when life and quality of life are at stake. Some decisions require such a valuation, and we often do better by making it explicit rather than implicit. But more often the practical choice is how much to pay to reduce the risk of injury by a small amount, which is somewhat easier. We all make such choices daily: when we cross the street, drive a car, engage in sports, use products that carry some risk of injury, and so on. In all these contexts, we voluntarily incur risks because they are outweighed by the benefits of the activities. Stoves and heaters protect from cold but contribute to the frequency of fires. Drugs and medicines reduce pain and disease but can also kill. Automobiles vastly reduce the costs of transportation but are associated with more than 40,000 deaths annually on U.S. highways.

As individuals we affect the level of our exposure to risk by our willingness to pay for greater safety, either by taking personal precautions or by purchasing products with enhanced safety features. By reading warnings and using products with care, consumers can reduce risks. Workers can reduce the risk of on-the-job injury by choice of a relatively safe occupation or workplace and by taking safety precautions such as wearing protective clothing and using protective devices.

Risk reduction typically entails costs, either financial or nonmonetary. To the extent that consumers and workers understand the risks they face and value risk reduction, market forces create powerful incentives for producers to provide risk-reducing features as long as they cost less than their value to the public. Products that offer warranties or have good safety records command higher prices, whereas products that are known to pose health hazards rapidly lose market share. Similarly, risky jobs must pay premium wages in order to attract workers, as has been documented in numerous studies,[3] and markets penalize employers for providing unsafe working environments. Conversely, the desire to avoid paying these wage premiums creates strong incentives for reducing the risk of workplace injury.[4]

In order for the market alone to achieve the "right" level of risk, unaided by regulation and market forces, it is not necessary that all consumers and workers be perfectly informed about all risks and base all decisions on a strictly rational cost-benefit calculus. Obviously no one lives that way all the time. Fortunately, the efficient operation of markets requires only that the marginal consumer or worker make the right decisions. For example, a substantial fraction of consumers may underestimate the risk of a product, but the product price is determined by the price that the marginal consumer is willing to pay. Therefore, provided that the marginal consumer or worker is reasonably well informed and making rational choices, market prices and wages will send correct signals to producers. Further, even if market signals are only approximately correct, because of imperfect information and nonrational decision making, it is important to remember that the alternatives of regulation and liability are also imperfect. Both regulation and liability also face high costs for obtaining the information necessary to make correct decisions, are subject to pressures that lead to uneven weighing of costs and benefits, and hence are prone to errors. Thus, the practical choice is not between imperfect markets and perfect regulation or liability, but among three imperfect systems.

In general, then, where consumers and workers are reasonably well informed and have options from which to choose that involve more or less risk, market forces can provide reasonably appropriate incentives to control risk. Regulation and liability are likely to be superfluous and may even reduce efficiency by generating overhead costs and distortions in resource allocation. The great advantage of an efficiently functioning market is that it tends to produce the right level of safety without wasting any resources on administration or litigation. Market forces create incentives for producers to supply the level of safety that consumers and workers are willing to pay for – no more and no less. And just as our economy relies mainly on consumer preferences to determine the optimal allocation of resources to produce other goods and services, it is appropriate that we rely mainly on consumer preferences to determine the correct level of investment in risk reduction and safety, provided that consumers have a reasonably accurate perception of the risks and there are no risks to unrelated third parties.

MARKET FAILURE

The invisible hand of the market induces optimal safety levels for consumers and workers only if the market provides all cost-justified alternatives and if market participants understand the risks they face. But if information on risk is costly to obtain or process, underestimation of risk encourages both the development of products that are inherently too risky and the excessive use of such products.[5] Similarly, if workers systematically underestimate risk, employers subject to competitive pressures will provide less than optimal job safety – that is, less than the level workers would be willing to "pay for" if they perceived the job hazards accurately.

Market failure because of imperfect information is most likely where risks are not immediately observable and the manifestation of injury is delayed, particularly if causal connections are not obvious – for example, if the injury or disease can also result from other factors. Carcinogens and cumulative stress are examples of latent hazards for which markets may fail. Another context in which markets may fail to create adequate incentives for safety involves injuries to bystanders or third parties who are not in a direct contractual relationship with the source of the injury. In such circumstances, the concern of potential victims for safety is not automatically internalized by producers through wage negotiations or product prices.

WHEN TO USE REGULATION AND LIABILITY

Where markets produce insufficient incentives for safety, the alternative policy tools of regulation and tort liability should be considered. However, market failure is a necessary but not a sufficient condition for imposing these alternative controls because both regulation and liability are very costly to implement, are inevitably imperfect, and often cause other resource misallocations. Thus, these additional corrective forces are worth implementing only if the costs are offset by comparable benefits in terms of risk reduction and compensation. Whether to use regulation or liability, separately or in combination, depends on the circumstances.

Regulation involves setting explicit, before-the-fact standards constraining the production process, monitoring compliance, and imposing fines for violations. It therefore tends to be very costly if a large number of separate activities must be regulated in order to achieve the desired result.

Imposing liability, in contrast, does not require detailed, before-the-fact standard setting and monitoring of producer actions. Rather, the rules – at least in theory – define broad principles that relate each party's liability in the event of injury to his or her conduct or level of care. The anticipation of potential liability if these standards are not met creates incentives for taking appropriate levels of care. Liability can, in principle, entail lower enforcement costs because extensive administrative monitoring of all production activities is not required. Rather, each potential victim has an incentive to monitor the products and services they use and to file a suit if an injury occurs due to violation of standards of care. Under liability, then, significant enforcement costs are incurred only in those instances where a violation occurs or is thought to occur and results in an injury.

These broad characteristics of regulation and tort liability imply that regulation is most appropriate in circumstances that call for uniform standards based on technical expertise beyond the competence of the typical plaintiff and the typical juror. Regulation is more likely to be cost-effective where the desired result can be achieved either by setting standards for a manageably small number of activities or by setting an overarching performance standard. It is the only practical alternative in circumstances where liability has no disincentive effects because potential defendants are or can become effectively judgment-proof.

Conversely, liability is likely to be the more efficient approach where uniform standards are inappropriate because of the idiosyncratic circumstances of each case. To be cost-effective, liability requires (1) that courts have the expertise needed to define appropriate standards of care and to accurately assess the defendant's actual conduct against these standards and (2) that the costs of litigation are small relative to the compensation payable to the injured party and the deterrence value of the suit. Liability is much less likely to be cost-effective if standards of liability or damages are prone to systematic bias or unpredictability, either because the courts are intentionally using the system primarily for compensation purposes or because technical complexity generates inconsistent outcomes across different jurisdictions. When liability standards are unpredictable or systematically wrong, they at best fail to send a clear deterrent signal and at worst induce wasteful defensive strategies and resource misallocation.[6]

The efficiency of tort liability also depends on selecting the right rule for the circumstances. For accidents that are solely within the control of producers – for example, contamination of canned food – making producers strictly liable for defective products is potentially efficient.[7] But where the user can influence the rate of injury, as is common for many product-related injuries, a rule of strict producer liability creates insufficient incentives for users to exercise care and is thus inefficient. More efficient in such circumstances are liability rules that specify strict liability with a defense of contributory negligence, negligence, or comparative negligence.[8] Although these three rules may be equally efficient for purposes of deterrence, consideration of the costs of litigation and insurance is likely to tilt the balance in favor of a negligence rule. Under an efficiently functioning negligence rule, liability is shifted only if the defendant was negligent and the plaintiff was not. There should therefore be fewer suits under negligence than under the rules of strict liability or comparative negligence and greater use of less costly first-party insurance rather than liability insurance with its higher overhead costs.

However, where information about risks is costly to both consumers and producers, any liability rule tends to work poorly, and regulation is likely to be the most efficient approach. For example, people tend to ignore very rare, low-probability events, acting as if they do not exist.[9] A potential role for a regulatory body in such circumstances is to undertake a systematic study of such hazards, collect information from multiple sources, and then set standards and disseminate information. It is worth pointing out, however, that although regulators may have a comparative advantage in gathering information about risk, to make efficient choices, they would need to know the incremental costs of producing greater safety and the preferences of consumers toward risk versus money or other goods and services. Mandated increases in safety standards almost always reduce consumer income because they increase the price of goods. If regulators set safety standards too high, consumers are made worse off. To regulate appropriately, we need to understand both the costs of improving safety and consumer willingness to bear risk. If these components of the problem are ignored, the potential efficiency gains from regulation will not be fully realized. The Delaney amendments to the FDA Act, for example, impose excessively high standards by requiring *complete* elimination of agents with *any* carcinogenic potential.

INHERENT INSTITUTIONAL BIASES

Obtaining and transmitting information is never costless, and markets can and do make mistakes. Because courts and regulators do not have automatic access to the information necessary for sound decision making, they can make mistakes just as markets do. But unlike markets, courts and regulators are prone to systematic bias in addition to random errors. In contrast with well informed, competitive markets, there are no automatic self-correcting forces in courts, legislatures, and regulatory agencies. Decisionmakers in these forums rarely have external incentives to consider and weigh fairly all the social costs and benefits of decisions that may affect literally millions of individuals.

Very few of the affected individuals have a sufficiently large stake in the outcome to make their concerns known. Thus, collective decision making through courts and regulation tends to be dominated by those individuals or groups who have a large stake in the outcome or who can bring pressure to bear at low costs. Although consumer and taxpayer groups do become involved in such issues, they are self-appointed and do not necessarily represent the broad interests of those they claim to represent. The resulting decisions may be against the interests of the great majority of consumers and taxpayers.

In the judicial process, for example, lawyers bringing and defending cases have few incentives to consider either the costs they impose on other litigants and the public or the benefits society derives from law enforcement. The bias could go either way, but the net effect is probably to generate a socially excessive level of litigation. Judges and juries also have few incentives to consider the full social costs and benefits of their decisions. When judges and juries focus on the benefits of compensation to an injured individual and believe the costs are easily and costlessly absorbed by society, there is an inherent bias toward expanding the scope of liability.[10]

Individual state legislators have weakened incentives to rein in the pro-plaintiff bias in the courts because the beneficiaries of this process –

plaintiffs, attorneys, and judges – are overwhelmingly in-state residents and voters, whereas the costs are borne largely by out-of-state corporations, employees, and shareholders.[11]

Finally, consider the incentives of regulators charged with setting safety standards and designing and enforcing the regulations to achieve those standards. Interested parties can and do influence regulators and distort this process to their own advantage, often at heavy social cost.[12]

It is reasonable to conclude that reticence of courts and legislatures to control the pressures to expand liability is hampering efficient allocation of resources. It is important to remember that a reasonably informed market is less prone to these inherent biases, and "if the market ain't very broke, don't try to fix it." Where regulatory and liability controls are clearly warranted, objective rules and guidelines should be used to the extent feasible to minimize the potential for bias in case-by-case decision making.

DEFECTS IN OUR SYSTEMS OF DETERRENCE

OVERLAPPING LIABILITY AND REGULATION

Our patchwork of regulatory and liability systems has developed in a largely haphazard and uncoordinated fashion. Of course some apparent overlap is not necessarily wasteful. Regulation and liability may operate on different aspects of the same activity, or liability may increase compliance with regulation. But without coordination, the simultaneous use of both regulation and liability can lead to duplicative and even conflicting standard setting, duplicative expenditures on litigation and regulatory enforcement, and distortions in production.

For consumer products, these excesses are most obvious in the case of pharmaceuticals. The FDA monitors new drugs and medical devices extensively prior to their general release to assure that they are both safe and effective and carry appropriate labeling and warnings. Since no drug is totally without adverse effects in some subpopulation of users, approval is based on a favorable ratio of benefits to risks for the population as a whole. After introduction, manufacturers of an approved drug must continue to report instances of possible drug-related adverse experiences and make modifications in labeling and warnings as required. Such information may be obtained from patients, physicians, or the worldwide medical literature. The costs and delays of premarket testing have increased over the years; it is now estimated to cost an average of $125 million to successfully bring a new drug to market.[13] The average regulatory delay increased between 1964 and 1984 from 4.5 years to 9.5 years.[14]

This cost estimate ignores the indirect costs to consumers in terms of delay in obtaining access to potentially beneficial drugs. Delay also reduces effective patent life and thus incentives to develop new products.[15]

Studies of FDA regulation have concluded that it has tended to err on the side of imposing unreasonably high delay costs on consumers in an attempt to achieve very low levels of risk and high standards of efficacy.[16] Nevertheless, compliance with this stringent system of FDA regulation does not protect a pharmaceutical manufacturer against liability claims, including punitive damages. Similarly, compliance with EPA warning requirements does not protect chemical manufacturers from liability. (See "Compliance with EPA Requirements: *Ferebee v. Chevron Chemical Co.*," below.)

COMPLIANCE WITH EPA REQUIREMENTS

Ferebee v. Chevron Chemical Co.

Even compliance with a government-prescribed warning label has been found to be inadequate warning. In *Ferebee v. Chevron Chemical Co.,* Chevron was found liable for damages caused by a chemical it manufactured, even though it explicitly followed the EPA's approved label for the chemical.

Richard L. Ferebee, a worker at a federal agricultural center, contracted pulmonary fibrosis, a serious lung disease, apparently as a result of his long-term exposure to dilute solutions of paraquat, an herbicide manufactured by Chevron. Under the Federal Insecticide, Fungicide and Rodenticide Act (FIFRA), EPA extensively regulates the sale and labeling of paraquat. After extensive scientific testimony, EPA approved the following wording for paraquat labels: "DANGER. CAN KILL IF SWALLOWED. HARMFUL TO THE EYES AND SKIN." The approved label also stated that in case of skin contact the area exposed to the chemical should be washed immediately and contaminated clothing removed. In addition, the label noted that "prolonged contact" would cause severe irritation and that "repeated contact" may increase the danger of absorption.

Chevron used this label on the paraquat alleged to have caused Ferebee's illness and death. Notwithstanding the fact that the defendant failed to read the label, the U.S. District Court of D.C. as well as a federal court of appeals decided that the warning was inadequate. Although FIFRA does not permit states to impose additional labeling requirements, and the courts conceded that Chevron had no legal right to add to or depart from the EPA-prescribed warning, both courts still found Chevron liable and awarded damages to Ferebee's estate.[17]

Workplace safety is another area where the superimposition of strict liability under workers' compensation, regulation, and now tort liability, in addition to strong market forces, can generate conflicting standards and excessive implementation costs. In the nineteenth century, employers were liable for workplace injuries under a negligence rule, with defenses of contributory negligence, assumption of risk, and negligence of a co-worker. Since 1911, all states have replaced this negligence rule with the workers' compensation system, whereby employers are strictly liable for work-related injuries regardless of employee contribution to injury. Since 1971 this system of strict liability has been reinforced by regulation through the Occupational Safety and Health Administration (OSHA), which sets standards for literally thousands of workplace conditions.

In the 1970s, courts, under newly affirmed doctrines of strict liability, began to allow workers to sue in tort for work-related injuries. Manufacturers of products used in the workplace have been sued both by the employees of another employer and by employers seeking reimbursement for their workers' compensation expenses. In addition, some employees have successfully circumvented the rule that workers' compensation was to be the sole remedy for work-related injuries by suing their employers directly on grounds of their dual capacity as manufacturers of products used in the workplace. The reintroduction of employer liability in tort has created an additional costly layer of controls and compensation that often undermines the incentives created by workers' compensation. The deterrence benefits from adding tort liability are likely to be minimal, given the powerful forces of the market, workers' compensation, and regulation (see Chapter 6). In these circumstances, tort liability is largely a duplicative and inefficient system of compensation.

Environmental hazards are an area where regulation is potentially the most efficient approach to controlling risk, and adding overlapping tort liability is wasteful. In this area, markets fail because of the absence of market connections between the affected parties. Liability is usually extremely costly and imperfect because of the large number of potential plaintiffs and defendants involved and the extreme difficulties of assessing risk and establishing causal connections long after the fact. For example, in the case of carbon monoxide emissions from automobiles, it would be prohibitively costly to rely on tort liability actions in which consumers attempt to establish relationships between the design of an automobile and pulmonary disorders allegedly associated with poor air quality. As in the case of drugs that comply with FDA standards, permitting courts to impose liability where products comply with EPA or other specific regulatory standards surely adds very little positive deterrence and may even be counterproductive.

INEFFICIENCIES IN REGULATION

Countless studies have been undertaken evaluating the costs and benefits of individual regulations and entire regulatory agencies. A recent review examined forty-four major regulations proposed and implemented by federal agencies.[18] The results of the study, which took the agencies' estimation of costs and risk reduction, are reported in Table 5.2. The most striking finding is the huge range in both initial risk levels and estimated cost per life saved, ranging from $100,000 per fatality avoided by NHTSA's auto steering column redesign to $92 million for EPA's arsenic regulation and $72 billion for OSHA's proposed formaldehyde standard. Inconsistencies in cost per life saved across different risk-reduction activities implies forgone opportunity: the total number of lives saved could be increased at no additional cost simply by reallocating resources from those areas with relatively low benefits per dollar spent to those with a greater payoff.[19] Further, costs of achieving the target level of risk are often needlessly high because of the way regulations are set. For example, it is common to require a uniform exposure level to a particular pollutant at each site or to mandate the uniform adoption of a specific technology at each discharge point without regard for differences in total cost and in the relative cost-effectiveness of different technologies at different sites. The total cost of achieving any desired level of risk can be lower if targets are set in terms of performance standards – which may vary by site – and industry is permitted to adopt the most cost-effective methods of achieving those standards.

A second significant point that emerges from Table 5.2 is that the process of administrative and judicial review of proposed regulatory standards has resulted in rejection or modification of some of the most costly regulations.[20] In contrast, the safety-related decisions of courts with respect to liability are not subject to the same scrutiny of their cost-effectiveness.

A third important conclusion is that the regulatory process is highly vulnerable to influence by interested parties. The adoption of standards that mandate adoption of certain technologies rather than setting performance standards (e.g., defining a target level of air quality) can result in competitive advantage to producers who have already adopted the technology or whose costs of adapting will be low at the expense of other domestic or international competitors.[21] The costs of these distortions are reflected in higher prices to domestic consumers and must be offset against any benefits of the regulation in terms of risk reduction.

INEFFICIENCIES IN TORT LIABILITY RULES

The key to the efficient functioning of tort liability as a system of deterrence is requiring each individual who fails to take cost-justified care to pay for the damages that he or she causes, no more and no less. This condition is quite general and applies to all areas of liability, not just product liability. It requires that courts define and apply appropriate standards of care and rules of damages. However, as the liability system has evolved in recent years, driven by the twin goals of internalizing the cost of injuries and compensating victims, it has departed in significant ways from the standards required to induce efficient levels of care. This is particularly true in the area of product liability, where standards of strict and even absolute liability have been carried farthest. By imposing liability where it is not appropriate and failing to impose it where it is, the tort system operates as a system of taxes and subsidies that distorts the allocation of resources. Because we have discussed these legal trends in depth in Chapter 2, what follows is a summary of specific rules that particularly distort the efficiency of incentives for risk management. Inefficiencies in tort damage rules are discussed in Chapter 6.

INADEQUATE INCENTIVES FOR CONSUMERS AND WORKERS

Traditional negligence law recognized the importance of care by potential injury victims through the doctrines of assumption of risk and contributory negligence: a plaintiff was barred from recovery if the hazards were open and obvious and he or she knowingly chose to use the product or if his or her own negligence contributed significantly to the injury. Imposing liability on a negligent defendant *unless* the plaintiff was contributorially negligent is a rule that provides both parties with appropriate incentives to take reasonable care.[22]

Although modern product liability law nominally retains defenses in cases of consumer misconduct, product misuse or alteration, and assumption of risk, these doctrines have been greatly restricted since the 1960s.[23] In practical application, strict liability has become increasingly a rule of absolute liability of manufacturers for product-related injuries. Absolute producer liability, even where users are careless or even reckless, creates incentives either to design products to guard against *any* potential misuse, which raises production costs and often reduces the performance of the product, or to withdraw products and services that cannot be made completely safe. The results are higher prices and loss of convenience to the great majority of consumers who are willing to be reasonably careful.

JOINT AND SEVERAL LIABILITY

The rule of joint and several liability creates a similar potential for imposing an excessive liability burden on parties contributing to an injury and can add enormously to the costs of litigation. This rule permits the injured victim to collect his entire recovery from any one of the defendants who have been found liable, even if that defendant played only a minor

TABLE 5.2

Analysis of Costs of Risk Reduction through Regulation

Regulation	Year	Agency	Status[a]	Initial Annual Risk[b]	Annual Lives Saved	Cost Per Life Saved (Thousands of 1984 $)
Steering Column Protection	1967	NHTSA	F	7.7 in 10^5	1,300.000	$100
Unvented Space Heaters	1980	CPSC	F	2.7 in 10^5	63.000	100
Oil & Gas Well Service	1983	OSHA-S	P	1.1 in 10^3	50.000	100
Cabin Fire Protection	1985	FAA	F	6.5 in 10^8	15.000	200
Passive Restraints/Belts	1984	NHTSA	F	9.1 in 10^5	1,850.000	300
Fuel System Integrity	1975	NHTSA	F	4.9 in 10^6	400.000	300
Trihalomethanes	1979	EPA	F	6.0 in 10^6	322.000	300
Underground Construction	1983	OSHA-S	P	1.6 in 10^3	8.100	300
Alcohol & Drug Control	1985	FRA	F	1.8 in 10^6	4.200	500
Servicing Wheel Rims	1984	OSHA-S	F	1.4 in 10^5	2.300	500
Seat Cushion Flammability	1984	FAA	F	1.6 in 10^7	37.000	600
Floor Emergency Lighting	1984	FAA	F	2.2 in 10^8	5.000	700
Crane Suspended Personnel Platform	1984	OSHA-S	P	1.8 in 10^3	5.000	900
Children's Sleepware Flammability	1973	CPSC	F	2.4 in 10^6	106.000	1,300
Side Doors	1970	NHTSA	F	3.6 in 10^5	480.000	1,300
Concrete & Masonry Construction	1985	OSHA-S	P	1.4 in 10^5	6.500	1,400
Hazard Communication	1983	OSHA-S	F	4.0 in 10^5	200.000	1,800
Grain Dust	1984	OSHA-S	P	2.1 in 10^4	4.000	2,800
Benzene/Fugitive Emissions	1984	EPA	F	2.1 in 10^5	0.310	2,800
Radionuclides/Uranium Mines	1984	EPA	F	1.4 in 10^4	1.100	6,900

Agent	Year	Agency	Status	Risk	Annual deaths per exposed population	Cost
Asbestos	1972	OSHA-H	F	3.9 in 10^4	396.000	7,400
Benzene	1985	OSHA-H	P	8.8 in 10^4	3.800	17,100
Arsenic/Glass Plant	1986	EPA	F	8.0 in 10^4	0.110	19,200
Ethylene Oxide	1984	OSHA-H	F	4.4 in 10^5	2.800	25,600
Arsenic/Copper Smelter	1986	EPA	F	9.0 in 10^4	0.060	26,500
Uranium Mill Tailings/Inactive	1983	EPA	F	4.3 in 10^4	2.100	27,600
Acrylonitrile	1978	OSHA-H	F	9.4 in 10^4	6.900	37,600
Uranium Mill Tailings/Active	1983	EPA	F	4.3 in 10^4	2.100	53,000
Coke Ovens	1976	OSHA-H	F	1.6 in 10^4	31.000	61,800
Asbestos	1986	OSHA-H	F	6.7 in 10^5	74.700	89,300
Arsenic	1978	OSHA-H	F	1.8 in 10^3	11.700	92,500
Asbestos	1986	EPA	P	2.9 in 10^5	10.000	104,200
DES (Cattlefeed)	1979	FDA	F	3.1 in 10^7	68.000	132,000
Arsenic/Glass Manufacturing	1986	EPA	R	3.8 in 10^5	0.250	142,000
Benzene/Storage	1984	EPA	R	6.0 in 10^7	0.043	202,000
Radionuclides/DOE Facilities	1984	EPA	R	4.3 in 10^6	0.001	210,000
Radionuclides/Elemental Phosphorous	1984	EPA	R	1.4 in 10^5	0.046	270,000
Acrylonitrile	1978	OSHA-H	R	9.4 in 10^4	0.600	308,000
Benzene/Ethylbenzenol Styrene	1984	EPA	R	2.0 in 10^6	0.006	483,000
Arsenic/Low-Arsenic Copper	1986	EPA	R	2.6 in 10^4	0.090	764,000
Benzene/Maleic Anhydride	1984	EPA	R	1.1 in 10^6	0.029	820,000
Land Disposal	1986	EPA	P	2.3 in 10^8	2.520	3,500,000
EDB	1983	OSHA-H	P	2.5 in 10^4	0.002	15,600,000
Formaldehyde	1985	OSHA-H	P	6.8 in 10^7	0.010	72,000,000

[a]Proposed, rejected, or final rule.
[b]Annual deaths per exposed population. An exposed population of 10^3 is 1,000.

SOURCE: John F. Morrall III, "A Review of the Record," *Regulation* (November–December 1986): 30.

role in causing the injury. If this arbitrary sharing rule tended to average out over cases, there would be no distortion in deterrence because the expected liability cost to each potential defendant could be correct. But in practice, defendants with the deepest pockets, including municipalities, corporations, auditors, and others, tend to bear a disproportionate share of the damages because individual defendants typically lack the assets or the high limits of liability insurance to pay for multimillion-dollar awards. (See "Joint and Several Liability: *Walt Disney World Co. v. Wood,*" below.)

Distortions in the assignment of liability and costs of litigation are exacerbated because the joint and several liability rule encourages plaintiffs to name in their suits any financially responsible party that could be considered to have contributed to the injury in even a most minor way. Such a defendant then has a choice between incurring large costs of litigation with a risk of having to pay the full damages or making a settlement offer well in excess of its real contribution to the plaintiff's loss. The operation of joint and several liability in the context of Superfund liability for the cleanup of hazardous wastes is a major cause of the vast litigation and delay in implementing cleanup and contributes significantly to the crisis in pollution liability insurance.

PROBABILISTIC CAUSATION[24]

The notion of probabilistic causation also makes it more difficult and costly for the tort system to achieve efficient deterrence. Under traditional tort rules, a plaintiff could not recover unless he could show that the conduct of a particular defendant was the cause of his injury. This requirement of a clear causal link between a particular plaintiff and a particular defendant has given way to a probabilistic notion of cause. For

---

JOINT AND SEVERAL LIABILITY

Walt Disney World Co. v. Wood
A recent case illustrating the unfairness of the application of joint and several liability is *Walt Disney World Co. v. Wood,* 515 So.2d 198 (Fla. 1987). The driver of a bumper car was injured when her car was struck by the bumper car driven by her fiancé. The jury found the fiancé 85 percent responsible for the injury, the plaintiff 14 percent responsible, and Disney World 1 percent responsible. Because her fiancé, who had become her husband by the time of the trial, was immune from suit by his wife under Florida law, Walt Disney World had to pay their 1 percent plus the fiancé/husband's 85 percent, or all of the damages not attributable to the plaintiff.

example in *Sindell v. Abbott Laboratories,*[25] the California Supreme Court adopted a market share approach to liability. Damages were shared among defendant pharmaceutical companies in proportion to their share of the market of the allegedly harmful product, the drug DES, thereby dispensing with the requirement of establishing any connection between a particular defendant and a particular plaintiff. In the class action case concerning Agent Orange, Judge Weinstein granted summary judgment despite conflicting expert medical testimony on the causation issue.[26]

This probabilistic approach corresponds roughly to modern scientific views of causation, but it is a major contributor to current problems with the liability system. It vastly expands the potential scope of liability, particularly in mass exposure cases (see Chapter 2), and the costs of this type of litigation are enormous (see Chapter 3). Here we are concerned with the potentially distorting effect on deterrence.

Appropriate deterrent incentives can be retained if there is a requirement of proof of the link between the conduct of a particular defendant and a class of plaintiffs, although determination of damages remains difficult (see Chapter 6). But if the sole requirement for liability is a probabilistic connection between the conduct of a class of defendants and a class of plaintiffs, deterrence incentives are seriously undermined. For example, under a strict market share allocation of liability, the potential liability of a particular manufacturer depends less on the safety of its own product than on the average safety of the products of the industry as a whole. Each firm's incentive to incur costs to enhance the safety of its own product is reduced in proportion to its market share. In practice, distortions in incentives may be much worse because the aggregate assessment of liability is likely to be inaccurate and volatile from case to case because of the difficulty of measuring the contribution of other factors, such as environment and lifestyle. Thus, in many of the contexts that give rise to these cases, regulation is in our judgment the more efficient solution.

RETROACTIVE STANDARDS

The rejection of the state-of-the-art defense and imposition of liability even where the court determines that the defendant could not have known of the hazards at the time of the allegedly harmful conduct has also been adopted with the intent of extending compensation.[27] By definition, such a retroactive imposition of liability can serve no positive deterrent purpose. In fact, it can have a negative effect by discouraging new technologies and products, particularly products that are expected to be long-lived or to entail some risk of having long-latent effects. Of course, such future risks should not be ignored. But current decisions must be based on an evaluation of expected benefits and costs, based on the best information available at the present and including the best assessment of risk of future harm and costs of withholding a product or delaying introduction until more information is obtained or safer technologies are developed. If manufacturers anticipate that future courts will base their judgments on newly developed standards of liability or damages, innovation will be overly deterred.

It is very hard to measure the distorting effects of retroactive imposition of liability, but such effects are almost bound to have grown in recent years and will continue to grow as a result of the interaction of several critical factors: the more frequent rejection by the courts of the state-of-the-art defense and a coincident acceleration of the rate of technological change; expanded understanding of the causes of disease and ability to trace minute exposures; and the vastly expanded scope of liability and size of damage awards. Thus, the net effect of these interacting factors is much greater than the sum of each operating separately.

The temptation to impose liability retroactively, regardless of the state of knowledge when the injury occurred, may arise out of the sense that someone other than the injured person should pay for the unanticipated injury. But there is little equity in imposing liability on the defendant if the risk was unknowable at the time of his or her action. This is particularly true in the case of a corporate defendant, where both management and shareholders may have undergone a complete turnover between the time of the allegedly harmful act and the imposition of liability. Where unanticipated risks emerge, there is a real need for compensation. In most cases, existing private and public insurance programs would cover such losses because they are designed to pay regardless of the cause or circumstances of the injury. However, we acknowledge that there are gaps in these insurance programs. (For a detailed discussion, see Chapter 6.) But to use the tort system purely to fill these gaps by imposing liability retroactively for risks that were unknowable at the time of the defendant's actions serves neither the purposes of efficient deterrence nor equity and indeed is likely to be counterproductive on both counts.

UNLIMITED DURATION OF LIABILITY

Statutes of limitations and repose define the length of time within which a plaintiff may bring suit. For most torts, traditional limitations are typically about two years. In cases of professional liability and product liability, concern that the existence of an injury and its cause may not be immediately obvious has led to the adoption of liberal discovery rules. These start the clock of the statute of limitations from the date the injury was, or should have been (with due diligence) discovered, rather than from the date of the allegedly harmful conduct. Thus a manufacturer who made a product fifty years ago could be held liable for injuries that occur today. In practice, long statutes primarily affect producers of capital goods and industrial equipment with long useful lives (and the potential for modification by successive users).

Allowing an unlimited time for discovery provides maximum protection to plaintiffs. It could also be consistent with efficient deterrence *if* potential future liability could be accurately predicted. This requires that the standards imposed at the time of discovery of the injury be those prevailing at the time of the action that allegedly caused it. Although some courts adhere to a state-of-the-art defense, there is clearly a risk that new standards will be applied retroactively, sometimes unintentionally. Moreover, even if liability is determined according to the knowledge and standards that governed the defendant's actions, the magnitude of damages is generally that prevailing at the time of disposition. Thus, a long duration of liability tends in practice to imply retroactive application of new standards, with all the adverse consequences already noted.

JUDICIAL LATITUDE

Some of the recent problems of the tort system can be traced to specific rules that are clearly inefficient, but even efficient rules will not produce sound results if they are not applied. In principle, judges control juries by making procedural and evidentiary rulings and by defining the substantive rules of law that juries are to apply. The role of the jury is to make findings of fact. In practice, many expert observers believe that judges are granting increasing latitude to juries and that this contributes to innovation and unpredictability in court decisions and the expansion of liability.[28]

BENEFITS AND COSTS OF REGULATION

The studies of the benefits and costs of health and safety regulation are too numerous to review here, but some salient findings are worth noting.[29] Litan and Nordhaus estimate that the costs of administering health, safety, and environmental regulations increased from $600 million in 1969 to $3 billion in 1981, changing the cost-per-family from approximately $11 in 1969 to approximately $50 in 1981. Estimates of the costs of compliance (altering production methods to meet required standards) are much larger, ranging from $20.8 to $55 billion in 1977, or 1.1 to 2.9 percent of GNP. That translates to a 1977 per-family annual cost of between $370 and $1,000.[30] Comparable costs are probably significantly higher now with the enactment of the Superfund program in 1981. An important point that emerges from detailed analyses of specific regulations is that initial government estimates of the costs of compliance are often much lower than actual costs. In particular, costs of complications and newly created risks tend to be underestimated.[31]

Evidence on the risk reduction benefits of regulation is more mixed. There is spotty but generally positive evidence that OSHA regulation has reduced injury rates in the workplace. Results are even more tentative for the effects of EPA controls on emissions and CPSC regulations of consumer products.[32] Although some of these studies use the best data and methodologies available, conclusions are necessarily tentative because of the limitations of the data on pollution levels and injury rates and the difficulty of adequately controlling for all other relevant factors in order to isolate the net effect of regulation. For example, emissions of some pollutants depend on cyclical levels of business activity, the industrial mix and shift to the service sector, the level of energy prices, and the relative use of petroleum versus coal. Imperfect control for these other factors can lead to biased estimates of the effects of regulation of pollutants. Thus, the conclusion on regulation is that the costs are significant but the evidence on benefits is mixed and unreliable because of the difficulty of measuring the number of injuries prevented.

BENEFITS AND COSTS OF TORT LIABILITY

A full evaluation of the liability system requires calculating total benefits minus total costs. In principle, on the benefit side of the ledger are the reductions in risk of injury and the increases in compensation. On the cost side are the increased resources absorbed in risk reduction, insurance, and litigation costs and the value of consumption and production opportunities forgone because of product withdrawal and loss of international competitiveness. Measures of both benefits and costs of liability must net out the effects of market forces and regulation.

The risk-reduction benefits and costs of tort liability have proved even harder to measure than those of regulation. For liability, there are no clearly defined standards, promulgated at a specific time, from which changes in the injury rate or in costs can be measured. The state-specific character of tort law muddies the identification of when particular rulings might affect specific firms, some of which operate locally and some nationwide. Thus, the unpredictability of liability standards that plagues corporate decision makers also defeats the analyst trying to evaluate the effects of the system. Moreover, existing data on injury rates are not well designed to measure changes that might result from the tort system.

In this chapter we are concerned particularly with the risk reduction or deterrence benefits and costs of tort liability. The compensation component is discussed in Chapter 6. On the benefit side, existing data on injury rates are inadequate to measure the deterrence effects of the tort system. The cost side is equally problematic. The litigation expense component was documented in Chapter 4; it is estimated at $11 billion in 1985 for nonauto torts. If this $11 billion is viewed as the cost of administering the tort system, it can be compared with the estimated $3 billion (in 1981 dollars) cost of administering federal health and safety regulation (see Table 5.2). The $3 billion includes only budgetary costs of federal agencies and therefore underestimates the total administrative cost of regulation. Nevertheless, even if we double the figure to allow for administrative costs to other parties, it seems safe to conclude that the administrative costs of tort liability are at least comparable in magnitude to the administrative costs of regulation and may be significantly greater.

In addition to the direct litigation costs of the tort system, there are indirect costs which are much harder to measure. The first component of indirect costs of liability, which is analogous to compliance costs in the regulatory context, includes the opportunity cost of additional resources devoted to risk reduction, due to increased expenditures on research and development to assess remote risks, modifications of product design, quality control, labeling, and warnings. The cost here is the value of the output that could have been produced if these resources had been devoted to other uses.[33] Only those costs that are incurred because of the threat of liability should be included. In practice, of course, it is very difficult to distinguish liability-induced changes from safety measures that would have been undertaken in response to either market incentives or regulatory requirements.

The second component of indirect costs is the loss that results from products being withdrawn or never brought to market because the costs of protecting against the liability threat are prohibitive. The resulting reduction in choice of products and services available to consumers and loss of employment and profit opportunities for workers and owners of capital are real social costs but are very hard to quantify. Such costs result, for example, when day-care centers and sports facilities close, and new contraceptives are not made available in the United States although they are marketed in Europe.[34]

IMPACT OF TORT LIABILITY ON PRODUCERS: SURVEY EVIDENCE

The difficulty in measuring indirect costs of liability to corporations stems from several factors. Present corporate accounting systems are not designed to measure these costs, particularly the additional effect of liability over and above market and regulatory effects.

Most of the evidence discussed here is therefore necessarily drawn from personal interviews or surveys.[35] General conclusions based on such evidence are very tentative because survey respondents may be unrepresentative of industry as a whole and because any single respondent in a large corporation is unlikely to have a complete picture of the total effect that is the sum of myriad small changes in the allocation of time and other resources throughout the firm. Thus, surveys of different corporate officers such as chief executives, risk managers, and general counsel may yield quite different pictures simply because each has a different and necessarily limited information base.

Survey-based estimates of the impact of liability are likely to have a systematic downward bias if liability is typically a significant but not dominant factor in many decisions. For example, the decision to introduce a new product or withdraw an established product depends on the expected rate of return, which in turn depends on many factors, of which liability is only one. In response to a question about how many products have been withdrawn or not introduced because of concern over liability, respondents may list only those where liability was the predominant factor, not the probably greater number where liability was significant but not the predominant factor. With these caveats, we summarize some of the main findings of these surveys.

INSURANCE COSTS

Survey evidence estimates that the cost of liability insurance averages under 1 percent of sales, although in some industries it is much higher: for example, 10 percent of the cost of general aviation aircraft production and 4.2 percent of sales for sporting goods.[36] Even if these direct costs appear small when measured as a percentage of sales, the 1 percent figure is about half the amount manufacturing companies spend on research and development, more than a quarter of all new expenditures on manufacturing plant and equipment, and twice undistributed profits in 1985.[37] Thus, direct liability-related costs are not negligible when measured as a percentage of net operating income or profit, and the variance of potential liability costs may add significantly to the variance of operating margins. This effect on expected return and the riskiness of that return is a more relevant benchmark than a percent-of-sales measure for assessing the impact of liability on international competitiveness and on broad corporate strategy, including whether to remain in or enter product markets at home and abroad.

INDIRECT COSTS OF INCREASED PRODUCT SAFETY

Both anecdotal reports and corporate surveys provide clear evidence of the existence of both types of indirect cost (increased resource use to reduce product risk and withdrawal from risky product lines) but the magnitude of the impact is impossible to gauge with information currently available in research libraries and corporate records. In a recent Conference Board survey, over one-third of responding chief executive officers of large firms report having improved the safety of products, redesigned product lines, and improved product usage and warning information (see Table 5.5).[38] However, the costs of these changes were not estimated.

The number of firms in the Conference Board study reporting forgone opportunities is substantial: 36 percent of the larger firms had discontinued product lines because of liability concerns, 30 percent had decided against introducing new products, and 21 percent had discontinued product research (see Table 5.5 for impact on smaller firms).[39] The survey did not attempt to obtain information on the actual or projected sales value of the products withdrawn or not introduced, or on whether a close substitute product had subsequently been introduced, possibly by a foreign competitor. As we noted earlier, these responses may reflect only those instances where liability is the overwhelming factor in a decision and thus may not reflect the pervasive but small effect on the expected rate of return on all new products and hence on the rate of innovation.

Whether or not liability leads to an excessive allocation of resources to the search for safer product designs cannot be determined from survey evidence. Some of the corporate responses to reduce product risk may be appropriate. However, distortions are likely in two areas. First, making firms strictly liable for injuries that result from product misuse, where the injury could be prevented at lower cost by the product user than by the firm, wastes resources in the assessment of risks of possible misuse and in design and manufacture to avoid them. Second, concern over potential liabilities that are very remote in the future may effectively force current consumers to pay for excessively high standards on long-lived products such as machine tools. Consistent with this expectation of a bigger impact for long-lived products, the Conference Board survey shows that a much larger percentage of firms in industries with long-lived products rate the impact of the liability system as major: 61 percent for consumer durables and 54 percent for industrial equipment and machinery compared with 38 percent for consumer nondurables and 39 percent for industrial materials and supplies.[40]

INTERFIRM ALLOCATION OF PRODUCTION

In many respects, small firms are particularly adversely affected by the liability system. Monitoring and complying with changes in liability entail fixed costs that are more burdensome, the smaller the volume of operations over which they can be spread. Small firms are less able to self-insure and face higher costs of obtaining insurance. Two-thirds of the CEOs of small firms rated the impact of the liability system on their industries as major,[41] and 15 percent were operating without insurance. The fixed costs of dealing with liability may also make large diversified firms less willing to enter risky product lines on a small scale, because the expected returns may not warrant placing the entire corporate assets at risk. Thus, liability is likely to increase concentration in risky product markets.

Firms higher up in the chain of production and distribution are monitoring the insurance coverage of suppliers more carefully.[42] This may be an example of the positive benefits of liability: it strengthens incentives for those connected in the chain of production and distribution to monitor each other. On the other hand, potentially beneficial transactions between firms will simply not be pursued if the costs of verifying financial responsibility or contracting for indemnification are high.

Similarly, companies are now much more concerned about the potential product and environmental liabilities of firms they may acquire. No

---

THE IMPACT OF PRODUCT LIABILITY

The Conference Board has conducted two studies of the effect of product liability on U.S. businesses. The most recent, *The Impact of Product Liability* (McGuire, 1988), investigated the extent to which business operations overall had been affected and was based on the responses of over 500 chief executive officers of both large and small companies. The Board also conducted a study entitled *Product Liability: The Corporate Response* (Weber, 1987) that sought specific information on the impact of liability such as the number of liability suits faced and the cost of liability insurance for companies. The 1987 survey has been criticized because of the limited number of issues it addressed and the limited perspective of its respondents (mainly risk managers). For this reason we focus mainly on the 1988 survey.

For the 1988 study, *The Impact of Product Liability,* CEOs of 2,000 of the largest U.S. manufacturers and CEOs of 2,000 U.S. manufacturers with fewer than 500 employees were surveyed for their views on the corporate impact of product liability. Approximately 270 usable responses were received from the large manufacturers, and approximately 280 were received from the smaller manufacturers. Tables 5.3, 5.4, and 5.5 were compiled from this report.

doubt there is some benefit from increased scrutiny of all aspects of an acquisition, including potential liabilities. But with necessarily imperfect information about hidden liabilities, there will be a reduction in liquidity of corporate assets. For example, interviewed firms cite concern over hidden hazardous wastes as a significant factor leading to a preference for developing new sites rather than purchasing existing plants.[43] This may lead to an excessive rate of new development and suboptimal reuse of sites already developed.

Overall, more than 40 percent of the CEOs of large firms and 59 percent of the CEOs of small firms believed that the U.S. product liability system has had a major impact on their firms, and over half of all the CEOs believed that the added costs are having a major impact on our international competitiveness.

EFFECT OF TORT LIABILITY ON U.S. COMPETITIVENESS

The present U.S. liability system is far more advantageous to plaintiffs in both procedural and substantive law than that of any other country. U.S.

TABLE 5.3

Impact of Product Liability on Industries

Degree of Impact Reported	Percentage Distribution	
	Fortune 2000 Co.[a]	Smaller Firms[b]
Major	45 %	66 %
Moderate	39	27
Minimal	16	7
Total	100	100

[a]Based on responses from 261 of the nation's largest manufacturers.
[b]Based on responses from 276 randomly selected manufacturing firms with fewer than 500 employees.

SOURCE: E. Patrick McGuire, *The Impact of Product Liability,* Research Report No. 908 (New York: The Conference Board, 1988), Table 7, 41, pp. 7, 31.

discovery rules are more liberal and can be used to impose huge costs on defendants. U.S. damage rules are more generous, particularly in determining awards for noneconomic loss. The concept of punitive damages is completely absent in most other countries.[44] Among the major industrialized countries, only the United States permits contingent fees that enable a plaintiff to bring a suit without paying legal costs up front. In the great majority of other countries, liability suits are decided by judges, not juries. These differences make it easier to sue and to receive higher awards in the United States. Although the European Economic Community has recently adopted a strict product liability directive that resembles U.S. law in many ways, implementation of similar rules may be quite different and far less expansive in Europe than it has been here, because of remaining differences in rules of procedure, damages, and legal fees.

U.S. firms selling abroad may be sued by foreign plaintiffs in U.S. courts. However, our courts may decline jurisdiction under the doctrine of *forum non conveniens* when it is determined to be more convenient,

TABLE 5.4

Impact of Product Liability on International Competitiveness

Degree of Impact Reported	Percentage Distribution	
	Fortune 2000 Co.[a]	Smaller Firms[b]
Major	49 %	68 %
Moderate	37	25
Minimal	14	7
Total	100	100

[a]Based on responses from 260 of the nation's largest manufacturers.

[b]Based on responses from 261 randomly selected manufacturing firms with fewer than 500 employees.

SOURCE: McGuire, *The Impact of Product Liability,* Tables 10, 44, pp. 8, 32.

given the required witnesses and documents, to have the case tried in another jurisdiction. U.S. federal courts typically do invoke this doctrine against foreign claims, but state courts are less reluctant to accept such cases because rules on state court jurisdiction are more liberal.[45]

In contrast, although foreign manufacturers selling in U.S. markets are in principle subject to the same liabilities as domestic firms, in practice foreign firms have significant procedural advantages. For example, the more restrictive discovery rules of the home country may apply even to litigation in the United States, at least with respect to the firm's records outside of the United States.[46] Similarly, the costs of collecting a judgment against a foreign firm are often higher. Many foreign firms operate in the

---

TABLE 5.5

Effects of Liability Cited by Responding Companies Based on Actual Liability Experience

Effect	Percent of Large Firms Reporting Effect[a]	Percent of Small Firms Reporting Effect[b]
Closed production plants	8 %	2 %
Laid off workers	15	9
Discontinued product lines	36	27
Decided against introducing new products	30	31
Decided against acquiring/ merging	17	11
Discontinued product research	21	18
Moved production offshore	4	2
Lost market share	22	25
Improved safety of products	35	17
Redesigned product lines	33	24
Improved product usage and warnings	42	29

[a]Based on responses from 180 of the nation's largest manufacturers except for the final 3 impacts cited which are based on 264 responses.

[b]Based on responses from 279 randomly selected manufacturing firms each with fewer than 500 employees.

SOURCE: McGuire, *The Impact of Product Liability,* Tables 28, 31, 59, 61, pp. 19-20, 34-35.

United States through independent export agents or wholly-owned sub-sidiaries whose assets may be insufficient to permit recovery of large damages. As a consequence, foreign firms face lower expected costs of being sued than their domestic competitors in the United States.

The net result of these two effects – that U.S. exporters may be subject to U.S. liability rules for their products sold abroad and that foreign firms are unlikely to be fully subject to U.S. law for their products sold in the United States – is that U.S. firms incur much greater insurance costs per dollar sales than their foreign competitors do.[47] For example, an insurance company has estimated that in terms of gross domestic product (GDP) devoted to liability insurance, the United States spends more than Japan, West Germany, France, Great Britain, Canada, Italy, and Australia by an average factor of four. Liability insurance expenditures in the United States exceeded Japan's insurance expenditures by a factor of fifteen.[48] Liability insurance constitutes as much as 15 percent of the cost of certain machine tools manufactured in this country.[49] Dow Chemical spent $100 million on legal and insurance costs for its domestic sales of $5 billion in 1986, but its $6 billion in overseas sales required only $20 million in such costs.[50] McDonnell Douglas Corporation, in selling aircraft in China, had to include an allowance for the insurance costs of protecting against possible claims in the United States of an air crash in China. Its European rivals would not face comparable costs. The premium charged foreign firms by their insurance companies for coverage for their goods sold in the United States is estimated to exceed premiums for their goods sold in their own or other countries by a factor between four and ten;[51] depending on the product, the rate for sales into the United States may be as much as a hundred times the rate for European sales.[52]

For some products, insurance costs that reflect the differential cost of the U.S. liability system can impose a damaging competitive disadvantage. Perhaps more important, the higher costs of both product and environmental liability in the United States lead domestic firms to adopt more costly production methods that place them at a disadvantage when competing abroad against firms with production costs that reflect less strict liability regimes and less litigious environments.[53] By the same logic, it might be argued that foreign producers selling products in the United States that are designed primarily for less safety-conscious foreign environments are at a disadvantage relative to domestic producers in U.S. markets. Like any barrier to imports, this could benefit domestic producers and reduce product choice for U.S. consumers. In practice, foreign firms probably still benefit overall because the disadvantage of selling in a safety-conscious environment is often outweighed by the lower probability of suit against foreign firms.[54]

It is sometimes argued that foreign producers face higher payroll taxes for social insurance programs and that this offsets the higher liability costs faced by U.S. producers. This argument is largely false. To the extent payroll taxes go to pay for social insurance programs that are valued by workers, the incidence of these taxes is likely to be largely on workers through an offsetting wage adjustment.[55]

The recent Conference Board survey of senior executives of small and large manufacturing companies found that many believe that if the United States is to maintain its position in the competitive world, consideration must be given to the international effects of the U.S. liability system. In that survey, 75 percent of the respondents expected that the impact of the liability system on U.S. competitiveness will grow in significance in the future.[56]

REFORM OF TORT LIABILITY FOR EFFICIENT DETERRENCE

FEDERAL PRODUCT LIABILITY STATUTE

We believe there is a need for a uniform federal product liability statute. Until recently, tort law was a state prerogative. For the traditional tort involving a dispute between two individuals from the same state, state autonomy made sense and continues to do so. Similarly, medical malpractice actions usually involve residents of the same state, so diversity of tort standards among states is not a problem.

However, product liability cases routinely involve litigants from different states. Diversity of state standards encourages forum shopping by plaintiffs and creates costly uncertainty for corporations that market goods and services nationwide. Multistate producers cannot practically develop multiple product lines depending on the standards of each state and so tend to view the most demanding state standards as applicable. Thus, states that set unreasonable standards for producers indirectly impose costs on consumers in states with more reasonable standards.

The problems created when diverse state laws apply to goods and services in interstate commerce have already led to federal standards for antitrust and other commercial law. The same logic argues for a federal product liability law.

Several federal product liability reform bills have been introduced in Congress in recent years, so far without success.[57] Frustrated by the obstacles to change at the federal level, at least thirty-nine individual states have enacted generic tort reform legislation since 1986.[58] Although many of these changes are useful, most do not address the fundamental issues.

State legislators have little incentive to adopt fundamental tort reform because they know that in-state residents would bear most of the cost and reap few of the benefits as long as other states have more liberal standards.

We believe that basic standards for product liability must be set at the federal level, but we recognize that there will always remain a role for state legislation to address issues that are specific to the individual state or raised by court decisions within that state.

FAULT-BASED STANDARDS

We believe liability should be based on some notion of fault or responsibility for harm. The fundamental standards of tort liability should be designed to encourage all relevant parties to take appropriate care.This means placing liability on *only* those parties who fail to take cost-justified care and placing some degree of liability on *all* parties who fail to take cost-justified care. This is quite general and applies to personal, professional, and municipal liability, for example, as well as to product liability. One of the most difficult issues in tort reform is defining a standard that achieves this result.

In the products context, courts have recognized that in order to avoid an unreasonable standard of absolute liability for every product-related injury, liability should be strict only when the product is "defective." Legal distinctions are made among defects in design, manufacturing, and warning. But the fundamental economic question is the same in all these cases: could the defendant have taken cost-justified measures, through the product design, the manufacturing specifications and quality controls, or the warnings and labeling, to reduce the risk of injury? A correct answer to this question presupposes that other parties involved, notably product users (either employers, workers, or final consumers) are also taking cost-justified levels of care. Although producers could modify products to guard against totally reckless use, such modifications are not cost-justified from a social perspective if reasonable care by product users could reduce risk at lower cost.

Courts sometimes grope toward this concept of weighing costs and benefits when they invoke a risk-utility standard for defining product defects. But the risk-utility standard is only one among several possible standards that may be applied, sometimes in the same case.[59] Even when applied, the concept is rarely accurately defined in a way that would lead a jury to make the appropriate decisions, even assuming it had the information and expertise required to apply the standard.[60] Determining the relevant costs and benefits from a product is not a matter of mechanically applying a simple formula. Both expertise and judgment are required to estimate the value users place on having the product despite its risks and the value they would place on reduction in risk of injury. Some of these concepts cannot be readily measured in monetary terms. And yet some implicit, if not explicit, balancing of these nonmonetary benefits against the more readily quantified costs is unavoidable for sound decision making regarding risk.

Regulators employ experts trained in these issues. Yet, as Table 5.2 illustrates, there is huge variation in the standards applied for different products, even with trained analysts and with rulings subject to a degree of public scrutiny. The situation is unlikely to be better for judicial decisions made by lay jurors who lack guidance and expertise and who are accountable to no one for the efficiency or consistency of their decisions. Indeed if a comparable table to Table 5.2 could be constructed showing the dollars per life saved implicitly required to be spent by different judicial decisions, it would surely show at least as much variation as regulatory practices and probably more. Regardless of the value placed on safety, inconsistency itself is inherently costly. Simply reallocating resources without spending any more would save additional lives.

Thus, an efficient standard for product liability must be based on a rule that can lead to an appropriate weighing of costs and benefits in a consistent manner across cases. This is particularly critical in cases involving alleged defects in design and warnings, where the absence of a clear standard of what constitutes a defective product readily degenerates into an arbitrary system of absolute liability.

The correct standard is clear in concept, but specifying such a standard in a way that can be applied in practice is less simple. Some advocate a return to a standard based explicitly on fault or responsibility for harm or negligence.[61] Others have advocated a clear cost-benefit test. Another approach is to ask whether the manufacturer could have practicably adopted some alternative design or production method that would have prevented the accident.[62] A complementary approach would supplement the basic standard with specific defenses, barring liability for unreasonable or unforeseeable misuse, for use contrary to explicit warnings, and for risks that are obvious.

Which of these or other possible formulations would lead to the best judicial decisions in practice is hard to determine beforehand because all formulations inevitably leave much discretion to judge and jury. Therefore, we avoid specification of details. However, we strongly recommend that the basic standard of liability be reformulated to place liability on, and only on, all parties who fail to take cost-justified measures to prevent injuries.

Consistent with this general principle, we make the following specific recommendations:

- **A state-of-the-art defense is essential to prevent retroactive imposition of liability.** Liability for risks that were unknowable at the time of the defendant's actions, given prevailing research and scientific knowledge, cannot usefully deter and may actually discourage valuable innovations. Retroactive application of new standards also is a very arbitrary and inequitable way of providing compensation. Moreover, it is an inefficient method of compensation because the persons who are retroactively held liable would not have reserved funds for this unanticipated liability. This defense would apply primarily to actions alleging a defect in design or warning.

- **A reasonable standard of repose to prevent retroactive application of new standards of liability and compensation to actions taken many years previously is consistent with the principle of a state-of-the-art standard of liability, and probably essential for its application in practice.** A reasonable statute of repose running from the date of the allegedly harmful act, combined with the standard two-year statute of limitations running from the date of discovery of the injury, provides a compromise between the conflicting goals of efficient deterrence, fair compensation, and preventing inefficient retroactive liability.[63] The statute of repose could vary, depending on the type of product or service and the age of the plaintiff. For example, potential liability should be longer – but not indefinite – for long-lived products, latent injuries, and plaintiffs who are minors at the time of injury.[64] Of course, a statute of repose should not apply if the defendant fraudulently conceals an injury.

There is a real and valid concern that a state-of-the-art defense combined with a fairly short statute of repose will leave some victims of unforeseeable risks without compensation. Such injuries should be compensated in a fair and efficient manner, but the tort system is grossly inefficient for this purpose. These injuries should be covered through workers' compensation, if work-related, or private first-party and social insurance programs which are designed to provide compensation on a no-fault basis, without regard to the cause of injury (see Chapter 6).

- **Joint and several liability should be eliminated.** Joint and several liability encourages the unprincipled use of the liability system for purposes of compensation. It assigns costs arbitrarily, systematically imposing excessive penalties on parties with assets or insurance and inadequately penalizing others. It encourages frivolous suits against parties who have only a remote chance of being held liable, adding to litigation costs and distorting settlements. It makes liability an unpredictable risk and contributes to the high cost and lack of availability of insurance.

- **Courts should recognize a defense if a product causes injury when it is unreasonably misused, altered, or used in a way against which the manufacturer had explicitly warned.** In such cases, the damages payable by the manufacturer should be reduced in proportion to the degree of the other party's fault.

ROLE OF REGULATORY APPROVAL

We believe regulatory approval should preempt and constitute a bar to tort liability. This bar should apply only to those aspects of product design or labeling that have explicitly been approved by a regulatory agency. The bar would not apply in cases involving fraud or suppression of evidence in obtaining regulatory approval.

Earlier we documented the substantial overlap between regulation and tort liability for product design and warnings. For these disputes, regulation appears to be the more efficient alternative. Courts have greater difficulty in resolving design and warning cases than manufacturing defect cases because the definition of a design or warning defect raises more complex issues and requires greater expertise to resolve correctly. Furthermore, the courts have a built-in bias toward placing absolute liability on the producer because liability is usually determined with the wisdom of hindsight and in the presence of an injured plaintiff.

Where latent hazards render market forces inadequate, regulation is potentially superior to liability because regulatory standards are subject to scrutiny and review and are set before the fact by an expert body. However, regulatory standard setting has its own biases. For example, the FDA's tendency to ignore the costs of delay in its premarketing requirements deprives some patients of valuable therapies. Moreover, there are limits to the cost-effectiveness of regulation. Regulating the design and labeling of *all* products would be prohibitively costly, and unnecessary for products where consumers can adequately assess the risks themselves.

Currently, regulatory approval can usually be introduced as evidence by the defense, but has no special status. There have been cases of pharmaceuticals approved by the FDA and chemicals approved by the EPA in which courts have nevertheless imposed liability. (See "Regulatory Approval: *Wells v. Ortho Pharmaceutical,*" on page 102, and "Compliance with EPA Requirements: *Ferebee v. Chevron Chemical Co.,*" on page 78.) Even if the manufacturer wins the majority of cases, the costs and uncertainty of such litigation can be a serious disincentive to introducing new drugs and have led to the withdrawal of approved drugs.[65] In view of the extensive effort and expertise that goes into regulatory standard setting, allowing courts to second-guess regulatory decisions may result in undue delay in introduction of new products and possibly unwarranted withdrawal of products that, although not risk-free, nevertheless are the products of choice for some purposes.

Exposing pharmaceutical manufacturers to liability for failure to warn about every conceivable side effect of approved drugs raises particularly difficult issues. A drug that is safe and effective for the majority of users may still pose remote risks to subpopulations with particular conditions. If manufacturers are potentially liable for failure to warn of every remotely possible but unsubstantiated adverse effect, they have an incentive to overload the labels with warnings. The net effect of attempting to warn of all the possible risks can be counterproductive. "Information overload" may lead physicians and patients to ignore the package inserts because they are not useful. Including all theoretical hazards as contraindications would result in such confusion that the value of drug labeling would be undermined. Recognizing this problem, the FDA explicitly limits the warnings to be listed. In its role as protector of all consumers, the FDA has some (admittedly imperfect) incentive to weigh costs and benefits to different groups and make a decision that is in some sense best for society overall. But a jury is more likely to focus on the interest of the particular plaintiff, without regard to how, for example, requiring a warning for a

---

REGULATORY APPROVAL

Wells v. Ortho Pharmaceutical

In *Wells v. Ortho Pharmaceutical*, 788 F.2d 2741 (11th Cir. 1986), the plaintiff was awarded $4.7 million against Ortho Pharmaceutical on the theory that Ortho-Gynol contraceptive jelly had caused her child's tragic birth defects. An FDA-appointed expert advisory panel had concluded that contraceptives such as Ortho-Gynol are "safe and effective for over-the-counter use" (45 Fed. Reg. 82, 014-49, 1980). In 1983 an FDA standing committee further reviewed the evidence on vaginal spermicides and found that the currently available evidence indicated no association between such products and congenital malformations. Nevertheless, appellate court upheld the verdict, ruling "Plaintiffs' burden of proving that Katie Wells' defects were caused by the product did not necessarily require them to produce scientific studies showing a statistically significant association between spermicides and congenital malformation in a large population." 788 F.2d at 745.

particular remote adverse reaction might harm the interests of the great majority of consumers.

Some advocates of reform have proposed that regulatory approval of a product should be a bar to punitive damages, and a few states have enacted such a change.[66] We believe that the logic for a regulation defense for punitive damages applies equally to compensatory damages. Because punitive damages are intended to deter inefficient risk taking, awarding such damages when a manufacturer is in compliance with regulatory specifications is grossly unfair and inefficient. By the same token, allowing liability when a manufacturer is in compliance with regulatory standards is to use the tort system solely to provide compensation that can be achieved at lower cost through other insurance mechanisms. Allowing tort suits in such cases wastes resources on litigation and may lead to withdrawal of products that conform to regulatory standards.

CONTRACTUAL AGREEMENTS

We believe courts should honor contracts entered into by informed parties. There is a growing tendency for courts to override contractual agreements.[67] In circumstances where the contracting parties are equally well informed and have equal bargaining power, there is no reason to believe that a jury would achieve a better allocation of risk and resources.

The overriding of contractual terms is particularly unwarranted for commercial liability insurance because the buyers of such coverage are often highly sophisticated repeat purchasers who are as familiar with the risks as their insurers are. Liberal judicial reinterpretations of liability insurance contracts, with the social aim of increasing compensation, have undermined the availability of insurance (see Chapter 3). The situation is particularly acute for pollution and, to a lesser degree, directors' and officers' liability. If insurers cannot be certain that the coverage defined by the insurance contract will hold up in court, they cannot price the coverage accurately and are thus less willing to provide it.

Similarly, manufacturers need to be able to bound their potential liability to those circumstances where the product is used according to instructions (thus shifting to the user those risks that result from misuse) in order to be willing to market those products. Enforceable contracts are a fundamental component in the functioning of markets and are equally vital in the efficient allocation of risk.

PUNITIVE DAMAGES

We believe punitive damages should be awarded only in cases of willful misconduct and should be limited to a modest multiple of the

compensatory award. Punitive awards are a significant component in the unpredictability of size and awarding of damages in tort liability cases. The potential for huge punitive awards encourages suits and distorts the settlement process. The lack of coordination of awards in different cases related to the same product or incident can make the total assessment excessive and totally arbitrary. Huge punitive awards can exhaust a defendant's assets, resulting in gross overcompensation to early plaintiffs and leaving later plaintiffs undercompensated.

The economic rationale for awarding punitive damages is to provide appropriate deterrence incentives in circumstances where the deterrence effects of compensatory awards are inadequate: for example, if few legitimate claimants file claims or if compensatory awards are less than the full social value of risk reduction.

However, to determine the right amount of punitive damages, the court must know how much has already been paid by this defendant on related cases and how much will be paid on future cases. Optimal punitive awards may also depend on the deterrent effects of market forces, regulation, adverse publicity, and loss of reputation that often accompany liability suits. Whether a punitive award is necessary for optimal deterrence also depends on whether potential defendants are risk-averse. Thus, even if compensatory awards are set at less than the full social cost of injuries, it does not follow that punitive damages are necessary to provide correct incentives.[68]

Although it is very difficult to define general criteria for awarding punitive damages that will be correct in all cases, some guidelines to limit the arbitrariness of the present system are essential. We recommend that punitive awards be permitted only in cases of willful misconduct and that the amount of the award be limited to a modest multiple of the compensatory award.[69] It should be noted that, under these conditions, legislatures, courts, regulatory agencies, and insurance companies would probably be inclined to disallow insurance as a matter of public policy.

To the extent feasible, court-assessed punitive damages in one case should take into account amounts already paid in punitive awards in related cases. If in class actions of general scope, participation in the class is voluntary with respect to compensatory damages, it should be mandatory with respect to punitive damages (see Chapter 4). These recommendations for reform of punitive damages are designed to preserve and reinforce incentives for prudent attention to risk without exposing potential defendants to unpredictable, catastrophic judgments that are out of proportion to damages suffered.

A difficult question remains: to whom should the punitive awards be paid? Assuming that compensatory awards are designed to provide optimal compensation, paying punitive awards to the plaintiff provides excessive compensation.[70] One proposal is to pay punitive awards to the state to defray the public costs of the courts. Paying the awards to the state would appropriately allow the activities that generate court costs to pay for them. But it could also make the state a party to any suit with a potential punitive award, possibly adding to the complexity of the litigation and creating a conflict of interest for the courts.

An alternative would be to limit the fee a plaintiff's attorney could receive out of a punitive award, which could discourage the excessive pursuit of punitive awards. On the other hand, if plaintiff attorneys were to receive no share, they would have no incentive to invest time and money to determine whether a punitive award was justified, and this could undermine the deterrent purpose of punitive awards.

Further study of these issues is needed to determine who should receive punitive awards.*

FOREIGN LITIGANTS AND MANUFACTURERS

We believe all U.S. courts should deny access to foreign litigants for injuries incurred outside the United States, as most federal courts already do. Moreover, foreign sellers of products in the United States should be subject to financial responsibility requirements as stringent as those applied to U.S. firms.[71] The distinctive attributes of the U.S. liability system place U.S. producers at a disadvantage in both foreign and domestic markets. The U.S. liability system is, of course, only one among numerous factors affecting our international competitiveness and trade deficit. Nevertheless, our liability system does have a significant effect on the competitiveness of U.S.-manufactured products, particularly pharmaceuticals, chemicals, machine tools, and general aviation.

Changes in the liability system need to be made to achieve a more level playing field between U.S. and foreign producers while still affording consumers in each country the protection to which they are accustomed. For example, foreign litigants against U.S. producers for injuries outside the United States should be given the same rights they would enjoy in their own country. This could be accomplished by denying foreign litigants access to U.S. courts for such claims, as most federal courts already do. The alternative of requiring U.S. courts that grant such access to apply the rules of liability damages and discovery of the plaintiff's home country is likely to be ineffective in practice because U.S. courts are unfamiliar with the standards of foreign countries.

It may also be worth exploring the feasibility of requiring foreign sellers of products in the United States to consent to being sued here for product defects and having some means of payment for potential liability

*See memorandum by LEON C. HOLT, JR. (page 169).

judgments in the form of sufficient attachable assets in the United States such as a line of credit or a liability policy. However, such financial standards should not be set higher than those to which competing U.S. firms are typically held in order to avoid creating what would amount to a new nontariff trade barrier.

IMPROVING THE PRACTICE OF RISK MANAGEMENT: THE CASE OF HAZARDOUS WASTE

The control of environmental hazards, including discharges into the air, groundwater, and surface waterways, poses some of the greatest challenges in risk management. The subject is too complex for a full analysis here; rather our discussion is intended to give an overview and sense of the magnitude of the problems and the issues we face.

Although control of hazardous wastes is only one component of the network of regulation and liability related to environmental hazards, it warrants particular attention because it illustrates the difficulties of defining acceptable risk levels and of making efficient compromises when the ideal standard of zero risk is unattainable. It demonstrates the enormous problems that result when retroactive changes in liability rules create vast, unfunded liabilities, and how unpredictability in legal rules makes risk uninsurable. It also illustrates the importance of distinguishing policies designed for prospective impact on future actions from policies that are retrospective and simply allocate costs for damage already incurred.

CLEANING UP INACTIVE SITES: THE LEGACY OF THE PAST

The original Superfund law, the Comprehensive Environmental Response, Compensation and Recovery Act (CERCLA) of 1980, established a $1.6 billion trust fund and a program to address the cleanup of unsafe hazardous waste sites. The EPA was empowered to develop a list of priority sites and, for each site, to set target standards, devise cleanup and containment procedures and technologies, and identify the parties potentially responsible for the cleanup. If the potentially responsible parties (PRPs) could not be found or failed to agree among themselves on strategies for cleanup and cost allocation, the EPA could use trust fund money to implement a cleanup and then sue the parties in court to recover costs.

CERCLA vastly underestimated the magnitude of the problem and the scientific, legal, and political obstacles to dealing with it. The original law envisioned a list of roughly 400 priority sites, but a 1985 Office of Technology Assessment report estimated that the number of sites requiring cleanup could exceed 10,000, with costs to Superfund of $100 billion and total costs several times higher.[72]

In 1986, the Superfund Amendments and Reauthorization Act (SARA) revised the program, addressing some of the criticisms concerning delays, lack of progress, and arbitrariness of cleanup standards. SARA established as a goal the standard of the Safe Drinking Water Act, which requires water-quality levels at which "no known or anticipated adverse effects on the health of persons can occur." This standard applies to all sites, including some that currently and for the foreseeable future are unlikely to affect drinking water. This provision virtually removes cost and techno-logical feasibility considerations from the cleanup program.

Moreover, the trust fund of $9 billion established in the Superfund reauthorization for a five-year cleanup effort is only a tiny fraction of the total projected cost. A recent General Accounting Office report estimates there are 425,000 potential sites.[73] With cleanup costs per site running in the tens of millions of dollars,[74] the estimates of the aggregate cleanup cost over the coming decades range from $100 billion to more than $1 trillion, depending on number of sites requiring remedial action, the cleanup standards applied, and the technology available.[75] Either cost figure, even if spread over many years, is clearly prohibitive compared with the annual U.S. GNP of roughly $4 trillion.

The massive real resource costs that will be required for a cleanup of this nature are being compounded daily by enormous costs of litigation over responsibility for this vast unfunded liability. Courts have held that individual PRPs are jointly and severally liable for cleaning up a site to specified levels, even if they can prove that their conduct was lawful, nonnegligent, and consistent with state-of-the-art standards. In addition to site cleanup costs, Superfund has been used to authorize equity and tort claims by state officials for groundwater contamination and private suits alleging harm from exposure to chemicals at the sites.[76]

With the enactment of Superfund, Congress imposed a vast retroac-tive liability on the private sector. A substantial legal debate rages in the courts as to whether this is covered in the language of general liability insurance policies. In any event, it was not adequately funded by either PRPs or their insurers. The inevitable litigation between tens or hundreds of PRPs on any site is compounded by litigation between each PRP and their multiple insurers and reinsurers. Thus, resources are being devoted to litigation which could otherwise be spent on additional cleanup activities.

Conflicting court decisions which are now emerging regarding insurance coverage of such liability are providing fuel for further litigation between manufacturers and insurers. Concern by the insurers that the terms of the insurance contract cannot reliably be used to define and bound the insurer's liability contributes to insurers' uncertainty in pricing this kind of coverage and hence to the lack of availability of such insurance coverage. Pending resolution of these issues, this vast potential liability encumbers the capital of insurers and producers alike that are involved and hampers both's ability to do business.[77]

REFORMING OUR SYSTEMS OF WASTE CLEANUP

The critical importance of preserving the cleanliness of the groundwater by cleaning up inactive waste sites is beyond dispute. Regulation clearly has an essential role to play in managing this risk, particularly for already generated wastes. However, the Superfund reauthorization's goal of cleanup to the point of zero risk to groundwater is clearly not feasible in the near term because of the enormous costs involved. Reaching a consensus on an acceptable level of risk and the means to achieve it requires better understanding of the nature of the risks, costs, and trade-offs (including a better understanding of carcinogens), as well as better communication among local communities, industry, and federal and local government.

Government officials should be aware of the distorting incentives created by the Superfund approach, which imposes off-budget liability on unidentified private parties. With off-budget financing, legislators, bureaucrats, and the general public tend to perceive cleanup as free. They therefore have every incentive to demand much higher cleanup standards than they would if they had to pay the cost directly, through earmarked tax levies. Moreover, although the benefits of the Superfund approach are received by local communities, the costs are often borne by out-of-state corporations and shareholders. This allocation of benefits and costs may reverse past inequities, but the correspondence between past and present gainers and losers is a very weak equity argument for the current method of financing.

Government regulation has a critical role to play in defining practical standards of acceptable risk while continuing to develop a greater knowledge base. Regulators need to set priorities for site cleanup and for pollutants to monitor. At least temporarily, different standards may have to be accepted at different sites. In general, standards should be defined in terms of an overall target quality level for a site or, preferably, for an area and should encompass not only hazardous waste sites but also agricultural and municipal discharges and mobile sources of pollutants, which are currently not subject to the same stringent standards as waste sites are.

Government regulators should not mandate the use of specific technologies. Such technology-forcing undermines the ability of industry to apply the minimum-cost technologies for meeting set standards in the short run. In the longer run it undermines incentives to develop new technologies, which are our greatest hope for achieving a clean environment at an acceptable cost.

Joint and several liability exacerbates the already arbitrary allocation of cleanup costs. It should be replaced by apportionment of costs in proportion to contribution. When contributing parties either cannot be traced or are not financially responsible, the difference should be made up through some mix of public funds. Joint and several liability not only contributes to the huge expenditures on litigation and to the riskiness of liability insurance, it also reduces the willingness of producers to share in waste disposal operations.

There is huge potential for savings to all parties involved if greater cooperation among potential responsible parties and their insurers at each site can be achieved through site-specific steering committees that could apportion liability and negotiate with the EPA over the nature of the cleanup remedy. Where negotiation fails, ADR mechanisms should be explored. Amalgamation of the decisions rather than site-by-site litigation should be adopted wherever feasible as a further strategy for reducing litigation costs.

CONTROLLING THE GENERATION AND DISPOSAL OF NEW WASTES

We cannot allow the dilemmas we currently face in correcting and paying for past mistakes to contaminate our policies for managing the future generation and disposal of wastes. Although regulation may be the best instrument for providing cleanup of existing wastes, market forces and liability can and should have a greater role to play in the control of future waste generation and disposal. By making producers or waste-site operators liable, the costs of disposal can be incorporated into the price of the products that entail the generation of wastes, creating appropriate incentives to economize on such products and to develop new technologies for treatment. In some ways, increased liability has given firms increased incentives. Many large firms, for example, are moving to methods of recycling and treatment rather than using land-based disposal of untreated waste. Prevention of waste through recycling and treatment is clearly preferable to storage in the long run.

However, the incentive effects of liability do not work if potentially liable parties are effectively immune because they can become judgment-proof if necessary by declaring bankruptcy. Many small operators are reportedly "going bare" rather than incur the costs of insurance, which are disproportionately higher for small operators because of the fixed costs of reducing risk and of having a risk assessment made by an insurer. In principle, site operators are required to prove they are financially responsible and adequately insured; but in many cases, these laws have not been enforced, in part because of the unavailability and high cost of liability insurance. Pooling of wastes, a possible solution to the small operator's high costs, is made much less attractive on account of joint and several liability.

ONE COMPANY'S RISK MANAGEMENT STRATEGY

The overlapping impact of regulation, liability, and market forces operating through reputation is illustrated in a recent case study of the response of a large chemical company to the Bhopal disaster.[78] Concern over health hazards to workers and associated liability suits led this company to support the Toxic Substances and Control Act of 1976, which required the testing of all potentially toxic chemicals. The company's search for new technologies for disposal of hazardous wastes (e.g., incineration rather than storing waste in landfills) had been influenced by a combination of concern over community relations surrounding their own landfills, the Love Canal publicity, and the costs associated with the Superfund legislation. Thus, even before Bhopal, the company had an active risk-management program focusing on risks associated with chronic illness and landfills.

Bhopal triggered a series of systematic steps to reduce the risk of a catastrophic disaster. These steps included a risk assessment at all the company's plants worldwide, focusing on risk to surrounding populations, and measures to decrease these risks by reducing inventories of hazardous chemicals, technological changes to reduce the need for such chemicals, and preparation of plans for community evacuation, in addition to the existing plans for worker evacuation at all plants.

Several interesting conclusions emerge from this case study. First, reputation and the need for good community relations are clearly potent forces leading to corporate concern over environmental risks to populations.[79] These forces operate only when the public is aware of risks. This awareness tends to be triggered by specific events, such as Bhopal and Love Canal, which may in fact lead to

SUMMARY OF RECOMMENDATIONS

The data are not available to make a full evaluation of the costs and benefits of the liability system as a whole, but through logical reasoning we have identified specific aspects of the system that are likely to generate costs in excess of benefits. To function as an efficient system of deterrence, tort liability must hold everyone to a reasonable standard of care and assess a penalty equal to the damages they cause on anyone who fails to take reasonable care. Many of the distortions of our current system result from legal rules that violate this basic principle: absolute liability, joint and

an overestimate of the risks. Because both underestimation and overestimation of risks tend to undermine the efficient operation of markets, there is clearly a need for greater public education. Companies that need good community relations (e.g., to obtain planning permission for siting an incinerator or landfill) are expending increased effort on such education.

Second, both public and corporate responses to a catastrophe such as Bhopal illustrate the difficulties we all have in making decisions in the face of uncertainty, particularly in the case of very low-probability, high-consequence events. Below a certain threshold of probability, we tend to assume "it cannot happen to me." But when such an event does occur, the normal reaction is "it can happen to me," and we may actually overestimate the risks and focus on avoiding worst-case scenarios, perhaps to the point of taking risk-avoidance measures that are not justified on an objective cost-benefit basis.[80]

Third, such disasters and the associated adverse publicity tend to increase the involvement of CEOs in the problem of risk management. The unpredictability of the liability system and its capacity to create unanticipated corporate disasters can result in liability absorbing a share of the CEO's time that is out of proportion to the share of liability in current costs. This may be one factor leading to the greater weight attached to liability by CEOs than by risk managers in the Conference Board surveys. By contrast, because regulation is more predictable, it may have less adverse impact on planning and strategic decision making, although compliance costs may be at least as great.

several liability, retroactive application of new knowledge or new legal standards, and penalties out of proportion to harm caused. There are also inconsistencies between legal and regulatory standards and between legal standards in different jurisdictions. More generally, courts are being used to set standards and engage in fact-finding in areas where the regulatory process is more efficient.

PRINCIPLES OF AN EFFICIENT DETERRENCE SYSTEM

A series of general principles underlies our recommendations.

- Individuals are the best judges of their own preferences, provided that they have reasonable access to needed information at reasonably low cost and that they understand the risks involved.

- Market forces can accurately control risk if individual choices reflect an informed understanding of the risk. Therefore, individual decisions and contractual agreements made by knowing parties should be honored.

- Overriding markets through regulation or liability is likely to produce a net gain only where markets are seriously distorted and the benefits of the regulatory or liability intervention clearly outweigh the costs of operating these systems or where there are third parties involved who are not in a direct contractual relationship to the source of injury. Obtaining the information necessary for sound decision making is costly for regulators and courts, just as it is for individuals.

- Regulation is likely to be more efficient than tort liability where there are economies of scale in having a single expert body assess risks or where liability appears remote and is an ineffective deterrent to potential injurers because possible injuries would not appear until the distant future.

- Tort liability is potentially more efficient than regulation where connections between defendant behavior and injury to plaintiff are reasonably easy to establish. Liability deters injuries that appear soon after exposure and have a limited number of factors and agents contributing to the injury.

- Deterrence should be the guiding principle in designing rules of tort liability and should override concern for compensation if these two goals conflict. Where compensation is the primary purpose, this can be provided for efficiently through other private and social insurance mechanisms.

- Liability laws should be designed to provide incentives for care for all parties who are potential contributors to risk.[81]

REFORM OF TORT LIABILITY FOR EFFICIENT DETERRENCE

In summary, our major recommendations concerning deterrence are:

- There is a need for a uniform federal product liability statute.

- Liability should be based on some notion of fault or responsibility for harm.

- A state-of-the-art defense is essential to prevent retroactive imposition of liability.

- A reasonable standard of repose to prevent retroactive application of new standards of liability and compensation to actions taken many years in the past is consistent with the principle of a state-of-the-art standard of liability and probably essential for its application in practice.

- Joint and several liability should be eliminated.

- Courts should recognize a defense if a product causes injury when it is unreasonably misused, altered, or used in a way against which the manufacturer had explicitly warned.

- Courts should honor contracts entered into by informed parties.

- Regulatory approval should preempt and constitute a bar to tort liability, except in cases of fraud or suppression of evidence.

- Punitive damages should be awarded only in cases of willful misconduct and should be limited to a modest multiple of the compensatory award.

- All U.S. courts should deny access to foreign litigants for injuries incurred outside the United States, as most federal courts already do. Foreign sellers of products in the United States should be subject to financial responsibility requirements as stringent as those applied to U.S. firms.

MANAGING RISKS POSED BY HAZARDOUS WASTE

Given our current understanding of this complex problem, we draw the following conclusions:

- Policies for managing the future generation and disposal of wastes should not be contaminated by the dilemmas we currently face in correcting and paying for past mistakes.

- Government has a critical role to play in developing knowledge about risk and setting standards for acceptable levels of risk. Even if the long-term goal is zero risk, efficient resource allocation requires recognition of the inevitability of compromise in the shorter term.

- **Government should not attempt to regulate the methods and technologies to be used in cleanup.** Standards should be defined in terms of acceptable water quality for a site or area. Over the longer term, we need to develop an integrated approach to controlling risks to groundwater that includes nonpoint sources of pollution.

- **Joint and several liability should be replaced by assessment of fault in proportion to contribution. Where contributing parties either cannot be traced or are not financially responsible, the difference should be made up through some mix of public funds.**

- **Every effort should be made to resolve funding disputes by negotiation and alternative methods of dispute resolution, rather than through the courts.** Amalgamation of the decisions rather than site-by-site litigation should be adopted wherever feasible as a further strategy for reducing litigation costs.

- **The private sector should make every effort to develop the information base necessary to make sound decisions on short-term priorities for cleanup, and on longer-term reform of the current institutional framework for regulating and managing environmental risk.**

CHAPTER 6

Recommendations for Change in our Systems of Compensation: Coordinating Private Insurance, Social Insurance, and Tort Liability

The sometimes implicit but often explicit desire to extend compensation has been a major force driving the recent expansion of the tort system. This expansion has included:

- Extending the circumstances in which compensation is awarded, through the shift from fault-based liability to strict and increasingly to absolute liability.

- Broadening the categories of damages that are compensable from measurable monetary loss to nonmonetary loss such as pain and suffering.[1]

- Increasing the amount of compensation for a given type of loss.

Between 1960 and 1984, for example, the average jury verdict in two sample jurisdictions increased over 300 percent in inflation-adjusted, 1984 dollars, with even more dramatic increases for product liability and medical malpractice than for other claims.[2]

This expansion of the tort system for purposes of compensation has occurred without public debate or consensus that this is a sound form of social insurance. Yet tort liability does entail a system of compulsory insurance, funded by hidden taxes on the goods and services that carry with them the right to compensation in the event of an injury. For example, with a rule of strict liability, a consumer who buys a product simultaneously buys the right to tort compensation as an inseparable tie-in to the product if it proves defective. However, unlike our other systems of social or mandatory insurance, many of the terms of this compulsory tort insurance, such as the circumstances of eligibility and the scope and level of benefits, are not determined by a vote of elected representatives.[3] Rather, the structure of tort benefits is the outcome of jury decisions on thousands of individual cases. In contrast with every other private and social insurance program, the tort system does not have to operate within an overall budget constraint, and there is no annual review of the bottom line.

A fundamental flaw of setting the terms of a social insurance program through the courts is that the jury has neither the information nor the incentives to weigh the costs of its decisions against the benefits. The benefits are immediate and visible: compensation to an often tragically injured individual who is present in the courtroom. In contrast, the magnitude of the costs and the bearer of those costs are largely invisible. Because the defendant is typically insured or is a large self-insured corporation, the costs appear remote and are distributed over a large, faceless mass of shareholders or consumers. If it is easy for courts to ignore the direct costs of compensation because they are diffuse, it is surely even easier to ignore the indirect costs (e.g., products withdrawn, loss of international competitiveness) which are extremely hard to measure (see Chapter 5).

In view of the circumstances in which tort benefits are determined, it is not surprising that tort compensation is far more generous than the compensation individuals choose to pay for when they purchase private insurance and bear the costs themselves. Tort compensation is also far more generous than the compensation provided through other social insurance programs, where legislators face the tax consequences of the benefit levels they select, and therefore have incentives to consider both costs and benefits in setting the level and structure of benefits.

If the tort system is to be efficient in its compensation function, it should be guided insofar as feasible by the fundamental principles of sound insurance that apply to other private and public insurance or compulsory insurance programs. In general, we in the United States have chosen to rely largely on private choices and private markets to provide insurance, as we do for the provision of most other goods and services. Individuals are generally the best judges of their own preferences, and private markets are generally the best guarantors of efficient provision. But because insurance is so essential to well-being, we have supplemented our systems of private insurance with social insurance programs targeted at circumstances where private markets alone are unlikely to achieve satisfactory results.

These social insurance programs should not ignore certain basic principles of efficient insurance. First, it is not a prudent use of resources to attempt to provide full insurance for all types of loss. Some losses are simply not worth insuring because the cost of insuring outweighs the value of the compensation if a loss occurs. In private insurance markets, consumers and insurers tend to choose policies that limit coverage in circumstances where costs of administration are high or moral hazard is severe, such that the benefits of insurance are low relative to the costs. If informed consumers decide that the benefits of insuring against certain losses do not justify the costs of that insurance, attempting to cover those losses through public programs is not a good use of scarce public funds, if public programs are subject to the same cost factors. The same principle applies to the compulsory coverage of the tort system.

Second, the structure of benefits should be designed to preserve incentives for reducing the risk of loss and control of the extent of loss. In the context of personal injuries, efficient loss control includes providing opportunities and incentives for prudent use of medical care and for rehabilitation and return to independence to the extent possible.

Third, if some government role to extend insurance coverage is considered desirable, we should adopt the lowest-cost form of intervention, other things being equal. Specifically, compensation provided through the tort system carries much higher overhead costs than other systems of private and public insurance. To justify these additional costs, the tort system should be used only in circumstances where it performs a useful deterrent function in addition to compensation.

Fourth, individuals differ in the value they place on having insurance. But social insurance programs tend to require everyone to buy the same or similar levels of coverage. Requiring some people to buy more coverage than they really want is an indirect cost of social insurance. Program design should recognize this and attempt to minimize this cost while meeting the goal of assuring a basic minimum level of coverage for everyone.

In order to determine the optimal compensation role for the tort system within the broad scheme of our private and social insurance programs, this chapter first reviews the population at risk and our other nontort systems of compensation for the losses associated with personal injury. We then identify where this network of nontort compensation is incomplete, outline the reasons for incomplete coverage, and discuss the circumstances in which government intervention can play a useful role and those in which it cannot. Third, we evaluate the compensation function of the tort system within this broad framework and make recommendations for reform. Fourth, we discuss issues that are specific to work-related injuries and nonoccupational mass torts. Finally, we examine ways of filling the gaps in insurance networks through social and private insurance markets.

THE POPULATION AT RISK

Everyone, regardless of age or circumstances, is at risk for personal injury or disability. Some groups are more at risk than others, depending in part on circumstances largely beyond their control, such as genetic factors, environmental risks, and workplace hazards, and in part on their own choices of goods, services, activities, occupation, and places of residence. This diversity of exposures is reflected in the diversity of the disabled population, which is a large and heterogeneous group of people ranging from small children to certain segments of the frail elderly.

In the face of such diverse circumstances there are solid reasons for the multifaceted approach to compensation that currently exists in the United States. The goals of public policy in compensating the disabled should be to assure an adequate standard of living and to encourage, to the extent possible, their return to a state of independence that can enhance self-worth and social contribution. In most circumstances, these goals can best be achieved through private medical and disability income insurance. Where necessary and appropriate, this private infrastructure ought to be supplemented by carefully designed and targeted public programs.

OVERVIEW OF NONTORT SOURCES OF COMPENSATION

The major private and public sources of medical and disability insurance are no-fault systems that pay benefits regardless of the cause of injury. Unlike the tort system, the primary focus of these programs is compensation, not deterrence of injury.

The public disability income programs can be understood only in the context of their often conflicting goals: (1) to provide a system of insurance in which an individual's benefits are related to an individual's contribution to the system and (2) to provide a universal public safety net of adequate income, regardless of contribution. In recent years, the emphasis has shifted from insurance to income transfer. The insurance origins are reflected in the focus on providing income replacement for injured workers who have made some contribution to the system, whereas noncontributors, who also tend to be nonworkers, are less well covered. However, benefits are increasingly based on need and are not calculated to yield a fair rate of return on each individual's contribution.

PRIVATE FIRST-PARTY INSURANCE

Employment-based private first-party insurance is the primary source of compensation for medical expense for the great majority of the population. A substantial fraction of employees also have wage-loss protection through sick pay, long-term disability income insurance, and pension plans that are intended primarily for retirement but may be activated in the event of serious disability at younger ages. There are clear advantages of economies of scale, protection against adverse selection, and favorable tax treatment when insurance is provided through large employment groups. Because of these cost advantages, the great majority of full time employees in medium-sized and large firms have private health insurance and some form of wage-loss coverage. Many retirees also have employ-ment-based pensions and employer-provided private health coverage.

Nongroup coverage is also available, but at much higher cost, due to higher administrative cost, adverse selection, and less favorable tax treatment. Very small firms face costs similar to those of the nongroup market and consequently are much less likely than large firms to provide coverage. The uninsured, therefore, tend to be people who are employed in small firms, self-employed, or out of the work force.

GENERAL PUBLIC INSURANCE PROGRAMS

Many individuals who have limited access to private group coverage are eligible for one or more public insurance programs. The great majority of the population over sixty-five receive retirement income support from the Old Age and Survivors Insurance (OASI) component of the Social Security system, which covers workers and their dependents subject to a minimum labor force participation requirement. OASI also provides income support for surviving dependents of covered workers. Medicare covers acute care medical expense of the over sixty-five population regardless of prior work experience.

For the nonelderly population, the largest general disability program is Social Security Disability Income (DI). This provides income support in the event of total disability to all workers who have some minimal period of work experience. Medical expenses of DI recipients are covered through Medicare after a two-year waiting period. Unlike the old-age component of Social Security, DI does not apply to disabled dependents of covered workers unless the worker is disabled. In December 1986, there were 4 million DI beneficiaries, and total annual expenditures amounted to $18.1 billion.[4]

The insurance origins of the Social Security system are reflected in its funding. Both OASI and DI are financed through a payroll tax on covered employees. However, the relation of individual benefits to individual tax contributions is largely a fiction: the system is now financed on a pay-as-you-go basis, with benefits to current retirees paid out of taxes on current workers. Funding of Medicare, which covers the medical expenses of DI recipients, comes from a payroll tax, general revenues, and premiums paid by beneficiaries, with by far the largest share being paid by current workers.[5] Wage-replacement rates under DI are typically around two-thirds of pretax earnings, higher for low-wage workers and less for high-wage workers. Because benefits are fully tax-exempt, a two-thirds replacement rate of pretax wages implies close to full replacement of after-tax wages.

The quasi-insurance Social Security system for covered workers and their dependents is supplemented by a public safety net of means-tested transfer programs that pay benefits based on need, regardless of the individual's payment into the system. These programs are targeted at subgroups of the low-income population whose ability to provide for themselves is limited. Supplemental Security Income (SSI) provides for the elderly, blind, and disabled. Aid to Families with Dependent Children (AFDC) is targeted primarily to single-parent families with children.[6] Recipients of these programs are eligible for coverage of acute care medical expenses through Medicaid. Medicaid also covers long-term nursing home care for persons in poverty regardless of categorical status.[7]

In all states, tax-supported public hospitals are the health care provider of last resort for those who cannot afford to pay. Most states also have a number of direct medical programs, financed by a mix of state and federal funds, that are typically targeted to specific medical conditions.

DISEASE-SPECIFIC SOCIAL INSURANCE PROGRAMS

In addition to these comprehensive social insurance programs that cover individuals regardless of the source of their illness or disability, special funds exist for specific conditions. By far the largest of these is the Black Lung program designed to compensate coal miners with pneumoconiosis. It was originally intended to be financed largely by levies on the responsible coal mine operators and by taxes on the coal industry, with general revenues as a backup of last resort. The experience has been that both total costs and the share coming from general tax revenues have far exceeded initial projections.[8]

Partly in reaction to this adverse experience with the Black Lung program, Congress has so far resisted several proposals for special compensation funds for occupational disease and for environmental injuries. However, the federal government recently established a federal vaccine injury compensation fund, spurred on by the crisis in availability of vaccines that has been attributed to the cost of liability insurance. Similarly, two states (Virginia and Florida) have established special funds to provide no-fault compensation to neurologically impaired infants, to ease the crisis in liability insurance for obstetricians.[9]

COMPULSORY PRIVATE INSURANCE

The largest mandatory private insurance structure is the workers' compensation (WC) system, which originated in 1911 and now covers the great majority of full-time workers.[10] The WC program provides coverage of wage loss, medical expense, and rehabilitation for injuries and diseases arising "out of and in the course of employment," without regard to fault. Temporary, permanent partial, and permanent total disabilities are covered.

The WC system provides a very interesting model to guide reform of the tort system. It evolved from voluntary contractual arrangements, and even today it retains an implicit element of consensual agreement despite its mandatory character. Benefit levels are set by statute at the state level and are the outcome of political dialogue among the interested parties. Wage replacement for temporary and permanent total disability is typically at two-thirds of the preinjury pretax wages, which implies roughly full replacement of after-tax wages because WC benefits are fully tax-exempt. Most states have minimum and maximum weekly benefits, under which the replacement rate of pretax income is more than two-thirds for low-wage workers and less than two-thirds for high-wage workers.[11] For permanent partial injuries that are not completely debilitating but that reduce the worker's earning capacity, benefits are determined by a formula that combines scheduled benefits (a fixed amount for specific injuries) with partial replacement of actual wage loss or lost earning capacity. These limits on wage replacement are designed to preserve incentives for rehabilitation and for injury prevention. Employer incentives for injury prevention are preserved through the system of experience-rating of WC insurance premiums which applies to all but the smallest firms.

WC premium costs have grown over the past decade from just over 1 percent of payroll in the early 1970s to almost 2 percent of payroll in the early 1980s.[12] This growth reflects higher benefits levels, expanded scope of coverage of permanent injuries and occupational disease, and higher claim rates.[13] Ironically, this expansion of WC benefits has coincided with but not prevented the expansion of tort claims by workers against employers, eroding the original intent of WC to be the "sole remedy" for employment-related injuries.

Private insurance has also become compulsory for some non-work-related injuries. Some states mandate coverage for automobile injuries. Some mandate that all drivers carry liability insurance; others mandate first-party no-fault automobile coverage, which requires drivers to insure against their own medical expenses. One state, Massachusetts, recently enacted mandatory employment-based health insurance, and similar proposals are under debate in several other states and at the federal level.

GAPS IN THE NONTORT PRIVATE AND SOCIAL INSURANCE NETWORK

Private insurance has grown rapidly in the past two decades. At the same time, the expansion of public insurance and transfer programs has been even more striking. Benefit payments through SSI, DI, and workers' compensation have outpaced the rate of growth of hourly earnings in recent years (see Table 6.1). Social insurance programs have been the fastest-growing component of public expenditures over the past two decades.

Although the great majority of the U.S. population has adequate insurance coverage for most sources of loss, certain groups of individuals and some types of loss currently have limited or no coverage. In some cases, there may be real unmet need that can and should be met; in other cases, the optimal policy may be to do nothing because the losses are not worth insuring, given the costs. Further study is needed to determine the best policy in each case.

- Seventeen percent of the population under age sixty-five lacks either private or public health insurance to cover acute medical care.

- Coverage through DI and Medicare in the event of total disability is conditional on having worked for a specified minimum period in covered employment.[14] Thus, disabled children or adults who have never been in the work force do not qualify for DI support and medical coverage unless the family spends down and becomes eligible for the means-tested SSI and Medicaid programs.

- Private long-term care insurance is still limited. However, the number of companies in the market has increased rapidly in recent years, and innovative new policies are being introduced.[15] For example, some private insurers now offer an employment-based long-term care benefit that covers not only the employee but also the employee's parents and dependents. Thus, although in the past the bulk of long-term care financing has come from out-of-pocket payments and Medicaid, it is too early to judge the potential for private insurance and the optimal role for the public sector.

- With the exception of the WC program, there is relatively little formal coverage of rehabilitation expense.

There is essentially no coverage of the special educational needs of disabled children other than the publicly provided services.

The working poor in intact two-parent families are typically ineligible for either cash assistance or Medicaid because of the categorical restrictions attached to the means-tested programs (i.e., eligibility is restricted to those who, in addition to meeting the means test, are elderly, disabled, or in single-parent families).[16]

Even persons who meet the categorical restrictions and have income below the poverty line may not qualify for benefits because the income-eligibility threshold in their state is set well below the poverty line.

TABLE 6.1

Percent Change in Benefit Payments and Adjusted Hourly Earnings 1975 - 1985

Percent Change — — — **Hourly Earnings**

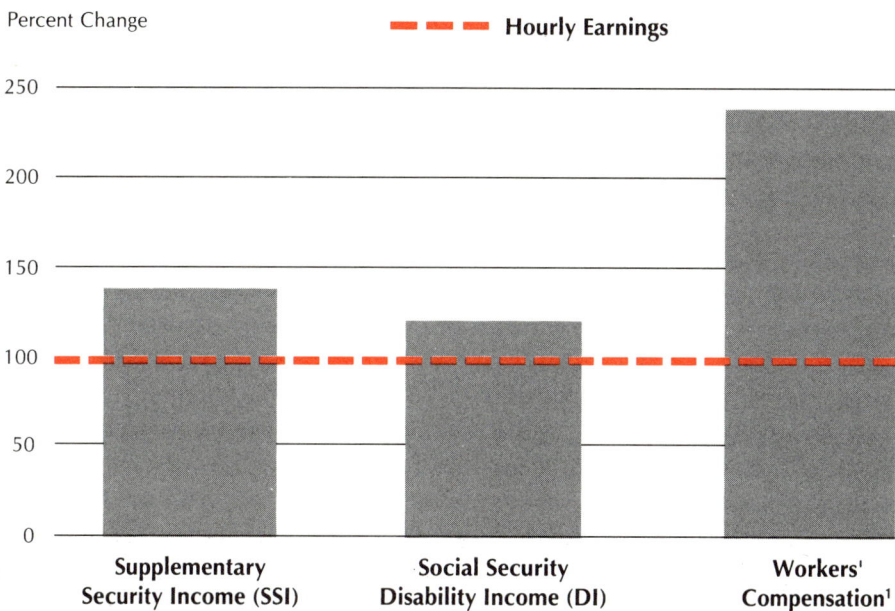

[1]This figure includes medical and hospital benefits and total compensation payments which include cash disability and survivor benefits. Also included is employer self-insurance.

SOURCE: U.S. Department of Health and Human Services, Socal Security Administration, *Social Security Bulletin, Annual Statistical Supplement, 1987* (Washington, D.C.: U.S. Government Printing Office, December 1987), p. 262 (WC Benefits), p. 275 (SSI benefits); *1988 Annual Report of the Federal Old-Age and Survivors Insurance and Disability Insurance Trust Funds,* Table 21, P.60 (DI benefits).

- Although most workers are covered for permanent total disability through DI and many have supplementary private coverage, permanent partial disability is covered only through workers' compensation, which applies only to work-related injuries.[17] The main problem facing both private and public insurance in providing compensation for partial disability is the difficulty of objectively measuring the true loss and hence controlling moral hazard (see glossary).

- No private or social insurance program other than the tort system provides coverage for nonmonetary losses.

Some of the apparent gaps in coverage are deceptive. For example, although only some 20 percent of employees have private long-term disability insurance, many of those without coverage could receive DI coverage to replace two-thirds of their income, a rate already at the maximum level permitted by private insurance. A significant number of the near-poor who lack health insurance would be covered through Medicaid if they incurred a significant medical expense.

Recent changes may significantly extend health insurance coverage in the near future. The Consolidated Omnibus Budget Reconciliation Act of 1985 (COBRA) requires employers to offer continued health care coverage for eighteen months at group rates to employees who either leave their jobs or have a change in marital status and to their dependents. As of 1990 all states are required to provide Medicaid coverage to all pregnant women (and children under one year of age) below the poverty line. This change and other recent Congressional actions sever the link between cash assistance and Medicaid, enabling states to raise eligibility thresholds for medical coverage without also having to provide cash assistance to poor households with incomes that exceed maximum state welfare benefit levels. Several states have enacted high-risk health insurance pools that offer health coverage to those who have been denied coverage in the private insurance market for medical reasons.

THE OPTIMAL ROLE OF GOVERNMENT IN PRIVATE INSURANCE MARKETS

Before evaluating the role of the tort system in supplementing this network of private and public insurance programs, it is wise to first review the factors that lead to incomplete insurance coverage, in order to identify more generally where the public sector can potentially perform a useful function in correcting failures in private insurance markets and where it cannot.

Several factors contribute to less than full private insurance coverage of all losses. Some of the factors that limit the purchase of private coverage apply equally to socially provided or mandated coverage. In such circumstances, attempting to fill apparent gaps in private insurance coverage is not an efficient use of resources. In other circumstances, the public sector can play a useful role in improving the equity or efficiency of insurance markets. Public intervention should be limited to such circumstances.

MORAL HAZARD

A major reason why we voluntarily choose less than complete coverage for many potential losses is what in insurance parlance is called moral hazard. (The term has no ethical connotations.) Moral hazard tends to occur when either the probability or size of loss is within the control of the insured and the insurer cannot measure the true loss or identify the contribution of the insured. Having insurance then tends to reduce the insured's incentives to control the actual loss or to exaggerate the reported loss. For example, moral hazard is probably a major obstacle in developing private coverage for long-term care, partial disability, and any non-monetary loss: it is simply impossible for the insurer to make an objective determination of the true extent of the loss. Insurance policies often include provisions to control moral hazard, such as copayments, utilization review (review of the need for expenses incurred), or other loss-control devices. In general, the government has no advantage over private insurers in controlling moral hazard. On the contrary, because private insurers are often closer to their policyholders and are more active in designing policy terms to control moral hazard, publicly provided insurance is often more exposed to moral hazard. Thus, where private insurance is not worthwhile because of moral hazard, social insurance may be equally undesirable.

MYOPIA AND FREE RIDING

Some individuals do not buy coverage because they underestimate the risk of loss (myopia) or because they count on receiving free care or public assistance of some form if they need it (free riding). In such circumstances, government *may* play a useful role by either mandating that everyone buy some minimal level of private coverage or providing universal coverage through a publicly funded program. Both myopia and free riding have been suggested as justifications for the Social Security program and mandatory automobile insurance. However, there are costs as well as benefits to mandating coverage, and these should be carefully considered before opting for mandatory coverage.

ADVERSE SELECTION

A third factor contributing to gaps in private coverage is adverse selection. This occurs when policyholders have better information about their own individual expected losses than insurers do. If the insurer cannot distinguish high and low risks and offers a common policy at a single price, the high risks are more likely to buy coverage and the price will be inadequate to cover losses.

When adverse selection undermines private insurance markets, a public role by either mandating coverage or providing it through a public program may be useful, provided that individuals are not required to purchase coverage greatly in excess of its value to them.

LOW INCOME

Insurance tends to be a luxury good; demand decreases more than proportionately as discretionary income falls. This implies that we only make the poor worse off if we force them to buy more insurance than they want. Thus, if we as a society wish to expand the insurance coverage of the poor, we should consider doing so through a program that is at least partially financed by the nonpoor, not by simply mandating that the poor buy unsubsidized coverage, either explicitly or implicitly as in the case of the tort system.

PRICE

The real price of insurance is the component of the premium that covers administrative expenses over and above the benefits actually received by the policyholder. The higher this administrative cost, the less worthwhile the insurance. The high administrative cost of providing coverage to individuals or small groups is a major contributing factor to the gaps in private health insurance coverage and for small firms. Purchasing either incomplete coverage or no coverage is a rational response when the price is very high relative to the expected compensation. Again, mandating coverage when individual choices indicate that consumers do not consider it worth the cost can only make them worse off.

NONMONETARY, IRREPLACEABLE LOSSES

Nonmonetary losses, such as pain and suffering and loss of faculties that affect the ability to enjoy life, are real and tragic. But by the nature of the loss, money cannot buy a replacement. Because insurance can only provide money, it may not be worth buying, particularly given the moral hazard associated with insuring such unquantifiable losses.[18] Optimal compensation for the nonmonetary aspects of personal injury varies with the type of injury and with the extent of compensation for economic loss. If compensation for economic loss already provides for special services, such as rehabilitation and educational aid, additional funds may buy little increase in well-being, and optimal compensation for noneconomic loss is low.[19] But if the compensation for economic loss provides strictly for wage replacement and acute medical care, compensation for noneconomic loss is one way of providing the funds to purchase worthwhile services.[20]

In summary, where gaps in private coverage are due to myopia, free riding, or adverse selection, making a minimum level of coverage compulsory can sometimes be a useful response. However, where gaps in coverage simply reflect the fact that individuals do not consider the coverage worth its cost because of high administrative costs, moral hazard, other more pressing uses of income, or the ability to cover the losses out of private savings, any government action that makes coverage compulsory makes people worse off.

HOW USEFUL IS THE TORT SYSTEM AS COMPENSATION?

When evaluated against this backdrop of private and social insurance programs and against these criteria for expanding coverage through government intervention, the tort system receives low marks for a number of reasons.

- It is necessarily incomplete in its scope of coverage.

- There is very substantial duplication of compensation from other sources.

- Some of the nonduplicative compensation is likely to be of low value, relative to the cost.

- The system is highly exposed to moral hazard.

- The unpredictability of tort compensation reduces its value as insurance.

- The system is inequitable. Some plaintiffs receive multimillion-dollar awards, others with similar injuries receive nothing, and persons with low incomes systematically receive less than persons with higher incomes, although all pay an equal share of the liability tax imposed through higher prices for goods and services.

- It is much more costly to operate than other private and social insurance programs (see Chapter 4).

SCOPE OF COVERAGE

In principle, the liability system provides compensation only for losses that are caused by the actions of someone else. If this principle is adhered to, tort liability can compensate only a small percentage of persons who are injured or disabled but are currently not covered through other programs. If the system deviates from this principle in order to provide wider compensation, it loses all deterrent value and any semblance of equity to potential defendants. The shift from negligence to strict liability and even absolute liability has the effect of expanding the reach of the tort system to injuries that are increasingly remote in their connection to the actions of a third party. But if the social goal is to extend insurance coverage to persons who are currently uninsured, this is a highly inefficient approach. Its reach as a compensation program is necessarily limited, it has very high overhead costs, and the imposition of liability out of proportion to damages caused can seriously distort resource allocation.

DUPLICATION

Much of tort compensation for medical expense and wage loss simply duplicates other private or social coverages, unless there is coordination of benefits. In such circumstances, the tort coverage at best provides no net benefits; at worst, it entails a net loss due to the costs of coordinating benefits and the moral hazard that results from duplicative coverage.

Coordination with other forms of coverage is not part of the traditional design of tort benefits. Indeed, the collateral source rule of traditional tort law explicitly rules out the introduction of evidence on the other collateral sources of compensation available to the plaintiff. This makes sense as long as the primary purpose of the tort award is to send a deterrent signal to the defendant, which requires that the defendant be fully liable for losses caused.

In principle, duplication can be eliminated while still requiring the tort defendant to pay the full loss if payments from the nontort insurer are secondary and are made only for losses not compensated through tort. In practice, such coordination of benefits is very hard to achieve because the nontort insurer may be unaware that the plaintiff has received a tort award and because tort payments have traditionally not been itemized to indicate the amount intended for medical expense, wage loss, and other items. Coordination is particularly difficult for long-term injuries because the tort compensation for all future losses has traditionally been paid as a lump sum at the time of verdict or settlement. A first-party health insurer or a public insurer such as Medicare cannot readily adjust its reimbursement to the plaintiff for medical expense to reflect a lump sum paid many years earlier.

TABLE 6.2

1985 Benefits Paid by Major Private and Social Insurance Programs

Insurance Program	Benefits Paid (in billions of dollars)
Social Security (OASI)	167.2
Private Health Coverage[1]	117.6
Medicare	70.5
Medicaid	37.5
Life Insurance Benefit Payments[2]	40.8
Workers' Compensation[3]	22.5
Disability Insurance	18.8
Supplementary Security Income	11.1
Private Pension Payments[4]	10.4
General Liability	8.2

Some of the benefit payments under these programs (particularly Social Security, private pension, and life insurance payments) reflect savings rather than pure insurance.

[1] This figure includes hospital-medical expense, dental expense, and loss of income payments by insurance companies, Blue Cross/Blue Shield, and self-insured plans. (See *1986-1987 Sourcebook of Health Insurance Data,* Table 2.1, p. 18.)

[2] This figure does not include policy dividends or surrender values.

[3] This figure includes private carriers, State funds, and self-insured plans.

[4] This figure represents only pension payments made by insurers and not the much greater amount paid by corporations through their own pension plans (1985 figures were not available).

SOURCES: *Statistical Abstract of the United States,* 108th Ed. (Washington, D.C.: U.S. Department of Commerce, 1988), Tables 564, 137, 575, 580, 555, pp. 341, 90, 347, 349, 351, 336; *1986-1987 Sourcebook of Health Insurance Data* (Washington, D.C.: Health Insurance Association of America, 1987), Table 2.1, p. 18; *1988 Life Insurance Fact Book* (Washington, D.C.: American Council of Life Insurance, 1988), pp. 41, 57; James S. Kakalik and Nicholas M. Pace, *Costs and Compensation Paid in Tort Litigation* (Santa Monica, Calif: The RAND Corporation, R-3391-ICJ, 1986).

Another possible mechanism for benefit coordination is for the private insurers to receive part of the tort award, through a subrogation action. States that have addressed this issue in their reform programs have opted for the simpler approach of reducing the tort award by the amount of collateral benefits. This goes some way toward elimination of duplicate coverage, but at the cost of undermining the deterrent aspect of the tort award.

Tort compensation for special needs, such as long-term nursing care, rehabilitation, and educational aids, is less duplicative of private coverage. But the absence of private insurance for such losses is surely due in part to the risk of moral hazard. This should be borne in mind in determining the optimal level of tort compensation and method of providing for these services.

COSTS OUTWEIGH BENEFITS

The standard of full replacement of pretax earnings tends to result in more than full replacement of after-tax earnings and hence is probably excessive, in the sense that it exceeds the level most people would choose to buy if faced with the full cost. The evidence from all private and other social insurance programs supports this view.

Further, a very substantial fraction of total tort compensation is designed to cover pain and suffering, a category of loss that is not covered by other private or public insurance. As we indicated earlier, it is impossible to determine by logical reasoning alone what would be the optimal compensation for nonmonetary loss. We must therefore turn to empirical evidence. All the evidence from other private and social insurance programs indicates that when faced with the cost, most people do not choose to buy such coverage voluntarily. The tort system is just as exposed to moral hazard for this type of loss as any private or public program – in fact more so. The plaintiff has every incentive to exaggerate the magnitude of the nonmonetary loss, and there is no objective evidence. The jury has little incentive to weigh the costs of generous compensation and operates without any budget constraint.

UNPREDICTABILITY

The purpose of insurance is to provide a steady flow of income and coverage of unexpected expenses. But tort awards are highly unpredictable in amount and are often received only after many months or even years of litigation. This unpredictability greatly reduces the value of tort awards as compensation.

INEQUITY

The large range of discretion left to the jury in determining tort awards necessarily results in very erratic outcomes and inequities among plaintiffs. Although tort compensation for wage replacement is proportional to income, payments into the system through the liability "tax" (i.e., the costs passed on via increases in prices to purchasers of goods and services) are unrelated to income. Thus, whereas private insurance tends to charge premiums at least roughly proportional to benefits received (so the rich get more out but also pay more in) and social insurance programs have features that redistribute from rich to poor, the tort system is likely to be regressive, with the poor getting lower benefits per dollar paid in than the rich.

REFORM OF THE STRUCTURE OF TORT COMPENSATION

If our concern is to fill inappropriate gaps in the network of private and social insurance for medical care and wage loss, a comprehensive program of either mandated private coverage or an extension of the existing public programs (DI, SSI, Medicare, and Medicaid) would probably be a better choice than an extension of the tort system. Although making specific recommendations on such complex issues would be beyond the scope of this policy statement, our review of the basic issues has convinced us that the tort system is not a cost-effective approach to this goal. It reaches only a tiny fraction of those potentially in need, at a much higher administrative cost than private or publicly funded insurance programs, with very considerable duplication of existing coverages, and at unusually high costs of coordinating benefits. The benefit structure is poorly designed, paying for losses that are not worth insuring. The large measure of discretion left to the courts in determining benefits in each case results in severe moral hazard and erratic and unpredictable awards that are inequitable and provide poor insurance. Overall, the system is likely to have a regressive effect on the distribution of income. Thus, the tort system fails as a compensation system by the criteria of target efficiency, economic efficiency, and equity.

The high overhead costs of the tort system make it worth retaining as a compensation system only in circumstances where it also performs a useful deterrent function, so that the high overhead costs effectively buy two services and need not be attributed solely to the compensation function. Even in such circumstances, however, incremental changes in the design of the tort benefit structure could do much to improve its cost-effectiveness as a system of compensation.

The tort damage award performs two functions. It provides compensation to the injured plaintiff, and it determines the penalty to be paid by the defendant, creating incentives for risk reduction. A policy dilemma arises because the same award level is unlikely to be simultaneously optimal for both purposes, particularly in the context of seriously disabling injuries. Consider an injury that results in the death of a bachelor with no heirs or dependents: the optimal compensatory award would be zero, whereas the optimal fine for purposes of deterrence could be very large. The optimal compensatory award is related to the amount of insurance that potential victims would have purchased voluntarily, whereas the optimal deterrent award is related to the amount they would want to spend to reduce the risk of injury (often referred to as willingness-to-pay for risk reduction). For serious personal injuries, the optimal penalty for deterrence may well be greater than the optimal compensatory award if there are no other mechanisms for controlling risk. Our recommendations here for restructuring compensatory tort awards are based largely on principles of optimal compensation, because market forces, regulation, and, in extreme cases, punitive damages are likely to provide additional deterrent incentives (see Chapter 5).

Based on general insurance principles, fundamental changes in the tort rules concerning damages are needed to improve their cost-effectiveness as a system of compulsory insurance. First, viewed from the standpoint of optimal compensation, the basic tort goal of making the plaintiff whole is almost certainly not optimal, in that it exceeds the level of insurance for which consumers are typically willing to pay. Benefit levels must permit an injured victim to maintain a reasonable standard of living and keep pace with inflation. Inadequate benefits are both inefficient and inequitable; they are also likely to generate pressures for alternative sources of compensation. For example, inadequacy of workers' compensation benefit levels has certainly been a factor in reopening the tort system for work-related injuries. But the evidence from both private and public insurance programs indicates overwhelmingly that compensation for wage loss should be limited to replacement of after-tax wages and that attempting full compensation for pain and suffering is not worth its cost because such losses are not replaceable by money.

Second, coordination of benefits from different insurance sources is critical to avoid unnecessary costs and overcompensation. Since the purpose of insurance is to provide for a stable income stream in the event of disability, narrowing the range of unpredictability of tort awards will increase its insurance value to consumers. Reducing unpredictability would also reduce incentives for expenditures on litigation and encourage prompter settlements. By making losses more predictable, it would reduce volatility in liability insurance markets (see Chapter 3). These considerations underlie our recommendations.

SCHEDULED AWARDS FOR MONETARY LOSS (SPECIAL DAMAGES)

In accordance with the principles adopted by the other major compulsory insurance systems (disability insurance and workers' compensation) more specific guidelines for determining tort damage awards should be set by statute, rather than leaving full discretion to the jury on a case-by-case basis. Guidelines could be specified with respect to certain parameters used in calculating wage loss: the replacement rate of pretax wages (e.g., two-thirds, or roughly full replacement of after-tax wages); the index of monetary inflation for calculating future wage growth (e.g., a state-specific wage index); an index of lifecycle wage growth; and the interest rate for discounting to present value (e.g., the one-year bond rate) if the payment is a lump sum. Guidelines should also be specified for compensation of persons who lack a current earnings history (homemakers, children, retirees). For example, future wage loss for children could be calculated at the median annual earnings in the state. Similar general principles should be applied for calculating compensation for medical, rehabilitation, and special educational expenses. Such guidelines would reduce the uncertainty of compensation to plaintiffs, decrease the exposure of the system to moral hazard in the form of delaying rehabilitation and exaggerating loss, discourage litigation expense by narrowing the range of possible outcomes, and, by making losses more predictable, increase the deterrent value of the system and reduce liability insurance risk and volatility.

SCHEDULED AWARDS FOR NONMONETARY LOSS (GENERAL DAMAGES)

The schedule of guidelines for determining compensation for monetary loss (special damages) should be extended to include limits on compensation for nonmonetary loss (general damages). In general, the optimal amount of compensation for general damages will vary with the age of the plaintiff, the type of injury, and the extent of compensation for other disability-related expenses, such as rehabilitation, special nursing, and educational needs. The preferred approach is to provide explicitly for such expenses in the schedule of compensation for special damages described above. Scheduled compensation for general damages should then be modest, to cover miscellaneous expenses, which will vary according to the age of the victim and the severity of the injury. Such an age-specific, injury-specific schedule would be far superior to the more common proposal of a single cap applied to all cases because the single cap results in a relatively more stringent limit on the young, severely injured plaintiff.[21] All scheduled amounts that are in nominal dollars should be pegged to a specified index of inflation such as the Consumer Price Index, in order to maintain the real value of compensation.

Moving to scheduled damages for both monetary and nonmonetary losses will represent a significant change from traditional tort law. Debate over such changes often assumes that scheduled benefits go hand in hand with a no-fault rule of liability, partly because the workers' compensation system introduced these two changes simultaneously for work-related injuries. However, neither economic efficiency nor equity dictates an automatic link between scheduled benefits and a no-fault rule of liability. As we have shown, scheduled benefits are consistent with sound principles of insurance and optimal compensation. They are the norm in every other private and social insurance program and would reduce the potential for inequity in tort compensation among similarly-placed plaintiffs. The design of an optimal structure of compensatory awards is distinct from the design of efficient standards of liability that was addressed in Chapter 5.

In fact, this proposal to establish schedules for monetary loss is not a radical departure from the way such losses are currently handled, at least in theory. Compensation for special damages is supposed to reflect wage loss, medical, and other out-of-pocket expenses. However, in practice the current method of determining such amounts leaves a large amount of discretion to the jury, particularly for future damages (where the choice of inflation and discount factors can lead to huge differences in estimates of future wage loss) and such expenses as private nursing care, education, and rehabilitation. A schedule would put the treatment of such issues on a more consistent basis and eliminate some of the uncertainties that currently generate expenditures on litigation and erratic and unpredictable outcomes.

Scheduling benefits will not be a panacea. It is unrealistic to expect to eliminate all uncertainty and all expenditures on litigation. Nevertheless the schedule approach offers promise of significant gains in efficiency and equity, provided that benefits levels are set and maintained at reasonable levels that provide fair and adequate compensation.

Moving to a scheduled approach to damages raises questions about the role of the jury and the possible use of an administrative forum for dispute resolution. The United States is unique in its use of the jury system for dealing with personal injury cases. These are important questions that need further study, but as a practical matter, change will necessarily occur in steps. The reforms proposed here would narrow the range of possible abuses of the jury system while leaving its basic structure intact. We recommend adopting these more limited reforms first and gaining experience with them in practice before addressing the issues of more radical alternatives.

PERIODIC PAYMENT FOR FUTURE DAMAGES

Under traditional tort damage rules, compensation for future damages is paid in a lump sum equal to the discounted present value of the expected future costs. Several states have enacted laws allowing or requiring periodic payment of awards that exceed some specified amount at the discretion of the court or the request of one of the parties.[22] The amount of future payments is determined at the time the case is resolved, rather than being contingent on the actual expenses incurred by the plaintiff.[23] The defendant typically provides for future payments through a trust fund, annuity, private insurance policy, or other financial instrument.

We propose adopting the periodic payment approach because it permits the provision of whatever stream of future payments is intended for the plaintiff at lower cost and with greater predictability and hence ultimately reduces the cost of the tort system to consumers. Basically, it takes advantage of financial instruments currently available in the market and removes from the court the need to determine the life expectancy of the plaintiff and the appropriate rates of inflation and discounting. Periodic payment through structured settlements using financial instruments are increasingly being used in out-of-court settlements but are less commonly used in court verdicts and should be encouraged.[24]

COORDINATION OF BENEFITS: THE COLLATERAL SOURCE RULE

The collateral source rule of traditional tort law prohibits presenting evidence to the jury of the plaintiff's potential compensation from other sources such as private and public insurance. There are two possible approaches to eliminating duplicative compensation. The alternative most commonly proposed, and the one that has been adopted in several states, reduces the amount of the tort award by the amount of compensation from other sources.[25] However, this approach requires the court to estimate the amount of future collateral benefits, and it may seriously undermine the deterrent value of the tort system. Under such an approach, given the prevalence of other sources of compensation described in this chapter, many potentially valid tort claims may simply not be worth bringing, particularly those involving temporary injuries where private and social insurance coverages would typically cover most medical expense and short-term wage loss.[26]

The second alternative is to reduce the payments from private and social insurers by the amount of the tort recovery or to give the other insurers the right to claim such funds from the tort defendant. This approach preserves the internalization of costs to the tort defendant and is thus preferable for purposes of deterrence, but it may entail higher costs of benefit coordination. Whether transactions costs are much higher under this approach, compared with the first alternative of collateral source offset, is an important but unresolved empirical question. Further research into the experience under currently operating statutes is required before we could recommend one alternative.

PAYMENT IN PROPORTION TO FAULT

The amount of the damage award should be reduced in proportion to the plaintiff's percentage of fault in contributing to the injury. This follows from the logic that where the efficient prevention of injuries requires care by both the user and the producer of the product, both should face incentives to take care. For example, consumer negligence is often a significant factor in product-related injuries, and employee negligence contributes to many workplace injuries. Awarding full compensation to the plaintiff in such circumstances undermines incentives for care by those exposed to risk. It also places an unfair and inefficient burden on defendants that creates incentives for inefficient resource allocation, including adding costly safety features that reduce product efficiency and withdrawing goods and services that cannot be modified to guard against consumer misuse.

Applying this principle of comparative negligence to reduce the award to the plaintiff where he or she has negligently contributed to the injury will inevitably result in awards that provide incomplete compensation. Other private and social insurance programs would normally pick up most of the shortfall because these coverages pay without regard to the cause of the injury, and this will inevitably undo some of the intended incentive effect of providing only partial coverage through the tort system. There is no simple, ideal solution to this problem. It is part of the inevitable tension between providing compensation and maintaining incentives for care.

WORK-RELATED INJURIES

Claims arising out of work-related injuries have mushroomed in recent years. The asbestos and the Agent Orange claims are the most prominent examples, each involving hundreds of thousands of claims, but injury claims by individual workers are also increasing. Some of these claims are brought by the individual worker against either his or her own employer. Others, the third-party employee claims, are brought by an employee of another employer against the manufacturer of a product or substance used in the workplace. Work-related product claims are also brought by employers of injured workers against manufacturers of workplace equipment seeking indemnity for payments made under workers' compensation. Almost one-third of all product liability claims are for work-related injuries.[27]

This growth in employment-related litigation runs counter to the original purpose of the workers' compensation statutes, which intended the WC system to be the sole remedy for work-related injuries and diseases. Employees gave up their common law rights to sue in return for the right to compensation without regard to the employer's or their own fault in causing the injury. But since the 1970s, the courts have sanctioned third-party claims against manufacturers under expanded doctrines of duty to warn, design defect, and failure in testing.[28] Courts have also permitted claims against employers under doctrines of dual capacity and willful misconduct.

Many of these employment-based tort claims are related to diseases rather than traumatic injuries, particularly slow-developing diseases that become apparent only twenty years or more after the toxic exposure. The WC system has not been able to handle these disease claims as smoothly as it handles traumatic injuries. Both the long latency and the fact that many of these diseases may arise from other, nonoccupational factors, have created difficulties in proving workplace causation. Also, the WC principle of full compensation is inappropriate in cases where occupational exposure is only a marginal contributing factor. The resort to the tort system has in part been an escape valve for the perceived inadequacy of the WC system.

This shift in the forum for work-related injuries has vastly complicated the issues by creating, retroactively, a new source of liability. For example, expanded tort doctrines have been applied to permit claims arising out of asbestos exposure in the 1930s, 1940s, and 1950s. At that time, an employee's sole remedy would typically have been a workers' compensation claim against his employer. Because this future tort liability was unanticipated, asbestos manufacturers purchased inadequate insurance coverage. Moreover, insurance contracts were written in language that leaves totally ambiguous the issue of whether the insurer is liable for latent injuries arising out of *exposure* in the policy period or for injuries *manifest* in the policy period. The fact that the asbestos claims arise out of a retroactive and therefore unanticipated change in liability rules is a major factor contributing to the inadequacy of funds for compensation and the enormous expenditure on litigation as manufacturers and insurers attempt to shift this unfunded liability among themselves.

This unprecedented confusion over the asbestos litigation tends to cloud the policy debate over compensation for occupational disease and injuries. The fact that the problems arise in part out of a retroactive change in liability rules is very instructive about the costs of such midstream shifts in policy. But it would be unfortunate if the problems arising out of this experience with unanticipated past liabilities were allowed to dominate the design of policy that is to have prospective impact.

The key issues in assigning liability for past losses are equity, fair compensation, and minimizing of the costs of litigation. But in designing policy that is to have prospective impact, which is our main concern here, the primary issues are to create efficient incentives for injury prevention; to provide for optimal compensation, through insurance or other funding mechanisms, for the injuries that may occur in the future; and to minimize transaction costs. Because there is often a tension between these three goals of prevention, compensation, and transaction-cost minimization, the efficient policy is a compromise that achieves the best trade-off.

In considering future-oriented policy for work-related injuries and diseases, there are three main options: (1) Make WC the sole remedy, in accordance with the original intent. (2) Supplement WC with tort claims under circumstances left to the discretion of the courts (i.e., the status quo). (3) Institute special public funds or programs, following the Black Lung model. The following section evaluates each of these measures by the criteria of prevention, compensation, and transaction-cost minimization.

OPTION 1: EMPLOYER LIABILITY UNDER WORKERS' COMPENSATION

Placing sole liability on employers through the workers' compensation system has advantages for prevention, compensation, and overhead costs. Employers are uniquely placed to make efficient choices for injury prevention and risk management. They have direct control over many aspects of workplace safety and indirect influence over other potential contributors (i.e., product suppliers and employees) through the terms and conditions of supply and employment contracts. It is a fundamental principle of the design of efficient liability rules that even when there are multiple contributors to the risk of injury (in this case, employers, product suppliers, and employees), dividing liability among the potential contributing parties is not necessary for providing each with the right safety incentives as long as the costs of contracting among the parties are low.[29]

For purposes of compensation, the WC mechanism of setting benefit levels before the fact by legislative decision at the level of the individual state is much more likely to lead to an efficient structure of compensation than the ad hoc, after-the-fact jury process is. Indeed, both theory and evidence suggest that the WC norms of replacement of after-tax earnings plus medical and rehabilitation expense are closer to optimal insurance than the tort principle of full compensation for all monetary and nonmonetary losses. The statutory determination of benefits provides greater consistency and predictability of the benefit structure, which increases its value as insurance to the employee and as a deterrent to the employer. Statutory determination of benefits also guards against retroactive changes in liability rules, with all the attendant costs of underfunded insurance and litigation. Moreover, overhead costs of litigation and providing insurance are lower under WC than under the tort system, in part because the statutory determination of benefits reduces the range of issues to be litigated, and in part because the process is handled through a specialized administrative agency, rather than by lay juries.

One common criticism of the WC system has been that benefit levels are inadequate. This may have been true in the early years of the system, but benefit provisions have increased since the early 1970s. The replacement rate for temporary and permanent total disability in virtually all states is now two-thirds of pretax, preinjury wages, which typically implies full replacement of after-tax wages. Medical expenses are covered for the duration of the injury. The fact that WC does not provide compensation of nonmonetary loss does not mean that the system is defective; both theory and the evidence from other private and social insurance programs suggest that such compensation is not worth its cost.

A second, more troubling criticism has been that some statutory definitions of occupational disease have acted as barriers to compensation through the WC system. There is an inevitable tension between, on the one hand, the principle that WC should be the sole remedy for work-related injuries and diseases, and on the other hand, the principle that only the appropriate level of liability should be imposed on industry. For many diseases, exposure to toxic substances while on the job is typically only one possible cause, in addition to genetic, environmental, personal health, and other factors. Consider a situation where occupational exposure raises the incidence of cancer from ten cases in a hundred workers to eleven cases. If employers are to bear only the incremental cost of the disease caused by occupational exposure, either only one of eleven workers should receive full compensation or all eleven should receive partial compensation. The former solution will appear arbitrary. The latter leaves all victims less than fully compensated, violates the sole-remedy principle, necessitates other sources of compensation, and causes attendant costs of coordinating benefits. The third alternative, of compensating all workers through WC, would impose an excessive tax on employment.

One possible solution to this dilemma is that WC should pay full benefits but only where the occupational exposure is the "predominant factor of causation."[30] Another alternative is for the employer to pay for only the share of the damages attributable to occupational exposure. In principle, this is the correct measure for purposes of equity and accurate deterrence. In practice, determining the marginal contribution in each case and coordinating benefits with the other insurance sources needed to complete compensation entails higher overhead costs.

Another difficult question that arises with long-latent diseases such as cancer is whether to place the full liability with the employer at the time the disease is manifest or to prorate liability over all employers that contributed to the exposure. Placing all liability on the last employer saves transaction costs but discourages employers from hiring older workers and taking adequate precautions to prevent diseases that are likely to appear only late in the worker's life. Prorating liability avoids distortions in incentives for hiring and risk reduction but entails higher transactions costs.

The best compromise, in our judgment, is to rely heavily on regulation to control workplace exposures to toxic substances and injurious processes and to leave the WC system free to focus on providing compensation at reasonable cost. We believe compensation should be limited to those injuries and diseases where occupational exposure is the predominant causative factor. For injuries that are compensable, WC benefit levels should provide an adequate level of compensation and be adjusted as needed to keep pace with inflation, although individual states may differ in the details of their benefit structures. WC should be the sole remedy. Where a compensable injury or disease is the result of exposure at several jobs, liability should be prorated among the contributing employers in proportion to their contribution.[31] Note that prorating liability in proportion to contribution should not normally generate litigation costs comparable to the costs of the current asbestos litigation, where costs are driven largely by the retroactive and therefore unanticipated nature of the liability. Such costs greatly exceed those of prorating if the prorating rule were clearly established, known at time of exposure, and enforced at time of manifestation.

Providing full compensation through WC but only for injuries where occupational exposure is the primary cause will necessarily appear to overcompensate some individuals and undercompensate others for their occupational exposure. This is a rough compromise intended to place approximately the right burden on the WC system. Drawing the line between diseases that are to be deemed occupational and hence compensable and those that are not compensable because occupation is a minor contributing factor will be very difficult in practice. But drawing such a line is essential in order to achieve the right internalization of occupational costs to the WC system. Unless such a line is clearly drawn there is a risk that the WC system will either become a general social insurance program, placing an excessive burden on employment, or provide inadequate deterrence of occupational risks.

Those employees who are not eligible for WC compensation because their diseases are not predominantly occupational in origin will normally be eligible for compensation through private first-party health and disability insurance and, if totally disabled, through the public disability programs (DI and Medicare). Because these private and public insurance programs are targeted at the employed population, the vast majority of workers are covered.

OPTION 2: TORT LIABILITY AS AN ADD-ON TO THE WORKERS' COMPENSATION SYSTEM

Tort liability suits against the worker's own employer cannot be justified for either deterrence or compensation reasons. The employer's strict liability under WC provides incentives for deterrence, and the WC benefit structure should provide appropriate compensation. Safety incentives are reinforced by market wage premiums for risky jobs and by OSHA regulation.[32]

Tort liability suits against the manufacturers of products used in the workplace are unnecessary for deterrence, because employers who are strictly liable through WC have strong incentives to monitor the safety of the products they purchase for use in the workplace. Regulation and market forces also provide additional risk control. Indeed, the employer's incentives for safety are undermined to the extent he or she can recoup the

WC benefits payable from the tort defendant, by placing a lien against the worker's tort recovery or subrogating to the worker's tort claim if the worker does not sue.[33]

Of course, from the standpoint of the individual plaintiff, pursuing a tort claim is attractive because tort compensation, when obtained, is higher. But from a societal point of view, it is simply not efficient to use tort as a supplementary system of compensation with a different benefit level and higher overhead costs, unless the supplementary system provides necessary additional deterrence incentives. Market forces, WC, and regulation all provide deterrence for work-related injuries. We believe, therefore, that the best solution is to set the benefits of the primary system – in this case, the WC system – at the desired level and make that system the sole remedy.

OPTION 3: SPECIAL PUBLIC FUNDS

There have been several proposals for special funds to replace or supplement the WC system for occupational disease. One common suggestion is to place all liability on the last responsible employer through WC but to set federal standards of compensation and provide for federally administered special funds if state benefits do not meet prescribed standards. Such a fund would probably be financed through a tax on the industry responsible for the exposure.

The case for a special federal fund is strongest if it were a temporary fund designed to address the problem of underfunding for past exposures caused by the retroactive change in liability rules. Such a fund would allow fair compensation for injuries already incurred and involve minimal litigation expense; in such cases deterrence is not an issue. But as the Black Lung experience has shown, even if a special fund is intended to be temporary, enforcing such a limitation is a practical impossibility.

A special fund that is permanent and therefore applies prospectively is likely to generate inappropriate incentives for prevention and for defining standards of compensation. Incentives for prevention are undermined because the costs of injuries are not borne by the firms that cause them. Similarly, incentives for setting efficient compensation standards are undermined because the costs and benefits of the compensation are no longer internalized. For example, the Black Lung program has created incentives for individual states to expand eligibility criteria but lower benefit levels, thereby shifting compensation of the maximum number of individuals to the federal fund. A replay of the cost explosion under the Black Lung program is likely under any federal program that sets a federal standard of compensation and promises unlimited federal funds to make up any shortfall between this federal standard and state-set standards.

NONOCCUPATIONAL MASS CLAIMS

Even with the removal of the mass occupational tort claims to the WC system, there remains a problem of potentially vast dimensions of mass claims that are not occupational but are related to consumer products or environmental exposures. One issue raised by mass claims is the cost of adjudication (see Chapter 4). Here our concern is with the appropriate measure of damages when a toxic exposure raises the incidence of an injury or disease above the normal rate for the population. The fundamental problem is the difficulty of attributing cause. Even if the issue of general causation can be resolved (how much a particular exposure raises the incidence of a disease in a population), the issue of specific causation (the contribution of the exposure for the individual case) is typically beyond the ability of existing scientific knowledge.

When the contribution of the multiple factors can only be determined in a probabilistic sense, determining damages that are appropriate in each individual case and in the aggregate over all cases is not a simple matter. As in the occupational disease context, if full damages for all claims are assessed against only one contributing factor or party, the result is an excessive tax on that activity. An excessive tax would also occur if potential victims are compensated before the fact for the increased exposure to risk, as some courts have recently permitted, and then are compensated possibly many years later when some of those at increased risk actually develop the disease in question.

In principle, the options are the same as those already discussed in the occupational disease context. If the environmental exposure raises the incidence of cancer in the exposed population from ten to eleven cases per hundred population, the polluter should: (1) pay full compensation to one in eleven cancer victims in the exposed population, (2) pay one-eleventh of the damages to each victim, or (3) compensate all one hundred exposed persons for the *ex ante* increased risk of cancer (or 1 percent of the cost per case). The first approach (full compensation of one in eleven cases) is unacceptably arbitrary. The third approach (compensation before the fact to the entire exposed population for the increased risk) would typically entail prohibitive transaction costs of determining the relevant population and the increase in risk, which would usually not be uniform for everyone exposed.

This leaves the second approach, compensation of all cases for the percentage of the damages equal to the marginal increment in risk. Even with this approach, transaction costs will be high and may not be worth incurring if the marginal contribution of the tort defendant is small and most compensation comes from other sources. Many potential small claims may not be filed unless class actions are brought, which have their own problems (see Chapter 4). Thus, the tort system is likely to yield poor deterrence and very high transaction costs in circumstances that involve a small loss to a large number of individuals.

Relying heavily on regulation to control such risks and on other systems of private and public insurance to provide compensation is the solution we prefer. Where a product is in compliance with regulatory standards, tort actions should be disallowed (see Chapter 5). Where this regulation defense does not apply, tort claims should be allowed only where the marginal contribution of the allegedly harmful substance exceeds some threshold.

SOCIAL INSURANCE PROGRAMS

As described earlier, the DI program provides for income replacement in the event of total disability, regardless of the circumstances or cause of the injury or disease. After two years on DI, an individual's medical expenses are covered through Medicare. However, eligibility for DI and disability-related Medicare coverage is limited to persons who have accumulated the required minimum amount of work experience and hence have contributed to the system through the payroll tax. Dependents of covered workers are not covered in their own right except that disabled dependents of covered retirees are covered. Thus, persons without the required work experience (homemakers and children) have no social insurance safety net other than SSI. This is a means-tested program, so it requires that the entire family spend down to the poverty level in order to qualify.

If our concern in expanding the tort system is to provide for a comprehensive system of insurance for serious disability, one possible option is to extend eligibility for DI to the entire population, regardless of work experience. A more limited approach would be to extend coverage to dependents of covered workers but also make contributions proportional to the number of dependents. This would greatly extend the reach of the program while retaining its link to employment. Linking contributions into the system to number of dependents as a precondition for extending benefits to dependents would preserve equity among families of different sizes.[34]

The advantages of relying on DI to extend disability coverage are its potential reach, lower overhead cost than the tort system, and lower costs of coordinating benefits with other programs. The major disadvantage of expanding DI is that it would require an increase in payroll taxes or other general revenue funding. If extended beyond dependents of covered workers to persons who have no work force connection or experience, it would turn employment-based insurance into a general social insurance program. Taxing employment is generally an inefficient and inequitable way of financing a general welfare program.

Revising the basic social insurance programs would involve major policy changes, and we are not in a position to make a recommendation without further analysis. However, we do believe that revisions of these programs are likely to entail lower real social costs and less regressive financing than using the tort system to fill gaps in the existing network of private and social insurance. Expanding social insurance programs may appear more costly, but that is because these programs appear as line items in budgets, whereas the costs of the tort system are diffuse and largely hidden.

In addition, the DI program itself requires review. For example, unstable benefit standards and inadequate use of rehabilitation undermine its cost-effectiveness. Detailed recommendations with regard to this program are beyond the scope of this statement but warrant serious attention.

EXPANDING PRIVATE INSURANCE COVERAGE

Recently, there has been renewed interest in expanding private health insurance coverage by mandating employment-based benefits. The Consolidated Omnibus Reconciliation Act of 1985 (COBRA) required employers who have health plans to offer continued health insurance coverage at group rates to employees and their dependents in the event of layoff, divorce, or some other major change in circumstances. Recent legislation makes employer health insurance, rather than Medicare, the primary payer for the working aged and certain other people. The Nondiscrimination rules in Section 89 of the 1986 Tax Reform Act are intended to make employers extend health insurance and other benefits to lower income employees.

Other measures are still on the drawing board. Voluntary State Health Insurance Risk-Pools Bill allow states to establish risk pools to provide health insurance for the high-risk uninsured, with losses to be subsidized by employers.[35] Senator Edward Kennedy (D-Mass.) and Representative Henry Waxman (D-Calif.) have introduced legislation that would require most employers to provide a minimum level of health coverage.[36] Massachusetts recently enacted legislation that essentially taxes employers who do not provide benefits, which has many of the same effects as mandating employer-provided benefits.

Attempting to expand health insurance coverage through employment has political appeal because a significant fraction of the uninsured could be covered at relatively low cost to public budgets. Of the 37 million uninsured Americans, almost three-fourths are either employed or are in households with at least one employed member. As we noted earlier, using the employment group as the criterion of eligibility can have advantages in the form of lowering administrative costs and reducing the risk of adverse selection, but these potential advantages apply only to medium-sized and large firms with at least fifty full-time employees. Even in large firms, these advantages are much less for new hires and part-timers. Yet, the great majority of employees who are currently not covered hold these types of jobs (either in small firms or as new hire and part-timers in large firms). Mandating coverage for these positions will entail significant costs and in the long run will result in lower wages for these workers and loss of job opportunities. Many of these workers are at or close to the minimum wage and are from low- and middle-income families. If the objective is to improve the lot of the uninsured, this is not the way to go about it.

A full evaluation of all the options for assuring reasonable access to health care for all Americans is beyond the scope of this statement, but our brief review suggests some important conclusions. Aside from the political appeal of off-budget financing, mandating employment-based benefits has few real advantages. The disadvantages are, first, that for the jobs where benefits are currently not provided, the costs are relatively high. Second, it is a fairly regressive form of financing and will entail indirect costs in the form of lost job opportunities and distortions in employment. Third, it will still leave some of the most needy individuals without coverage. An alternative approach that we believe deserves serious consideration involves a system of refundable tax credits for the purchase of health insurance. Such credits could be applied to employment-based coverage or to individually purchased coverage, thereby extending the existing tax subsidy to those without employment-based coverage. CED discussed this idea in a 1987 policy statement, *Reforming Health Care: A Market Prescription.*

SUMMARY OF RECOMMENDATIONS

Our examination of fundamental insurance principles and of the evidence from private and public insurance programs has led us to conclusions that should guide reforms of tort and other systems of compensation. These considerations and the proposed reforms of tort compensation apply to all types of liability for personal injury, including medical malpractice, municipal, and personal liability, and are not limited to product liability.

There is an inevitable tension between the goal of providing compensation and the goal of preserving incentives for preventing or minimizing loss. Where there is a severe risk of moral hazard (taking inadequate precautions or exaggerating the reported loss), purchasing only partial coverage or a policy with copayments is often the best choice – and one that we as individuals continually make in our private insurance purchases. Other valuable strategies for controlling overutilization of medical care include utilization review and various forms of prepayment of providers. In addition, the experience of large private employers with innovative programs of disability management shows some success in achieving speedy rehabilitation and reducing the total costs of disability. Skimping on expenditures for rehabilitation and retraining of disabled workers can be penny wise and pound foolish, yet neither the public disability programs nor the tort system pay much attention to disability management.

This nation's pluralistic approach to compensation is worth retaining. It has its justification in the diversity of circumstances in which injuries occur, the importance of deterrence in some circumstances but not in others, and the differing abilities of people to pay for private insurance and obtain it at reasonable cost.

But an inevitable side effect of a pluralistic approach is the potential for overlaps and gaps in coverage. These deserve more attention.

Overlapping benefits create overinsurance, encourage overutilization of medical care and prolonged dependency, and hence imply waste and unnecessary costs. Benefit coordination is critical, particularly between tort and nontort coverages. It can be done in different ways, and the preferred choice depends on the effects on incentives for prevention and on overhead costs.

On the other hand, the network of private and public coverages leaves some people without basic coverage. How best to fill these gaps is an important issue that should be addressed but goes beyond the scope of this report. However, because it is not cost-justifiable to provide full coverage for all types of loss, government should not attempt to fill all apparent gaps in coverage, either through the tort systems or through other social insurance programs.

Insurance is far more valuable to consumers if compensation is prompt and predictable. The desire for a stable income stream is the reason people buy insurance. The delays and unpredictability of tort benefits and the recent instability of federal policies with respect to DI benefits greatly reduce the value of these programs as insurance. Having said this, we recognize that perfection is not a realistic goal. No system of insurance for personal injury, either private or public, can be expected to deliver just the right amount of compensation, in the right circumstances, and without delay. The reason is that the nature and extent of most personal injuries and the potential for rehabilitation are rarely amenable to precise, prompt, and objective measurement. Both private and public insurance systems therefore can and should devote some time and resources to determining the extent of the loss, and some errors are inevitable. Our goal should be to design systems that minimize the potential for error and conserve on the overhead costs of making benefit payment decisions.

These considerations have been taken into account in the policy recommendations developed in this chapter. Those recommendations are summarized below.

TORT DAMAGE AWARDS

- **Statutory schedules should be established for determining compensation for monetary and nonmonetary losses, while retaining a fault-based rule of liability (see Chapter 5).**

- **Compensation for nonmonetary loss should be limited according to age and severity of injury.**

- **Greater use should be made of periodic payments for future loss using appropriate financial instruments such as annuities.**

- **Further study is needed of alternatives for coordinating tort awards with other sources of insurance (collateral source coordination).**

- **Damages should be levied in proportion to fault.**

WORK-RELATED INJURIES AND DISEASES

- **Tort actions against product suppliers and employers should be disallowed.**

- **We should rely to a greater extent on regulation to set standards for workplace hazards, with modifications to improve cost-effectiveness.**

- **Workers' compensation should be the sole remedy for compensation for injuries and diseases where occupational exposure is the predominant cause.**

- **Liability among contributing employers should be prorated in proportion to their contribution to the worker's exposure.**

- WC benefit levels and eligibility criteria should be set by statute at the state level, to the extent possible, to minimize litigation on individual cases.

- Benefit levels should be set to assure a reasonable standard of living and should be indexed to keep pace with inflation.

- Existing private and public insurance programs should be relied upon to cover injuries and diseases where occupational exposure is not the predominant cause.

- Further research is needed to better understand the extent to which certain diseases are job-related.

NONOCCUPATIONAL MASS TORTS

- Regulatory standard setting should be the primary instrument for controlling environmental health and safety hazards (see Chapter 4).

- Tort claims should be permitted only where the contribution of the tort defendant exceeds some threshold.

FILLING INSURANCE GAPS

- Further study is needed to determine the optimal approach to filling gaps in our nation's network of private and social insurance.

* * *

The policy recommendations found in this statement will not remedy all of the problems with our systems of dealing with risk, but we believe they would lead to a significantly improved balance of benefits relative to costs – for consumers, producers, employees, and for our society as a whole. Until our courts, regulatory agencies, and insurance programs are better designed and coordinated, their actual and potential beneficial effects will continue to be handicapped by the excessive costs they are generating for our economy and society – raising prices, deterring the provision of certain vital goods, discouraging innovation, and damaging U.S. international competitiveness.

We believe a more economical and equitable way of dealing with risk can be devised. We believe that the policy recommendations on these pages provide a constructive framework for doing so.

ENDNOTES

CHAPTER 1

1. In this policy statement we use the term efficient to mean costs and benefits to society as a whole, and not just to certain individuals, or in an operational sense of the word efficient. (See the introduction of Chapter 5 for further clarification.)

2. James S. Kakalik and Nicholas M. Pace, *Costs and Compensation Paid in Tort Litigation* (Santa Monica, Calif.: The RAND Corporation, R-3391-ICJ, 1986).

3. U.S. Department of Justice, Tort Policy Working Group, *An Update on the Liability Crisis* (Washington, D.C.: U.S. Government Printing Office, March 1987), pp. 45-46.

4. Deborah R. Hensler, Mary E. Vaiana, James S. Kakalik, Mark A. Peterson, *Trends in Tort Litigation: The Story Behind the Statistics* (Santa Monica, Calif.: The RAND Corporation, R-3583-ICJ, 1987).

5. Mark A. Peterson, *Civil Juries in the 1980s: Trends in Jury Trials and Verdicts in California and Cook County, Illinois* (Santa Monica, Calif.: The RAND Corporation, R-3466-ICJ, 1987), pp. 17, 22, 35.

6. Patricia M. Danzon, "Medical Malpractice Liability" in *Liability: Perspectives and Policy,* ed. Robert E. Litan and Clifford Winston (Washington, D.C.: The Brookings Institution, 1988), p. 107.

7. U.S. Department of Justice, *Report of the Tort Policy Working Group on the Causes, Extent, and Policy Implications of the Current Crisis in Insurance Availability and Affordability* (Washington, D.C.: February 1986). In particular, see Chapter 1, "The Crisis in Insurance Availability and Affordability," pp. 6-15.

8. See *Insuring Our Future: Report of the Governor's Advisory Commission on Liability Insurance* (New York: April 7, 1986); and U.S. Department of Justice, *Report of the Tort Policy Working Group,* pp. 14-15.

9. Kakalik and Pace, *Costs and Compensation Paid in Tort Litigation,* pp. 72, 74.

10. Patricia M. Danzon, *Medical Malpractice: Theory, Evidence, and Public Policy* (Cambridge, Mass.: Harvard University Press, 1985).

11. For a discussion of these issues, see Paul Slovic, "Risk Perception, Risk Communication and Hazardous Waste Management" (Paper presented at Wharton School, The University of Pennsylvania, May 1985).

12. F. N. Merck & Co., Inc., *Health Care Innovation: The Case for a Favorable Public Policy,* 1988.

CHAPTER 2

1. The data in this section pertain only to claims for which lawsuits are filed. In addition, a substantial number of claims are filed with defendants and insurers but disposed of prior to filing a suit. Because data on such claims are not available on a comprehensive basis, they are omitted from this analysis.

2. U.S. Department of Justice, Tort Policy Working Group, *An Update on the Liability Crisis* (Washington, D.C.: U.S. Government Printing Office, March 1987), pp. 41-42.

3. National Center for State Courts, *State Court Caseload Statistics: Annual Report, 1984* (1986).

4. Deborah R. Hensler, Mary E. Vaiana, James S. Kakalik, and Mark A. Peterson, *Trends in Tort Litigation: The Story Behind the Statistics* (Santa Monica, Calif.: The RAND Corporation, R-3583-ICJ, 1987).

5. U.S. Department of Justice, *An Update on the Liability Crisis,* pp. 45-46.

6. Hensler, Vaiana, Kakalik, and Peterson , *Trends in Tort Litigation.*

7. Mark A. Peterson, *Civil Juries in the 1980s: Trends in Jury Trials and Verdicts in California and Cook County, Illinois* (Santa Monica, Calif.: The RAND Corporation, R-3466-ICJ, 1987). See also other reports cited therein. This report includes data from other California jurisdictions which suggest that San Francisco is reasonably representative of other urban jurisdictions, although smaller-city and rural jurisdictions have lower median and mean awards.

8. For estimates of the relation between settlements and potential verdicts, see Patricia M. Danzon and Lee A. Lillard, "Settlement Out of Court: The Disposition of Medical Malpractice Claims," *Journal of Legal Studies* 12 (June 1983): 345-377.

9. In both Cook County and San Francisco, the number of verdicts has not increased in proportion to the number of filings since the 1960s, implying that parties are settling an increased proportion of cases. Cases tried to verdict may therefore include fewer small claims in later years. However, changes in the characteristics of cases in which a verdict is reached apparently are not sufficient to explain the increasing size of jury awards. See Peterson, *Civil Juries in the 1980s,* p. 16.

10. The post-1980 trend in San Francisco may be upwardly biased by the change in case load composition noted above.

11. Peterson, *Civil Juries in the 1980s,* p. 37.

12. Peterson, *Civil Juries in the 1980s,* pp. 17, 29. The proportion of plaintiffs' victories varies by jurisdiction and type of case, but the trend is upward for most types of cases.

13. Peterson, *Civil Juries in the 1980s,* p. 26.

14. Mark Peterson, Syam Sarma, and Michael Shanley, *Punitive Damages: Empirical Findings* (Santa Monica, Calif.: The RAND Corporation, R-3311-ICJ, 1987).

15. Peterson, Sarma, and Shanley, *Punitive Damages,* pp. 46, 13, 25, 35.

16. Michael G. Shanley and Mark A. Peterson, *Posttrial Adjustments to Jury Awards* (Santa Monica, Calif.: The RAND Corporation, R-3511-ICJ, 1987).

17. *MacPherson v. Buick Motor Co.,* 217 N.Y.382, 111 N.E.1050 (Ct. App. 1916). For differing views of the evolution of modern tort law, see George L. Priest, "The Invention of Enterprise Liability: A Critical History of the Intellectual Foundations of Modern Tort Law," *Journal of Legal Studies* 14, no. 3 (December 1985): 461-527; William M. Landes and Richard A. Posner, "A Positive Economic Analysis of Products Liability," *Journal of Legal Studies* 14, no.3 (December 1985): 553-566; and Gary T. Schwartz, "Old Products, New Products, Evolving Law, Retroactive Law," *New York University Law Review* 58 (1983): 796.

18. *United States v. Carroll Towing Co.,* 159 F.2d 169 (2d Cir. 1947).

19. For an economic analysis of legal rules, see Richard A. Posner, *Economic Analysis of Law,* 3d ed. (Boston: Little-Brown, 1986); John Prather Brown, "Toward an Economic Theory of Liability," *Journal of Legal Studies* 2 (June 1973): 323-349; and Richard A. Epstein, *Modern Products Liability Law: A Legal Revolution* (Westport, Conn.: Quorum Books, 1980).

20. For example, "The purpose of liability is to insure that the costs of injuries resulting from defective products are borne by manufacturers rather than by injured persons who are powerless to protect themselves." *Greenman v. Yuba Power Products Inc.,* 59 Cal.2d 57, 63, 377 P.2d 897 (1963). See also Priest, "The Invention of Enterprise Liability."

21. See, for example, Peter Huber, *Liability: The Legal Revolution and Its Consequences* (New York: Basic Books, Inc., 1988); and Priest, "The Invention of Enterprise Liability."

22. *H. Rosenblum, Inc. v. Adler,* 93 N.J. 324, 461 A.2d (1983). Other recent decisions include *Citizens State Bank v. Timm, Schmidt & Co.,* 113 Wis.2d 376, 335 N.W.2d 36 (1983); *International Mortgage Co. v. John H. Butler Accounting Corp.,* 177 Cal. App. 3d 806, 223 Cal. Rptr. 218 (Cal. Ct. App. 1986); and *Touche Ross & Co. v. Commercial Union Ins. Co.,* No. 56, 753 (Sup. Ct. Miss. Aug. 26, 1987).

23. *Ultramares v. Touche Ross,* 255 N.Y. 170 (1931) established the original standard for accountants' liability. This decision was reaffirmed by *Credit Alliance Corp. v. Arthur Andersen & Co.,* 65 N.Y.2d 536 (1985).

24. See, for example, Utah Code Ann. 78-15-6(1), (2) (1977); South Carolina Code 15-73-10, -30 (1976).

25. For example, *Greenman v. Yuba Power Products, Inc.,* 59 Cal.2d 57, 27 Cal. Rptr. 697, 377 P.2d 897 (1963).

26. See Priest, "The Invention of Enterprise Liability."

27. See, for example, Steven Shavell, "Strict Liability vs. Negligence," *Journal of Legal Studies* 9 (January 1980): 1-25; Charles E. Phelps, "Liability and Regulation: When to Use Which and When to Use Neither" (Research paper prepared for the CED Subcommittee on Risk Management, Dispute Resolution, and Injury Compensation, February 1987).

28. Brown, "Toward an Economic Theory of Liability"; Shavell, "Strict Liability vs. Negligence"; and Phelps, "Liability and Regulation." See also George L. Priest, "The Disappearance of the Consumer from Modern Products Liability Law," in *The Frontier of Research in the Consumer Interest,* ed. E. Scott Maynes (Columbia, Mo: American Council on Consumer Interest, 1988).

29. *Beshada v. Johns-Manville Corp.* 90 N.J. 191, 447 A.2d 539 (1982). See also U.S. Department of Justice, *Report of the Tort Policy Working Group on the Causes, Extent, and Policy Implications of the Current Crisis in Insurance Availability and Affordability* (Washington, D.C.: U.S. Government Printing Office, February 1986), p. 31, footnote 23. How much was known or should have been known in the 1930s regarding the risks associated with asbestos is not the issue here. Rather, the point here concerns the principle of retroactive liability and rejection of the state-of-the-art defense.

30. Patricia M. Danzon, "Tort Reform and the Role of Government in Private Insurance Markets," *Journal of Legal Studies* 13 (August 1984): 517-549. Since the medical malpractice crisis of 1974-1975, many states have adopted statutes of repose, which set a limit running from the date of injury for medical malpractice cases.

31. See Peter Huber, "Environmental Hazards and Liability Law," in *Liability: Perspectives and Policy,* ed. Robert E. Litan and Clifford Winston (Washington, D.C.: The Brookings Institution, 1988), pp. 128-154.

32. *Sindell v. Abbott Laboratories,* 26 Cal. 3d 588, 607 P.2d 924, 163 Cal. Rptr. (1980). Cert. denied, 101 S.CT. 286 (1980). Two recent cases modify the potential impact of *Sindell.* In *Brown v. Abbott Laboratories,* 44 Cal. 3d 1049, 751 P.2d 470, 245 Cal. Rptr. 412 (1988), the court held that strict liability does not apply to prescription drugs in California. The court stated that the costs created by unpredictable liability which results from the application of strict liability have in turn raised the cost of available drugs, encouraged manufacturers to withdraw drugs from the market, and discouraged research. The court also held that joint and several liability does not apply when the plaintiff recovers under a market share theory. In *Jolly v. Ely Lilly & Co.,* 44 Cal. 3d 1103, 751 P.2d 923, 245 Cal. Rptr. 658 (1988), the court rejected the argument that the statute of limitations should begin on the date that the court adopts a theory that would allow recovery under a market share theory. See Huber, *Liability,* p. 81, for a discussion of the first DES case.

33. Huber, "Environmental Hazards," p. 143.

34. Workers' compensation as an alternative to tort is discussed in Chapter 6.

35. W. Kip Viscusi, "Occupational Accidents and Illnesses," in *Liability: Perspectives and Policy*, ed. Robert E. Litan and Clifford Winston (Washington, D.C.: The Brookings Institution, 1988), p. 179. Viscusi is quoting Government Research Corporation, *Victim Compensation: The Policy Debate* (Washington, D.C.: Government Research Corp., 1983), for figures on numbers of asbestos suits and Paul MacAvoy, *The Economic Consequences of Asbestos-Related Disease*, Working Paper No. 27 (New Haven: Yale School of Organization and Management, 1982), pp. 66, 77-78, for figures on costs of litigation.

36. Richard A. Epstein, "Manville: The Bankruptcy of Product Liability," *Regulation* (September-October, 1982): 14-19, 43-46.

37. Greater use of expert witnesses to calculate the present value of future wage loss and medical expenses may have corrected previously inadequate levels of compensation.

38. See Gary Schwartz, "American Tort Doctrine Since 1960" (Research paper prepared for the CED Subcommittee on Risk Management, Dispute Resolution, and Injury Compensation, January 1987).

39. Patricia M. Danzon, *New Evidence on the Frequency and Severity of Medical Malpractice Claims* (Santa Monica, Calif.: The RAND Corporation, R-3410-ICJ, 1986).

40. For example, U.S. Department of Justice, *Report of the Tort Policy Working Group*, pp. 61-62.

41. See, for example, Priest, "The Invention of Enterprise Liability."

42. See, for example, Landes and Posner, "A Positive Economic Analysis of Products Liability."

43. J. Robert S. Pritchard, "A Systematic Approach to Comparative Law: The Effect of Cost, Fee, and Financing Rules on the Development of the Substantive Law," *Journal of Legal Studies* 17 (June 1988): 451-475.

44. The evidence that courts award different amounts for similar injuries, depending on the defendant, is suggestive on this point. See Audrey Chin and Mark Peterson, *Deep Pockets, Empty Pockets: Who Wins in Cook County Jury Trials* (Santa Monica, Calif.: The RAND Corporation, R-3249-ICJ, 1985).

CHAPTER 3

1. U.S. Department of Justice, *Report of the Tort Policy Working Group on the Causes, Extent, and Policy Implications of the Current Crisis in Insurance Availability and Affordability* (Washington, D.C.: U.S. Government Printing Office, February 1986), pp. 7-13.

2. Similar conclusions are reached in *Insuring Our Future: Report of the Governor's Advisory Commission on Liability Insurance* (New York: April 7, 1986), pp. 32-33 (hereafter referred to as *New York Report*).

3. With an occurrence policy form, the tail reflects delay in both filing and disposition of claims. The length of the tail therefore depends directly on the statute of repose for the insured's acts. With the claims-made form, the tail is much shorter, reflecting only delay in the disposition of claims.

4. Neil A. Doherty and H. B. Kang, "Interest Rates and Insurance Price Cycles," *Journal of Banking and Finance*, forthcoming; and J. David Cummins and F. Outreville, "An International Analysis of Underwriting Cycles," *Journal of Risk and Insurance* (June 1987).

5. U.S. Department of Justice, Tort Policy Working Group, *An Update on the Liability Crisis* (Washington, D.C.: U.S. Government Printing Office, March 1987); and U.S. General Accounting Office, "Product Liability: Extent of `Litigation Explosion' in Federal Courts Questioned," GAO/HRD 88-36BR (hereafter referred to as *GAO*).

6. U.S. Department of Justice, *Report of the Tort Policy Working Group,* pp. 7-13. Other examples are cited in *New York Report*, pp. 32-33.

7. U.S. Department of Justice, *Report of the Tort Policy Working Group,* p. 23, using Insurance Services Office data, shows that total commercial lines premium volume fell each year between 1977 and 1983 when measured in constant dollars. Assuming that the volume of coverage increased over this period, the decline in total premiums written understates the decline in premium rates.

8. Rate increases for surgical specialties have been higher than for medical specialties. Patricia M. Danzon, "Medical Malpractice Liability," in *Liability: Perspectives and Policy,* ed. Robert E. Litan and Clifford Winston (Washington, D.C.: The Brookings Institution, 1988).

9. "Average 1985 prices charged to a given class of insureds, when placed on a price curve upon which the last previous point was average 1979 prices, usually do not appear to indicate any major perturbation in the market." *New York Report*, p. 72.

10. See, for example, U.S. Department of Justice, *Report of the Tort Policy Working Group,* p. 6; *New York Report* ; *GAO*.

11. *GAO.*

12. The problems in EIL insurance arise both from the provisions of the Superfund legislation and from the implementation of that legislation by the courts.

13. See Patricia M. Danzon, *Medical Malpractice: Theory, Evidence and Public Policy* (Cambridge, Mass.: Harvard University Press, 1985), pp. 97-117.

14. U.S. Department of Justice, *Report of the Tort Policy Working Group,* p. 24.

15. Scott E. Harrington, "Prices and Profits in the Liability Insurance Market," in *Liability: Perspectives and Policy,* ed. Robert E. Litan and Clifford Winston (Washington, D.C.: The Brookings Institution, 1988).

16. Delay in closing out claims for a given policy year are especially long with the traditional occurrence form of policy, which covers all claims arising out of incidents occurring in the policy year, regardless of when in the future the claims are filed. Until the recent crisis, occurrence coverage was the norm for most commercial lines, with the notable exception of some medical malpractice and other professional liability policies.

17. Harrington, "Prices and Profits in the Liability Insurance Market," pp. 58-59, Table 3-6; *New York Report.*

18. Higher reported losses mean lower surplus and hence the possibility of exceeding allowable premium-to-surplus ratios. The premium-to-surplus ratio is monitored by regulators as a measure of leverage.

19. *New York Report,* p. 82b.

20. Because these data refer to number of occurrences, they are not contaminated by possible changes in the number of defendants named per claim.

21. Richard N. Clarke, Frederick Warren-Boulton, David D. Smith, and Marilyn J. Simon, "Sources of the Crisis in Liability Insurance: An Economic Analysis," *Yale Journal on Regulation* 5 (Summer 1988): 374, 394. Total litigation expense, including both plaintiff and defense costs, absorbs roughly 40 percent of the liability insurance premium dollar. See Chapter 4.

22. Underwriting profits are measured by the combined ratio of losses plus loss-adjustment expense to premiums written plus the ratio of underwriting expense to premiums earned. Although a ratio greater than 1 is sometimes interpreted as an underwriting loss, it does not necessarily imply that the insurance is underpriced because of investment income on the loss and unearned premium reserves. Under statutory insurance accounting, losses and adjustment expense have traditionally been reported undiscounted, whereas premiums in competitive markets will reflect the expected investment income over the period between premium collection and claim payment.

23. *New York Report,* p. 70a, shows that the cycle in operating return on equity for the property-casualty insurance industry is not perfectly synchronized with, and has greater amplitude than, the comparable measure for the Standard & Poor's 400.

24. See, for example, Clarke, Warren-Boulton, Smith, and Simon, "Sources of the Crisis in Liability Insurance;" Ralph A. Winter, "The Liability Crisis and the Dynamics of Competitive Insurance Prices," *Yale Journal on Regulation* 5 (Summer 1988): 463; and George L. Priest, "The Current Insurance Crisis and Modern Tort Law," *Yale Law Journal* 96 (1987): 1521.

25. The competitiveness of the liability insurance market has been called into question by the antitrust suit filed by several state attorney generals in 1988. The suit alleges collusive action between several large insurers, reinsurers, and the Insurance Services Office (ISO) related to modifications of the traditional insurance policy form, particularly the introduction of the claims-made form, the exclusion of pollution coverage, and the inclusion of legal expense in the overall policy limits. Elsewhere we note that changes in liability rules could account for problems in availability of pollution coverage and the attempt to switch more generally to claims-made. The true circumstances that gave rise to the attempt to effect these changes in the policy form are still unknown, and litigation will no doubt drag on for years.

26. A competitive premium reflects the discounted present value of expected loss and loss-adjustment expense, plus taxes and a markup for risk-adjusted return on equity. See Stewart Myers and Richard Cohn, "Insurance Rate Regulation and the Capital Asset Pricing Model" in *Fair Rate of Return in Property-Liability Insurance,* ed. J.D. Cummins and Scott E. Harrington (Norwell, Mass: Kluwer Academic Publishers, 1987). Thus, the higher the expected rate of return on invested funds and the longer the delay between collection of premium and payout on claims, the greater the interest sensitivity of premiums. If changes in nominal interest rates were paralleled by changes in the expected rate of inflation of losses, premiums would be sensitive not to changes in nominal interest rates but to real interest rates.

27. Tails on reinsurance are even longer than those on direct insurance because the large claims that penetrate the reinsured limits of coverage tend to take longer to settle. Reinsurers report that even excluding asbestos risks, they do not know of as much as 75 percent of the losses that will arise from a commercial general liability reinsurance policy until the thirteenth year after the policy was in force. See *New York Report,* p. 77.

28. Emilio C. Venezian, "Ratemaking Methods and Profit Cycles in Property and Liability Insurance," *Journal of Risk and Insurance* 52 (September 1985): 477-500.

29. Similarly, the flow of capital into the worldwide reinsurance market contributed to the very soft prices and expansion of coverage in the early 1980s.

30. Winter, in "The Liability Crisis and the Dynamics of Competitive Insurance Prices," develops a model of insurance cycles based on shocks to capacity and adjustment costs.

31. The early warning system applied by the National Association of Insurance Commissioners is described in Scott E. Harrington and Patricia M. Danzon, "An Evaluation of Solvency Regulation in the Property-Liability Insurance Industry" (Report to the Alliance of American Insurers, American Insurance Association, and National Association of Independent Insurers, University of Pennsylvania, Wharton School, June 1986). Insurance rating agencies such as A. M. Best use a similar set of financial ratios.

32. Changes in surplus and its components in the recent and prior cycles are described in Insurance Services Office, *The Coming Capacity Shortage* (February 1985). This study considers a premium-to-surplus ratio above 4 critical.

33. For some evidence, see Clarke, Warren-Boulton, Smith, and Simon, "Sources of the Crisis in Liability Insurance." For a comparative analysis of the Canadian liability insurance crisis, see Michael Trebilcock, "The Social Insurance-Deterrence Dilemma of Modern North American Tort Law: A Canadian Perspective on the Liability Insurance Crisis," *San Diego Law Review* 24 (1987): 929.

34. The ruling read, in part: "The health and safety of the people of this state must outweigh the express provisions of the insurance policy in issue. As a result, the exclusion clause in the policy which pertains to excluding coverage where the damage is to the policyholder's land must be held inapplicable where the danger to the environment is extreme." This case is on appeal.

35. We do not wish to enter the debate over whether coverage was knowingly sold below cost in the early 1980s. The debate begs the unanswerable questions of what was a reasonable projection of losses, investment income, and markup for risk and how a firm should balance those costs against the real costs of losing market share. Regardless of whether or why errors were made, the point remains that the potential for error varies directly with the length of the exposure and the unpredictability of sociolegal trends.

36. The fact that rulings by one court are often overturned by a higher court or that courts in different jurisdictions do not all immediately follow precedents from other jurisdictions simply modifies the positive correlation; it does not eliminate it.

37. See Patricia M. Danzon, "Tort Reform and the Role of Government in Private Insurance Markets," *Journal of Legal Studies* 13 (August 1984): 517-549; and Neil A. Doherty and Georges Dionne, "Risk Pooling, Contract Structure and Organizational Form of Insurance Firms" (Department of Insurance, The Wharton School, University of Pennsylvania, August 1988).

38. Usually, the retroactive period is the period during which the insured was covered by the insurer. When a policyholder switches carriers, an earlier retroactive period may be specified in the new policy. This provides the insured with an alternative to buying tail coverage from the prior carrier.

39. However, the initial policy may set some bounds on that price. There has been disagreement over the reinstatement of aggregate policy limits for tail coverage and the effect of defense cost inclusions. U.S. Department of Justice, *Report of the Tort Policy Working Group*, p. 53.

40. Roberta Romano, "Directors' and Officers' Liability and the Insurance Crisis" Research paper prepared for the CED Subcommittee on Risk Management, Dispute Resolution, and Injury Compensation, February 1988, p. 19.

41. Risk-retention groups are also exempt from certain Securities and Exchange Commission registration requirements and other regulations in raising capital. The provisions of the Act and some of its ambiguities are described in Jon Harkavy, "The Risk Retention Act of 1986: The Options Increase," *Risk Management* (March 1987).

42. "Give it a Chance," *National Underwriter,* November 9, 1987, at 22, col. 2.

43. This is discussed further in Danzon, *Medical Malpractice,* p. 109.

44. Lyda Phillips, "Insurance Group Warns of Crisis in Industry," *The Washington Post,* November 30, 1988. See also "Managing Insurer Insolvency" (Prepared for the National Association of Insurance Brokers by Stewart Economics, Inc., November 1988).

45. Patricia M. Danzon and Dennis Smallwood, "Solvency Regulation in the Property/Casualty Insurance Industry," *Bell Journal* (Spring 1980).

46. Similarly, the existence of federal deposit insurance has tended to increase the degree of risk taking and rate of insolvencies of savings and loans. See, for example, *The Wall Street Journal*, February 1, 1989, p. A14.

47. Of course if the tort system levies excessive liability costs on some activities, a subsidy to liability insurance through a JUA provides an offsetting effect. However, if the rationale for the JUA subsidy is that the tort system imposes excessive costs, a more efficient solution would surely be to adopt other policies to eliminate excessive liability costs directly, rather than to attempt an offsetting subsidy that itself introduces other distortions.

48. Of total shareholder suits, 74 percent are closed without payment to the claimant, but these claims have consistently above-average defense costs and size of awards.

49. For example, Wyatt Company, *1987 Wyatt Directors and Officers Liability Insurance Survey* (Chicago, 1987). The results of these surveys and the trends in law pertaining to directors and officers are summarized in Romano, "Directors' and Officers' Liability and the Insurance Crisis."

50. An important exception is *Smith v. Van Gorkum,* 488 A.2d. 858 (Del. 1985), in which the Delaware Supreme Court found directors grossly negligent in accepting a bid for their firm, although the bid substantially exceeded the firm's market value. The business judgment rule was not rejected but held inoperative because the directors were found to have not properly informed themselves concerning the firm's value.

51. For example, insurers have not been permitted to litigate the applicability of the dishonesty exclusion (*Pepsico v. Continental Casualty Co.,* 640 F. Supp. 656 S.D.N.Y. 1986) or to exercise their cancellation rights when the insured is bankrupt (*Minoco Group v. First State Underwriters Agency,* 799 F. 2d 517, 9th Cir. 1986). Related transactions have been found to constitute "separate loss occurrences" (*North River Insurance v. Huff,* 628 F. Supp. 1129, D. Kan. 1985), and misrepresentations in financial statements have been held not to void policies (*Federal Insurance Co. v. Oak Industries,* 1986 CCH Sec. Law Rep. para. 92,519 S.D. Cal. 1986). See also other cases cited in Romano , "Directors' and Officers' Liability and the Insurance Crisis."

52. Romano, "Directors' and Officers' Liability and the Insurance Crisis."

CHAPTER 4

1. See, for example, "The Coming Showdown in Car Insurance," *The New York Times,* November 6, 1988.

2. James S. Kakalik and Nicholas M. Pace, *Costs and Compensation Paid in Tort Litigation,* (Santa Monica, Calif.: The RAND Corporation, R-3391-ICJ, 1986). The study includes estimates of claims against insured and self-insured entities. It excludes claims that did not involve a lawsuit, claims in courts of limited jurisdiction, and small claims (under $1,000). Separate estimates were derived from insurance industry sources and from the University of Wisconsin's survey of 1,649 lawsuits that included in-depth interviews with lawyers and litigants. These two independent methods yielded very similar estimates. The simple average is reported here.

3. Estimates of tort claims covered under commercial multiperil and homeowners' multiperil liability policies are also included.

4. Kakalik and Pace, *Costs and Compensation Paid in Tort Litigation,* p. 62.

5. Patricia M. Danzon, *Medical Malpractice: Theory, Evidence, and Public Policy* (Cambridge, Mass.: Harvard University Press, 1985). The plaintiff's share of the liability insurance premium dollar is lower than the share of the total litigation expense reported in Table 4.1 because the estimate of the plaintiff's share of insurance premiums includes insurers' purely business costs such as brokerage fees, agents' commissions, and other overhead expenses but excludes the public costs of operating the courts and the litigants' time costs.

6. Andrew Schotter and Janusz Ordover, *The Cost of the Tort System* (New York: Starr Center for Applied Economics, New York University, March 1986).

7. Kakalik and Pace, *Costs and Compensation Paid in Tort Litigation,* p. 35. Total tort filings have been increasing at 3.9 percent a year, with a higher rate of increase for product liability (see Chapter 2). Since 1981, compensation paid per claim has been increasing at about 12 percent a year for auto and 17 percent a year for nonauto tort claims.

8. James F. Henry, "Use of Mini-trial Seeks to Ease Burden of Corporate Litigation," *The Washington Post,* October 13, 1985.

9. Patricia M. Danzon and Lee A. Lillard, "Settlement Out of Court: The Disposition of Medical Malpractice Claims," *Journal of Legal Studies* 12 (1983): 345-377; W. Kip Viscusi, "The Determinants of the Disposition of Product Liability Claims and Compensation for Bodily Injury," *Journal of Legal Studies* 15 (June 1986): 321-346.

10. See Peter W. Huber, *Liability: The Legal Revolution and Its Consequences* (New York: Basic Books, Inc., 1988), p. 102, and footnote 67, Chapter 5.

11. For a more complete description of alternative dispute resolution systems, see Jonathan B. Marks, Earl Johnson Jr., and Peter Szanton, *Dispute Resolution in America: Processes in Evolution* (Washington, D.C.: National Institute for Dispute Resolution, 1984).

12. See, for example, William M. Landes and Richard A. Posner, "Adjudication as a Private Good," *Journal of Legal Studies* 8 (March 1979): 235-284.

13. Peter H. Kaskell, Senior Vice President, Center for Public Resources, personal interview, January 20, 1988.

14. *Making Alternative Dispute Resolution Work* (Washington, D.C.: EnDispute Inc., 1987), p. 14.

15. CPR Legal Program, reprinted from *Across the Board,* October 10, 1984.

16. Much of the factual information in this section is drawn from Mark Peterson and Molly Selvin, "The Resolution of Mass Torts: Toward a Framework for Evaluation of Alternative Procedures" (Research paper prepared for CED Subcommittee on Risk Management, Dispute Resolution, and Injury Compensation, June 1987). The interpretation and recommendations are CED's. See also Frances E. McGovern, "Toward a Functional Approach for Managing Complex Litigation," *University of Chicago Law Review* 53 (1986): 440; and "Resolving Mature Mass Tort Litigation," *Boston University Law Review,* forthcoming.

17. Peterson and Selvin, "The Resolution of Mass Torts."

18. For example, in *Jenkins v. Raymark,* Judge Parker of the U.S. District Court for the Eastern District of Texas certified a voluntary class to decide common issues for all asbestos-related personal injury claims in that jurisdiction. The class included 755 individuals, all of whom had already filed individual claims; another 52 existing claimants opted out.

19. Dan R. Anderson, "Financing Asbestos Claims: Coverage Issues, Manville's Bankruptcy and the Claims Facility," *Journal of Risk and Insurance* 54, no.3 (1987).

20. *Business Insurance,* October 17, 1988.

21. Asbestos Claims Facility, news release, Princeton, N.J., June 15, 1988.

22. Judge Weinstein subsequently granted a motion to dismiss claims of opt-out plaintiffs, partly because of the weakness of the case on causation.

23. The experience of Florida, which adopted and subsequently dropped the English rule for medical malpractice cases, was that in practice the rule was unenforceable against individual plaintiffs.

CHAPTER 5

1. These groups are not mutually exclusive. Any individual may interact with firms and be exposed to risk in his or her capacity as a product consumer, a worker, or a member of the general public.

2. Small firms are exempt from some of these standards.

3. See, for example, W. Kip Viscusi, *Risk by Choice: Regulating Health and Safety in the Workplace* (Cambridge, Mass.: Harvard University Press, 1983), and studies cited therein.

4. Of course, although the existence of positive wage premiums for risk does prove that market forces provide incentives for risk reduction, it does not necessarily prove that those incentives are optimal.

5. See, for example, Michael Spence, "Consumer Misperceptions, Product Failure and Producer Liability," *Review of Economic Studies* 44 (October 1977): 561-572.

6. See, for example, Richard Craswell and John E. Calfee, "Deterrence and Uncertain Legal Standards," *Journal of Law, Economics and Organisation* 2 (Fall 1986): 279 - 303.

7. This assumes that damages are appropriately set.

8. See, for example, Steven Shavell, "Strict Liability versus Negligence," *Journal of Legal Studies* 9 (January 1980): 1-25. Charles E. Phelps, "Liability and Regulation: When to Use Which and When to Use Neither" (Research paper prepared for the CED Subcommittee on Risk Management, Dispute Resolution, and Injury Compensation, February 1987). The conditions stated in the text are necessary but not sufficient for efficiency. A negligence rule may not be efficient if consumers underestimate the average level of risk of a product; they tend to buy too much or use the product too frequently. Further, theoretical analyses of effects of different liability rules on incentives for care often ignore costs of implementation and insurance. In general, strict liability is likely to be more costly to operate than a negligence standard simply because more injuries are compensable. Liability insurance, which plays a larger role under strict liability, is more costly than first-party insurance, which plays a larger role under a negligence standard. Theoretical analyses also often assume that all victims bring suits and are correctly compensated in all appropriate circumstances.

9. See, for example, Daniel Kahneman and Amos Tversky, "Prospect Theory: An Analysis of Decision Under Risk," *Econometrica* 47 (March 1979): 263-291.

10. The evidence that juries tend to award higher amounts for similar injuries when the defendant is a deep-pocket defendant is consistent with this. See Audrey Chin and Mark Peterson, *Deep Pockets, Empty Pockets: Who Wins in Cook County Jury Trials* (Santa Monica, Calif.: The RAND Corporation, R-3249-ICJ, 1985).

11. See Richard A. Epstein, "The Political Economy of Product Liability Reform," *American Economic Review* 78 (May 1988). The same point is made with respect to bias in incentives of judges, in Richard Neely, *The Product Liability Mess: How Business Can Be Rescued From State Court Politics* (New York: The Free Press, 1988). Nevertheless, at least 39 states have enacted tort reform legislation since 1985. See note 58.

12. See, for example, Bruce Ackerman and William T. Hassler, *Clean Coal/Dirty Air or How the Clean Air Act Became a Multibillion-Dollar Bail-Out for High Sulfur Coal Producers and What Should Be Done About It* (New Haven, Conn.: Yale University Press, 1981.) Bruce Yandle, "The Riskiness of Regulatory Risk Reduction" (Research paper prepared for the CED Subcommittee on Risk Management, Dispute Resolution, and Injury Compensation, February 1988), and references cited therein.

13. Steven N. Wiggins, 1987. *The Cost of Developing a New Drug* (Washington , D.C.: Pharmaceutical Manufacturers' Association, June 1987), p.17.

14. Nancy Mattison, A. Gene Trimble, and Louis Lasagna, "New Drug Development in the United States, 1963 through 1984," *Clinical Pharmacology Theory* (March 1988): 290-301.

15. See, for example, Henry G. Grabowski and John M. Vernon, 1983, *The Regulation of Pharmaceuticals: Balancing the Benefits and Risks* (Washington, D.C.: American Enterprise Institute, 1983). The 1984 Drug Price Competition and Patent Term Restoration Act restores up to five years to patent life for time lost during the approval process.

16. Some of the FDA testing requirements have recently been modified and are now closer to those used in European countries (Fed. Reg. 8798, 1987).

17. *Ferebee v. Chevron Chemical Co.*, 736 F.2d 1529 (1984). See also Peter W. Huber, *Liability: The Legal Revolution and Its Consequences* (New York: Basic Books, Inc., 1988), p.55, for a discussion of this case.

18. John F. Morrall III, "A Review of the Record," *Regulation* (November-December 1986): 25-34.

19. Strictly, efficent allocation requires benefits per dollar spent, including reductions in morbidity as well as mortality, or quality-adjusted life years. It is highly unlikely that a more complete tally of benefits in the calculations in Table 5.2 would change the conclusions.

20. For example, the original EPA-proposed grain dust standard was significantly modified on the basis of review by the Council on Wage and Price Stability. See Yandle "The Riskiness of Regulatory Risk Reduction," p. 21.

21. See, for example, Bruce Ackerman and Hassler, *Clean Coal/Dirty Air*; and Yandle "The Riskiness of Regulatory Risk Reduction."

22. See, for example, John Prather Brown, "Towards an Economic Theory of Liability Rules," *Journal of Legal Studies* 2 (June 1973): 323-349.

23. For example, *Heil Co. v. Grant*, 534 S.W.2d 916 Ct.App. Tex. 1976. See also George L. Priest, "Modern Tort Law and Its Reform," The Monsanto Lectures on Tort Law Reform and Jurisprudence, *Valparaiso University* Law Review (Valparaiso, Indiana: Valparaiso University *Press*, 1987), and cases cited therein.

24. For a discussion of probabilistic causation and the legal system, see Troyen A. Brennan and Robert F. Caster, "Legal and Scientific Probability of Causation of Cancer and Other Environmental Diseases in Individuals," *Journal of Health Politics, Policy and Law* 10 (Spring 1985): 33-80.

25. *Sindell v. Abbott Laboratories,* 26 Cal. 3d 588, 607 P. 2d 924 163 Cal. Rptr. 132, cert. denied, 449 U.S. 912 (1980). Two recent cases modify the potential impact of Sindell. See Chapter 2 of this statement, note 32.

26. Peter H. Schuck, "The New Judicial Ideology of Tort Law," *The Public Interest* 92 (1988): 101.

27. For example, *Beshada v. Johns Manville* 90 N.J. 191, 447 A.2d 539 1982; *Barker v. Lull Engineering Co.,* 20 Cal. 3rd 413, 573 P.2d 443, 143 Cal.Rptr. 225 1978.

28. See, for example, Schuck, "The New Judicial Ideology of Tort Law," pp. 101-103.

29. For a review of some of the recent studies, see Yandle, "The Riskiness of Regulatory Risk Reduction."

30. Robert E. Litan and William D. Nordhaus, *Reforming Federal Regulation* (New Haven: Yale University Press, 1983), p.19, 23. In constant 1972 dollars, the annual cost on a per-family basis rose from $13 in 1969 to $33 in 1981. These costs are discussed further in Yandle "The Riskiness of Regulatory Risk Reduction," pp. 13-14.

31. See examples in Yandle "The Riskiness of Regulatory Risk Reduction."

32. U.S. Environmental Protection Agency (EPA),*Environmental Progress and Challenges: An EPA Perspective,* (Washington, D.C.: U.S. EPA, 1984); The Conservation Foundation, *State of the Environment* (Washington, D.C.: The Conservation Foundation, 1982); W. Kip Viscusi, "Consumer Behavior and the Safety Effects of Product Safety Regulation," *Journal of Law and Economics* 28 (October 1985): 527-553; and other studies cited in Yandle, "The. Riskiness of Regulatory Risk Reduction."

33. This assumes that the resources would have been otherwise employed. Thus, it would be a mistake to count jobs created as an offsetting benefit. Similarly, the increase in resources used per unit of output is the counterpart of loss of productivity. It would be double-counting to also include a measure of decreased productivity.

34. For example, Koenraad Wiedhaup, "View of Contraceptive Development," Netherlands, Organon International (Paper presented at the March 7-8, 1988, meetings of the National Academy of Sciences Committee on Contraceptive Development, Washington, D.C).

35. For a review of some of these sources, see Peter Reuter, "Expanded Liability of U.S. Corporations: Responses and Consequences (Research paper for CED Subcommittee on Risk Management, Dispute Resolution, and Injury Compensation, December 1987).

36. Douglas J. Besharov, *The Lesson of Bhopal: The International Trade Consequences of American Tort Liability,* Washington Legal Foundation, Critical Legal Issues Working Paper Series, 15 (June 1987): 14-15, 17.

37. Kenneth McLennan, representing the Machinery and Allied Products Institute (MAPI) in a written statement to the Subcommittee on Commerce, Consumer Protection and Competitiveness, House of Representatives, May 27, 1987, p. 4.

38. An earlier Conference Board survey of corporate risk managers and general counsel shows similar results. Roughly a third of respondents reported taking actions to improve product safety design and labeling. Although the report concluded that product liability has not had a major impact on management decision making, critics of this survey have correctly pointed out the limited number of issues addressed and the limited perspective of the respondents. See Victor Schwartz, "Product Liability: A Crisis Well With Us," *Across the Board* (October 1987): 14-22.

39. E. Patrick McGuire, *The Impact of Product Liability,* Research Report No. 908 (New York: The Conference Board, 1988) Table 28, p. 19.

40. McGuire, *The Impact of Product Liability,* Table 9.

41. McGuire, *The Impact of Product Liability,* Table 41.

42. Based on personal interviews and Reuter, "Expanded Liability of U.S. Corporations."

43. Reuter, "Expanded Liability of U.S. Corporations."

44. Douglas J. Besharov, *Liability for Foreign Torts: Whose Law Should Apply?* (Paper prepared for a Round Table Conference on The Impact of U.S. Product Liability Laws on U.S. Export Trade and International Competitiveness, The Fletcher School of Law and Diplomacy, Tufts University, October 4-6, 1987), p. 3.

45. Besharov, *Liability for Foreign Torts,* pp. 2, 18.

46. Indeed, in many countries outside the United States, disclosure of corporate records is a crime. See Besharov, *Liability for Foreign Torts,* p. 11.

162

47. It should be noted that making precise country-to-country comparisons of insurance costs is extremely difficult because of differences in policy limits and terms among countries.

48. March 7, 1988, letter from George Zacharokow, President, Marine and International Group, Continental Insurance, to J.H. Bretherick of Continental Insurance, forwarded to Charles F. Barber. These expenditures excluded auto liability insurance, for which the United States also led.

49. Besharov, *Liability for Foreign Torts*, p. 9.

50. Reuter, "Expanded Liability of U.S. Corporations," p. 10.

51. Ulrich Sturmer, "The Competitive Advantage of German Products in U.S. Markets" (Paper presented at a Round Table Conference on The Impact of U.S. Product Liability Laws on U.S. Export Trade and International Competitiveness, The Fletcher School of Law and Diplomacy, Tufts University, October 4-6, 1987); December 21, 1987, letter from Gary K. Brown, CPCU Deputy Managing Vice President, Alexander & Alexander, to D. A. Kline, Director of Insurance, Sun Company, Inc.; December 28, 1987, letter from Powell McHenry, Senior Vice President and General Counsel, Procter and Gamble, to Robert C. Holland; and Frank A. Orban, "Product Liability and International Trade and Politics" (Preconference working paper, edited proceedings *Product Liability Tort Law*, sponsored by the National Legal Center for the Public Interest, April 20-21, 1982, A-107).

52. Jean L. Fuchs, Managing Director, Hunter, Bowring, and Co. Ltd., N.V., Antwerp, Belgium, "Product Liability and International Trade" (Preconference working paper, edited proceedings *Product Liability Tort Law*, sponsored by the National Legal Center for the Public Interest, April 20-21, 1982, A-120).

53. Because of economies of scale, it is not cost-effective for many U.S. firms to have distinct product lines or distinct policies regarding risk, one for domestic and one for foreign markets, although for many large firms this is feasible. International firms tend to have uniform policies worldwide, so that liability-induced improvements are executed even in places where the liability may not apply. See Reuter, "Expanded Liability of U.S. Corporations"; and Edward Bowman and Howard Kunreuther, "Post-Bhopal Behavior at a Chemical Company," *Journal of Management Studies* 25 (July 1988).

54. See Paul Oreffice, "The Year Tort Reform Must Happen," *Imprimus* (July 1987).

55. Essentially, in the long run, there is a substitution of insurance benefits for cash compensation. Total labor costs rise by only the difference between the cost of the insurance benefits and their value to workers. At the limit, if benefits are valued at cost, total labor costs are unaffected by an increase in social insurance payroll taxes. By contrast, since most of the costs of liability insurance cover potential compensation to consumers and other third parties, there is no reason why employees would be willing to accept any wage reduction to offset an increase in liability costs to the firm. Thus there is far more pressure to shift liability costs forward in higher prices. But to the extent consumers either do not perceive or do not value the effects of increased producer liability, the costs cannot be shifted forward in higher prices without some reduction in output. Costs that are not shifted forward must ultimately be shifted back, through lower rates of return to capital, lower wages or loss of jobs. The incidence of payroll taxes is discussed in Samuel Brittain, "The Incidence of Social Security Payroll Taxes," *American Economic Review* (March 1971). See also Martin Feldstein, "The Incidence of the Social Security Payroll Tax: Comment," *American Economic Review* 62 (1972).

56. McGuire, *The Impact of Product Liability*, pp. 8, 35.

57. Perhaps the first federal product liability bill introduced was H.R. 5626, 96th Cong., 1st Sess., 125 *Congressional Record* 28, 678 (1979). More recently, see H.R. 1115, 100th Cong., 1st Sess. (1987); S.554, 100th Cong., 1st Sess. (1987); S.666,100th Cong., 1st Sess. (1987); and S.1999, 99th Cong., 1st Sess. (1985).

58. *Liability Alert* 3 (July 15, 1988). For example, New Jersey S.B. 2805, now codified at New Jersey Stat. Ann. 2A58C *et seq.*; Ohio H.B. 1, now codified at Ohio Rev. Code Ann. 2307.71 *et seq.*; Iowa S.B. 2265, Iowa Code Ann. 668.12.

59. For example, *Barker v. Lull Engineering Co., Inc.,* 143 Cal. Rptr. 225, 573 P.2d 443 (1978). Another prominent standard is the consumer expectation standard, which asks whether the product design deviated from the reasonable expectations of consumers with regard to safety features.

60. A widely adopted standard is that of John W. Wade, which lists seven factors to be considered in determining whether a product is abnormally dangerous. John W. Wade, "On the Nature of Strict Tort Liability for Products," *Mississippi Law Journal* 44 (November 1973): 825.

61. Robert H. Malott, Testimony before the Subcommittee on Commerce, Consumer Protection and Competitiveness of the Committee on Energy and Commerce. U.S. House of Representatives, May 5, 1987 (p. 11 of printed testimony); U.S. Department of Justice, *Report of the Tort Policy Working Group,* p. 61.

62. George L. Priest, "Modern Tort Law and Its Reform," The Monsanto Lectures on Tort Law Reform and Jurisprudence, *Valparaiso University Law Review* (Valparaiso, Indiana: Valparaiso University Press, 1987).

63. To the extent that this retroactive application of new standards is prevented by strict adherence to a state-of-the-art defense and unpredictability of changes in damage awards is reduced by scheduling damages with indexation to inflation (see Chapter 6 of this statement), the distortions resulting from a long statute are reduced and the optimal statute of repose would be longer.

64. Consistent with these general principles, most states have adopted fairly short statutes of repose of six years or less for medical malpractice, with extensions for minors. Colorado recently adopted a ten-year statute of repose for manufacturing equipment.

65. For example, in 1985, Merrell Dow took Bendectin off the market solely for liability reasons. In 1980, an FDA-appointed panel of independent experts had reviewed all the available evidence and concluded that the available data did not demonstrate an association between birth defects and Bendectin. *HHS News,* U.S. Department of Health and Human Services, FDA, P80-45, October 7, 1980. The FDA agreed. Nevertheless, over 1,000 claims have been filed. As of July 1987, of the 17 jury verdicts, Merrell Dow has won 12, plaintiffs, 5. But the overwhelming scientific consensus in the FDA and all respectable scientific circles remains that Bendectin does not cause birth defects. See also Huber, *Liability,* p. 102.

66. For example, New Jersey S.2805 contains a defense to punitive damages for drugs, devices, foods, and food additives that comply with FDA requirements. Compliance with FDA requirements also creates a rebuttable presumption that a warning or instruction is adequate. See also Oregon S.B. 323 (1987).

67. See cases cited in Schuck, "The New Judicial Ideology of Tort Law": 96-98.

68. The structure of compensatory damages that we recommend in Chapter 6 of this statement may result in compensatory awards that are less than the willingness to pay for risk reduction.

69. For example, Colorado Rev. Stat. 13-21-102 (1987) provides that punitive damages cannot exceed compensatory damages. At least twenty-eight states have enacted legislation since 1985 modifying their laws governing punitive damages. Some of these statutes raise the burden of proof from a "preponderance of the evidence" to "clear and convincing evidence" [e.g., Alabama Acts 87-185; Alaska Stat. 09-17.020 (1987)].

70. Spence, "Consumer Misperceptions, Product Failure and Producer Liability," shows that optimal compensatory awards are often less than optimal deterrent awards.

71. Within the broad term, "financial responsibility requirements," we mean to include those practices private or public contracting parties could decide upon as appropriate guarantees that foreign sellers can fulfill their liability responsibilities in connection with their products sold and used within the U.S. For example, a foreign seller without substantial assets in the U.S. could be required to take out a liability insurance policy payable in the United States to meet product claims on such products.

72. Office of Technology Assessment, Superfund Strategy, (Washington, D.C.: U.S. Government Printing Office, April 1985). See also Robert H. Harris and Grover C. Wrenn, "Making Superfund Work," *Issues in Science and Technology* (Spring 1988): 54 -58.

73. *Superfund: Extent of the Nation's Potential Hazardous Waste Problem Still Unknown* Washington, D.C.: U.S. General Accounting Office, Report No. GAO/RCED-88-44, December 1987.

74. James M. Seif and Thomas C. Voltaggio, U.S. Environmental Protection Agency, "Risk Management Strategies Used in Cleaning Up Hazardous Waste Sites" (Paper prepared for a Conference on Risk Assessment and Risk Management Strategies for Hazardous Waste Storage and Disposal Problems, The Wharton School, University of Pennsylvania, May 18-19, 1988). p.5. (Conference proceedings forthcoming.)

75. Leslie Cheek III, "Insurance Issues Associated with Cleaning Up Hazardous Waste Sites" (Paper prepared for a Conference on Risk Assessment and Risk Management Strategies for Hazardous Waste Storage and Disposal Problems, The Wharton School, University of Pennsylvania, May 18-19, 1988, p. 5. (Conference proceedings forthcoming.)

76. See cases cited in Cheek, "Insurance Issues Associated with Cleaning Up Hazardous Waste Sites."

77. It is not our intention to take sides on this matter. Our purpose is simply to point out that uncertainty in connection with the current debate as to how courts should interpret insurance contracts contributes to problems in insurance availability.

78. Edward Bowman and Howard Kunreuther, "Post-Bhopal Behavior at a Chemical Company," *Journal of Management Studies* 25 (July 1988). The study was based on in-depth interviews with over twenty corporate executives.

79. This suggests that the presumption of simple theory – that markets fail totally in the case of risks to third parties – is too strong. Bowman and Kunreuther, "Post-Bhopal Behavior at a Chemical Company," did not attempt the perhaps impossible task of distinguishing the effect of direct concern over adverse publicity from the effect of the expected cost of liability suits arising out of a catastrophe such as Bhopal.

80. The use of simple heuristics that emphasize the importance of memorable events such as severe disasters is discussed in Daniel Kahneman, Paul Slovic, and Amos Tversky, eds. *Judgement Under Uncertainty: Heuristics and Biases* (Cambridge: Cambridge University Press, 1982).

81. This is less critical if the parties can contract around the legal assignment of liabilities at low cost and such contracts are honored by the courts. This principle underlies our recommendations for reliance on the workers' compensation system for controlling risk in the workplace (see Chapter 6 of this statement).

CHAPTER 6

1. Compensation has recently been allowed for increased risk of injury, without any evidence of actual injury. This can result in overcompensation and overdeterrence, if the same individuals are compensated when the injuries actually manifest themselves. See cases cited in Leslie Cheek III, "Insurance Issues Associated with Cleaning Up Hazardous

Waste Sites" (Paper prepared for a Conference on Risk Assessment and Risk Management Strategies for Hazardous Waste Storage and Disposal Problems, The Wharton School, University of Pennsylvania, May 18-19, 1988). Conference proceedings forthcoming.

2. Mark A. Peterson, *Civil Juries in the 1980s: Trends in Jury Trials and Verdicts in California and Cook County, Illinois* (Santa Monica, Calif.: The RAND Corporation, R-3466-ICJ, 1987), pp. 22, 24, 29, 30, 35. See Chapter 2 for more information on jury verdicts.

3. A few states did adopt strict product liability by statute. Even in these cases, however, the court-driven evolution of product liability law probably goes far beyond what could have been anticipated by the legislatures that adopted these statutes.

4. Committee on Ways and Means, U.S. House of Representatives, *Background Material and Data on Programs within the Jurisdiction of the Committee on Ways and Means,* 1987 Edition, March 6, 1987, pp. 30-31. Of these 4.0 million DI beneficiaries, 2.73 million were disabled workers receiving an average monthly payment of $488, 0.3 million were spouses of disabled workers receiving an average monthly payment of $131, and 0.97 million were children of disabled workers receiving an average payment of $141.

5. Part A, which covers inpatient services, is financed through a payroll tax. The funding of Part B, which covers physician and outpatient services, is split between general revenues (75 percent) and individual contributions (25 percent). Under the 1988 Catastrophic Illness legislation, coverage was improved under both Parts A and B. Hospital coverage was extended from 60 days to 1 year and a dollar ceiling was placed on the amount that beneficiaries pay out-of-pocket for physician services and other services outside of the hospital. This package of benefit improvements is funded in two ways — through higher beneficiary premiums and through an income tax surcharge on higher income Social Security recipients.

6. An estimated 4.2 million persons receive SSI benefits. Of these, 2.7 million people (about 2.2 million of whom are under sixty-five) receive benefits on the basis of disability. There appears to be a sharp increase in the number of working-age people receiving benefits on the basis of disability. About 40 percent of the disabled SSI beneficiaries are eligible on the basis of mental impairments, and another 20 percent have circulatory disorders. See Committee on Ways and Means, *Background Material,* p. 508.

7. Additional in-kind support for the low-income population is provided through food stamps and housing and energy assistance. Because SSI, AFDC, and Medicaid are federal-state programs, there is substantial variation across states in income thresholds for eligibility.

8. Costs of the black lung program grew from $150 million in 1970 to more than $1 billion by the late 1970s. See W. Kip Viscusi, "Liability for Occupational Accidents and Illnesses," in *Liability: Perspectives and Policy,* ed. Robert E. Litan and Cliff Winston (Washington, D.C.: The Brookings Institution, 1988), p. 180.

9. Va. Code Ann. 38.2-5001 (Supp. 1987).

10. Starting in the 1900s, all states adopted WC statutes that replaced employer liability under common law negligence rules with a system of strict liability without regard to fault administered through special agencies. Initially, industries with a large proportion of small firms and casual or part-time workers (notably agriculture and services) were excluded, but coverage has been expanded over the years. Employers are required either to meet financial responsibility standards or to purchase insurance to cover their potential liability. In most states, workers' compensation insurance is provided by the private insurance industry. A few states have either competitive or exclusive state funds.

11. At first glance, this low replacement rate for above-median wages may seem suboptimal; but on closer inspection, it is probably a rational choice given the other private and public coverages available. See Patricia M. Danzon, "The Political Economy of Workers' Compensation: Lessons for Product Liability," *American Economic Review, Papers & Proceedings* (May 1988).

12. U.S. Department of Health and Human Services, Social Security Administration, *Social Security Bulletin: Annual Statistical Supplement, 1987* (Washington, D.C.: U.S. Government Printing Office, December 1987), p. 262.

13. Richard J. Butler and John D. Worrall, "Workers' Compensation: Benefits and Injury Claims Rates in the Seventies," *Review of Economics and Statistics* 65 (November 1983): 580-589, conclude that higher WC benefit levels have been a significant factor contributing to higher WC claim rates.

14. The minimum period is less for younger workers.

15. The number of companies selling long-term care insurance has jumped from sixteen to eighty within the past five years. See *Health Care Competition Week*, May 23, 1988.

16. States can extend their AFDC programs, with federal matching funds, to cover families with an unemployed primary breadwinner. A few states have adopted this optional program.

17. A small fraction of the population has accidental death and dismemberment coverage (ADD) that pays a fixed amount in the event of the loss of specific body parts.

18. Here the moral hazard is overreporting of loss.

19. See Patricia M. Danzon, "Tort Reform and the Role of Government in Private Insurance Markets," *Journal of Legal Studies* 13 (1984): 517-549.

20. The optimal level of compensation for noneconomic loss is such that the marginal utility of income is equal before and after the injury.

21. In the 1970s, several states enacted caps on noneconomic damages for medical malpractice cases. Since 1985, such caps have been enacted for other types of cases in several states. In 1986, the state of Washington enacted a cap based on a formula that includes the injured person's life expectancy prior to injury and the state average wage. The constitutionality of this cap is under challenge in *Sofie v. Fibreboard Corp.*, No. 54610-0.

22. See, for example, Connecticut S.B. 6134 (1986), which allows a judge to establish structured payments when future economic damages exceed $200,000; Michigan H.B. 5154 (1986) requires structured payments when future damages exceed $250,000.

23. Periodic payments that are contingent on the actual losses incurred by the plaintiff undermine incentives for rehabilitation and prudent use of medical and other resources.

24. There are also tax advantages in using structured settlements rather than lump-sum payments.

25. States vary in whether the offset applies to all collateral sources, whether it is mandatory or at the discretion of the court, and whether the plaintiff is credited for premiums paid to purchase the coverages.

26. Patricia M. Danzon, *New Evidence on the Frequency and Severity of Medical Malpractice Claims* (Santa Monica, Calif.: The RAND Corporation, R-3410-ICJ, 1986), reports evidence that collateral source offset for medical malpractice claims has reduced both the frequency and severity of claims.

27. Viscusi, "Liability for Occupational Accidents and Illnesses."

28. For example, *Borel v. Fiberboard Paper Products Corporation,* U.S. Court of Appeals, Fifth Circuit (1973). (See the discussion of these doctrines in Chapter 2 of this statement.)

29. Ronald Coase, "The Problem of Social Cost," *Journal of Law and Economics* 3 (October 1960): 1- 44.

30.This standard has been proposed in the *Crum and Forster Report* authored by Leslie Cheek III. The definition of occupational disease proposed in this report is one that arises out of employment and the nature of the job through "ingestion of, inhalation of, contact with, or other exposure to harmful substances." This leaves questions of defining job-related stress unanswered.

31. Contribution is most easily measured by duration of employment. However, such a rule eliminates incentives to reduce exposure per employee or to hire employees who are at relatively low risk, which may be an efficient way of reducing risk, although it may also raise issues of discrimination and equal protection. For example, in light of conflicting evidence about whether exposure to video display terminals adversely affects a developing fetus, this risk might be reduced by excluding women of child-bearing age from certain jobs.

32. W. Kip Viscusi, *Risk by Choice: Regulating Health and Safety in the Workplace* (Cambridge, Mass.: Harvard University Press, 1983); and Chapter 5 of this statement.

33. The tort defendant may in some states bring an action for contribution or indemnity against the employer. Thus, tort litigation becomes an expensive way of shifting costs of workplace injuries from one employer to another.

34. A similar proposal for the retirement component of Social Security is laid out in Laurence J. Kotlikoff, "Reforming Social Security for the Young: A Framework for Consensus," in *Controlling the Cost of Social Security*, ed. C. Campbell (1983).

35. Several states have already established such pools. Financing is typically from an assessment on insurance companies because the Employee Retirement Income Security Act preempts state regulation of self-insured employers.

36. Senator Kennedy introduced S.1265 (100th Congress) which proposed mandated health benefits for all employees who worked 17 1/2 hours or more. Representative Waxman introduced a similar bill, H.R.2508 (100th Congress). Both plan to introduce legislation on mandated health benefits in the 101st Congress.

Memoranda of Comment, Reservation, or Dissent

Page 2, by JAMES Q. RIORDAN

I agree with the statement. It is excellent. My only suggestion is that we should give more emphasis to the issue of international competitiveness. The statement indicated we are diverting a significant portion of our GNP to more costly methods of compensation and deterrence than are used in other industrialized nations. If this is the case, and I believe it is, we will surely pay the price in competitiveness. The money spent on wasteful litigation is not available for productive investment. If we saved and invested the money now being wasted, we would have a stronger, more competitive economy and a better standard of living for all.

Page 8, by JOHN DIEBOLD, with which ROY L. ASH, ROBERT W. LUNDEEN, and HAROLD M. WILLIAMS have asked to be associated

The cost and consequences of good intentions are nowhere more vividly illustrated than in the issues we have chosen to address in this policy statement. Yet these problems must be considered as only one example of a much more fundamental condition that transcends abuse of the concept of tort liability and affects us in many other ways.

The political attraction of mandating a risk free society is as clear as are the unintended and often unexpected consequences of such governmental intervention. Until there is a willingness to address head-on in legislation and governmental regulations the necessity to talk in terms of an acceptable level of risk, rather than in absolutes, we will continue to build into our lives problems of the kind addressed in this statement.

The American people are usually very good at understanding and responding to realities when they are honestly presented to them. No amount of after the fact adjustment is half as good as addressing the issue properly in the first instance. Political leadership at its best is largely public education. Facing the issue rather than yielding to the temptation to legislate the unattainable is an ideal opportunity to demonstrate political leadership.

Page 9 (first bullet), by RODERICK M. HILLS

We should rely on market forces. Whether the McCarran-Ferguson law should be repealed or whether the antitrust laws should be more broadly applied to the insurance industry are matters not within the scope of the study. I believe, however, that such matters when studied could be relevant to many of the matters and recommendations covered by our report.

Page 9 (third bullet), by RODERICK M. HILLS

Our support of "standards setting" rather than by expanding tort liability does not, I believe, suggest that we are opposed to market incentives that encourage safer and cleaner environments.

Page 105, by LEON C. HOLT, JR.

The discussion on punitive damages does not go far enough. The report should define willful misconduct so as to mean deliberate intent to harm. Most states now use willful conduct as a standard, but leave its interpretation open to the jury. This approach contributes to the lottery style award system that punishes a defendant for less than egregious conduct.

GLOSSARY

Absolute liability: A standard of liability that holds a producer responsible for losses associated with its products, without proof of defect in the product or a causal link between the product and the injury.

Adverse selection: Tendency for an insurer to unknowingly attract a disproportionate share of the high risks in the population. Occurs when the policyholder is better informed than the insurer about his or her own risk type. If an insurer offers all risks the same policy at a common rate, it tends to attract only the worst risks, for whom the policy is very advantageous. In such circumstances, where insurers cannot observe policyholder risk type and properly tailor rates to the risk of each policyholder, they may have to limit coverage in order to break even.

Agent Orange: An herbicide used by U.S. forces during the Vietnam War that contains dioxin, a poison. In 1979, veterans and their families sued seven chemical companies and the U.S. government for damages they said were caused by Agent Orange. The case became the largest class action suit filed to date.

Alternative dispute resolution: A range of practices aimed at managing and resolving disputes more cost-effectively and expeditiously than through formal court proceedings. Includes arbitration, mediation, mini-trials, and other procedures.

Arbitration: The submission of a dispute to one or more neutral persons for a final and binding decision; usually displaces trial by judge and jury, but is based on the same substantive rules of law.

Asbestos: A mineral whose nonflammable fibers have been used as insulation in buildings, furnaces, hair dryers, and other products and that has been linked to increased risks of lung cancer and other diseases.

Assumption of risk: A standard of liability that bars a plaintiff from recovering damages and places responsibility for an injury through fault of defendant, third person, or fault of no one on the plaintiff when he or she voluntarily exposed him or herself to a known danger.

Captive insurance company: An alternative insurance mechanism in which a corporation, hospital, or group of such entities form their own insurance company. These captives are typically capitalized by their parent(s), professionally managed, and issue insurance policies modeled after those used in the commercial market to risks including but not limited to the founding parents. Captives are typically located off-shore and have favorable tax and regulatory treatment compared to domestic insurers.

Cash flow underwriting: The reduction of premiums by insurers when earnings are high on their investments relative to the expected rate of inflation of claim costs.

Claims-made insurance policy form: Covers claims filed during the policy period, arising out of incidents that occurred in the policy period or within a time limit defined by the policy. Claims filed after the policy period may be covered by a reporting endorsement.

Class action suit: A suit brought on behalf of a group of persons who are similarly affected by an issue. Persons included in the class defined by the court may be allowed to opt in and participate in the class action or opt out and sue independently.

Collateral source rule: Traditional tort rule that prohibits presenting evidence to the jury of the plaintiff's potential compensation from other sources such as private and public insurance.

Compensable damages: Compensation for the injured party, including reimbursement for lost wages, medical expenses, or other damages such as pain and suffering, awarded to compensate for the injury sustained and nothing more (in contrast with *punitive damages,* which are awarded specifically to punish wrongdoing).

Contributory negligence: A liability rule that bars recovery by a plaintiff in a tort suit if he or she contributed by an act, or omission, amounting to want of ordinary care to his or her own injury, even if the defendant was also negligent. This is not synonymous with *assumption of risk.*

Dalkon Shield: An intrauterine contraceptive device produced by the A. H. Robins pharmaceutical company which has been linked to increased users' risk of contracting pelvic inflammatory disease and other problems. It was introduced before medical devices were subject to FDA regulation. Faced with hundreds of thousands of suits, A.H. Robins filed for Chapter 11 bankruptcy.

Deep-pocket defendant: A defendant with relatively large financial assets or insurance.

Diethylstibestrol (DES): A synthetic form of the hormone estrogen used to prevent miscarriages; it has been alleged to have caused cancer.

English rule for awarding costs: A practice used in English courts whereby the losing party pays the legal costs of both sides. The rule is intended to deter frivolous suits and cost-increasing legal strategies by parties that have little chance of winning in court.

First-party insurance: Insurance that pays benefits in the event of injury to the policyholder.

General causation: Proof that a type of product is harmful to humans (in contrast to *specific causation,* which is proof that a particular product harmed a particular person).

Joint and several liability: A rule that permits a plaintiff to collect the full amount of damages from any single defendant, in cases where multiple defendants are found to have contributed to the injury, regardless of the relative fault of each defendant.

Long-tailed lines of insurance: Lines of insurance in which there is a lag of several years between the time the policy is written and the time all claims under the policy are ultimately closed. The lag may be due to delay in filing claims (occurrence coverage) or the delay in disposition of claims (claims-made and occurrence coverage).

Mediation: The submission of a dispute to an outside facilitator, often with specialized expertise, for assistance in reaching a mutually acceptable settlement. The procedure is private, voluntary, and nonbinding.

Mini-trials: A nonbinding procedure designed to encourage settlement of business disputes without going to court. Lawyers present arguments before business executives from both sides, allowing them to evaluate the costs and benefits of going to trial and to reach a realistic agreement.

Moral hazard: The risk that having insurance will make a policyholder less likely to prevent or minimize loss. To control this risk, insurance policies often include copayments (deductibles, co-insurance) or other direct controls.

Mutual: A form of insurance company in which policyholders own the company, in contrast to a stock company which is owned by equity owners.

Occurrence insurance policy form: Covers all claims arising out of incidents in the policy period, regardless of when in the future the claims are filed.

Probabilistic causation: A concept of causation that is defined in terms of the probability of a causal link between, say, a particular product and an injury to a particular plaintiff. Used when direct mechanical connections are not observable.

Punitive damages: Damages awarded in a tort case to punish the defendant for wrongdoing (in contrast with *compensable damages,* awarded to make up for the financial and psychological loss incurred by the plaintiff).

Specific causation: Evidence that a specific product harmed a particular person (in contrast with *general causation,* evidence that a product is harmful to humans).

State-of-the-art defense: A defense which bars suits if the defendant complied with standards of care or a product was not defective, given the state of knowledge and what was reasonably knowable at the time of the defendant's action.

Statute of limitation: A statute prescribing a specified period of time in which a lawsuit can be filed, sometimes running from the date at which the plaintiff discovered (or should have discovered) the injury.

Statute of repose: A limit on the time within which a suit may be brought, with the limit defined from the date of the defendant's alleged harmful act, as opposed to the date the plaintiff discovered the injury (see statute of limitation).

Strict liability: Liability without fault. Case is one of strict liability when neither care nor negligence, neither good nor bad faith, neither knowledge nor ignorance will save defendant *(Black's Law Dictionary).* As applied to products, strict liability places liability on producers for product-related injuries if the product is found defective in design, warning, or manufacture. Thus at issue are the characteristics of the product, not the behavior of the manufacturer, as in a negligence case.

Subrogation: The lawful substitution of a third party in place of a party having a claim against another party. An insurance company often has subrogation rights that enable it to recover costs incurred on behalf of its policyholders (medical expense or disability payments) from another party – say, a tort defendant – who was responsible for these costs being incurred.

174

Superfund: A federal law (the Comprehensive Environmental Response, Compensation and Recovery Act) enacted in 1980 and amended in 1986 that gives the Environmental Protection Agency the responsibility for identifying and cleaning up toxic waste sites, allowing the EPA to sue and recover costs from responsible parties as necessary.

Tort: A private or civil wrong or injury other than breach of contract for which redress in the form of damages can be sought under common law.

Willful misconduct: Conduct which intentionally and voluntarily disregards the safety of others, such as failure after knowledge of an impending danger to exercise ordinary care to prevent it.

Following is a list of the research papers prepared as background for the CED Subcommittee on Risk Management, Dispute Resolution, and Injury Compensation.

American Tort Doctrine since 1960
Gary T. Schwartz, Professor, U.C.L.A. School of Law (October 1986)

Liability and Regulation: When to Use Which and When to Use Neither
Charles E. Phelps, Professor of Political Science and Economics, University of Rochester (February 1987)

The Resolution of Mass Torts: Toward a Framework for Evaluation of Alternative Procedures
Mark Peterson and Molly Selvin, Institute for Civil Justice, The RAND Corporation (June 1987)

Expanded Liability of U.S. Corporations: Responses and Consequences
Peter Reuter, Institute for Civil Justice, The RAND Corporation (October 1987)

Directors' and Officers' Liability and the Insurance Crisis
Roberta Romano, Yale University Law School (February 1988)

The Riskiness of Regulatory Risk Reduction
Bruce Yandle, Alumni Professor of Economics, Clemson University (February 1988)

OBJECTIVES OF THE COMMITTEE FOR ECONOMIC DEVELOPMENT

For over forty years, the Committee for Economic Development has been a respected influence on the formation of business and public policy. CED is devoted to these two objectives:

To develop, through objective research and informed discussion, findings and recommendations for private and public policy that will contribute to preserving and strengthening our free society, achieving steady economic growth at high employment and reasonably stable prices, increasing productivity and living standards, providing greater and more equal opportunity for every citizen, and improving the quality of life for all.

To bring about increasing understanding by present and future leaders in business, government, and education, and among concerned citizens, of the importance of these objectives and the ways in which they can be achieved.

CED's work is supported strictly by private voluntary contributions from business and industry, foundations, and individuals. It is independent, nonprofit, nonpartisan, and nonpolitical.

The over 225 trustees, who generally are presidents or board chairmen of corporations and presidents of universities, are chosen for their individual capacities rather than as representatives of any particular interests. By working with scholars, they unite business judgment and experience with scholarship in analyzing the issues and developing recommendations to resolve the economic problems that constantly arise in a dynamic and democratic society.

Through this business-academic partnership, CED endeavors to develop policy statements and other research materials that commend themselves as guides to public and business policy; that can be used as texts in college economics and political science courses and in management training courses; that will be considered and discussed by newspaper and magazine editors, columnists, and commentators; and that are distributed abroad to promote better understanding of the American economic system.

CED believes that by enabling business leaders to demonstrate constructively their concern for the general welfare, it is helping business to earn and maintain the national and community respect essential to the successful functioning of the free enterprise capitalist system.

CED COUNTERPART ORGANIZATIONS IN FOREIGN COUNTRIES

Close relations exist between the Committee for Economic Development and independent, nonpolitical research organizations in other countries. Such counterpart groups are composed of business executives and scholars and have objectives similar to those of CED, which they pursue by similarly objective methods. CED cooperates with these organizations on research and study projects of common interest to the various countries concerned. This program has resulted in a number of joint policy statements involving such international matters as energy, East-West trade, assistance to developing countries, and the reduction of nontariff barriers to trade.

CE	Círculo de Empresarios Serrano Jover 5-2°, 28015 Madrid, Spain
CEDA	Committee for Economic Development of Australia GPO Box 2117T Melbourne 3001, Australia
CEPES	Vereinigung für Wirtschaftlichen Fortschritt e.r. Weissfrauenstrasse 9 6000 Frankfurt a.M. 11, West Germany
IDEP	Institut de l'Entreprise 6, rue Clément-Marot, 75008 Paris, France
経済同友会	Keizai Doyukai Japan Association of Corporate Executives Japan Industry Club Bldg. 1-4-6 Marunouchi, Chiyoda-ku, Tokyo 100, Japan
PSI	Policy Studies Institute 100 Park Village East, London NW1 3SR, England
SNS	Studieförbundet Näringsliv och Samhälle (Center for Business and Policy Studies) Sköldungagatan 2, S11427 Stockholm, Sweden